KIERKEGAARD, THE MYTHS
AND THEIR ORIGINS

KIERKEGAARD, THE MYTHS AND THEIR ORIGINS

Studies in the Kierkegaardian Papers and Letters

HENNING FENGER
Translated from the Danish by George C. Schoolfield

NEW HAVEN AND LONDON   YALE UNIVERSITY PRESS

A Danish version of this book was published
in 1976 by Odense Universitetsforlag
under the title *Kierkegaard-Myter og Kierkegaard-Kilder*.

Designed by Sally Harris
and set in VIP Zapf International type.
Printed in the United States of America by
Murray Printing Co., Westford, Mass.

Library of Congress Cataloging in Publication Data

Fenger, Henning.
    Kierkegaard, the myths and their origins.

    Translation of Kierkegaard-myter og
Kierkegaard-kilder.
    Bibliography: p.
    Includes index.
    1. Kierkegaard, S øren Aabye, 1813– 1855—
Addresses, essays, lectures. I. Title.
B4377.F3613   198'.9   80-277
ISBN 0-300-02462-2

10   9   8   7   6   5   4   3   2   1

De omnibus dubitandum est.
Johannes Climacus

CONTENTS

PREFACE TO THE SECOND EDITION

This is an English version of my book *Kierkegaard-Myter og Kierkegaard-Kilder*, which was published in October 1976. Save for the omission of the chapter "P. L. Møller, H. P. Holst, og Søren Kierkegaard indtil 1843" (pp. 171–254 of the original), it presents the material of the Danish first edition essentially unchanged; in a few small instances, the text has been abridged or brought up to date. I would like to express my gratitude to Statens humanistiske Forskningsråd and to the Yale University Press, which have made it possible for these opinions about Kierkegaard research to appear in a major language.

H. F.

Normandy
July 1979

PREFACE TO THE FIRST EDITION

Es blies ein Jäger wohl in sein Horn
Wohl in sein Horn,
Und alles was er blies das war verlorn.

It is depressing to be obliged to write about Kierkegaard myths and sources. Of course, the two things are closely connected. If one does not form a solid opinion concerning the source material, defensible from the scholarly point of view, one runs the risk of being a fabricator of myths. But is that so bad? The answer depends upon the extent to which one thinks that the historical facts and probabilities—I would not dream of saying "historical truth," for who has ever seen that bluebird?—have any value in and of themselves. Objectively. Readers who can believe only in the truth that edifies are requested to alight at this point. For—with a few worthy exceptions—Kierkegaard scholars have never been on friendly terms with the sources for the master's life and teaching. Most frequently, the source critics have had to warm the benches until the season's last dance, while theologians, philosophers, jurists, and men of letters of every imaginable creed have whirled around the floor.

Whoever might wish to take a closer look at the Kierkegaardian sources cannot avoid getting into a quarrel with what may be called official Kierkegaard scholarship. That is something which depends on inbreeding for its very existence. In 1900, X wrote postulate A, which Y uses as a support for postulate B in 1910, which in turn forms the basis of postulate C, proposed by Z in 1920. Do I need to continue? The sad part is that X, Y, and Z are all honorable men and that they have dedicated a great part of their lives to the study of Søren Kierkegaard. Criticizing them gives one a bad conscience, for one is quite aware that they know infinitely more than oneself about a great many matters. They read Hebrew,

Greek, and Latin without difficulty, and they are completely at home with the Greek philosophers, the mystics, and Hegel. Beset by inferiority complexes, one grows morose. One has known various members of this band of Kierkegaard scholars, one has looked up to them and admired them. All the same, one feels a certain obligation to say what must be said: that Kierkegaard research has been erected upon a foundation so porous that it crumbles at the very touch. It crumbles, at any rate, when it is touched by a hand that knows how to apply a modern, historic point of view, a point of view which, if you will, may be called neopositivistic.

I have no intention of embracing the whole Kierkegaard. If I remember correctly, it was Hans Brix who employed the metaphor of the polar explorer: no matter how far he penetrated into the ice of the interior, he found cairns put there by someone else, by Kierkegaard. Of the manifold Kierkegaards, I am fascinated by the young, the aesthetic one. Just as I was enchanted earlier by the young Voltaire, the young Brandes, the young Johan Ludvig Heiberg. The explanation is simple: they are most exciting in their youthful years, the formative period in which they absorb impressions and impulses, and when their taste and view of life are being formed. The aging, the institutional personalities—Voltaire as the patriarch of Ferney, Heiberg as the director of the Royal Theater amidst the applause of an ecclesiastical and literary court, Brandes as Europe's elite critic and hero worshiper—have never been any more appealing to me than Kierkegaard is in his role as persecuted martyr in the market town of Copenhagen.

For the rest, I frankly confess that I am unable to follow Kierkegaard as he leaps out over a sea 70,000 fathoms deep—I am glad if I can survive the yard-and-a-half which was the depth of Søborg Lake in 1835. Let others map the whole of the Kierkegaard continent. My own ambitions will be richly fulfilled if I can delineate certain contours of the province which bears the name *Aesthetica kierkegaardiana*. "It is impossible to exaggerate the involvement of Kierkegaard in the intellectual life of Copenhagen in the years 1830–50," declared Paul V. Rubow, a man whom I—using Kierkegaard's words—can call "the enthusiasm of my youth," albeit neither "the mighty trumpet of my awakening" nor "the desired object of my mood." Just the same, it is with a good conscience toward the *manes* of Rubow that I have allowed the following pages to be shot through with quotations, direct and indirect.

The harrying, teasing, and tormenting of theologians was a veritable fountain of youth for Rubow, and he is correct, of course, in his statement about Kierkegaard's intimate connections with the intellectual life of Copenhagen in the Golden Age. Georg Brandes was also aware of the relationship; yet the Kierkegaard scholar Frithjof Brandt, who made these connections the particular object of his work, never really grasped the nub of the matter. He arrives at the same conclusions as does Rubow but proceeds from premises which are completely askew. Brandt was tied to the apron strings of P. A. Heiberg, and their mutual results—which we have lately learned to call "output," have we not?—have been shipped around the whole world, and no one can figure out what is what any longer: points of view, opinions, theories, hypotheses, guesses, and so forth and so on. It is easier to deal with facts. In the case of the two Kierkegaardians just named, the facts shine by their very absence. False conclusions and sins against the sources do not grow less because they are repeated "with tongue and mouth and from the bottom of the heart," to quote Kierkegaard when he is quoting Kingo.

Granted: Kierkegaard is difficult to read, very difficult indeed. That was his intention, and he got his way. Here neither speed-reading nor diagonal reading will help; only close reading will do. Slowly. Again and again. Was this not exactly the method of reading which P. A. Heiberg and Brandt employed? Yes and no. They steeped themselves in Kierkegaard's basic writings, but it is doubtful that they read them in the spirit in which they were written and in the historical context to which they belong. The whole of Kierkegaard's work is often more national, more a part of Copenhagen, more private and intimate, than Heiberg and Brandt realized. Their net was woven too large to catch the facts which, after all, ought to be very informative when viewed with something as ordinary as good common sense. It is a strange spectacle to see later scholars with a Marxist orientation, such as Ljungdal and Peter P. Rohde, refer to archivists and philosophers as if they had been exegetes authorized by the state to interpret the texts. Danish historical research (which has done such solid work on the Heiberg family and on H. C. Andersen) has a mission in the present case which it cannot simply disregard. It has a duty toward the poet-philosopher and religious figure who, in the nineteenth century, towers like a mountaintop in those reaches of the sky where otherwise only Hegel, Marx, and Nietzsche are to be found. The historians do not need to have it pounded into them; it should be sufficient to remind them that the Heibergs had the good fortune of stumbling upon A. D. Jørgensen, P. Munch, and Aage Friis, while Kierkegaard had the bad luck of leaving behind a relative by the name of Troels-Lund. It is my pious wish that Danish historical research will accept its mission, with its assets and liabilities, vis-à-vis Kierkegaard scholarship, so that—in the presence of the world at large—we need not be ashamed of the condition of its very foundations, the sources themselves.

If this little book has a thesis, it is simply that Kierkegaard research went down the wrong track at the outset and that "the mistake," to a certain extent—to a great extent—goes back to Kierkegaard himself. But, like anyone else, of course, Kierkegaard had the right to suppress, rewrite, misrepresent, distort, erase, destroy, and lead astray, and to arrange the interpretation of his life and his works. In precisely whatever way he pleased. It can scarcely be doubted that he enjoyed doing it. In the same fashion, the existential Kierkegaard reader has the plain right to believe Kierkegaard or not to believe him. To choose, to reject, to do as he likes in accordance with his own subjective needs.

Can this also be called research, research with scholarly pretensions? I leave the reply to the historians.

And with these words the introduction is at an end. If I may quote Kierkegaard. When he quotes Poul Møller.

"Postscript for those readers who might perhaps suffer damage by reading the foreword: they can of course jump over it, and if they jump so far that they jump over the treatise too, that's all the same" (*SV*, XIII:x).

Before the gentle reader makes such a broad jump, I should like to be allowed to thank the University of Odense, in particular its Nordic Institute, under the direction of Mogens Brønstedt, for choosing to include this work in its literary series. I wish also to thank Professor Tage Kaarsted for advice, encouragement, and guidance in my work on this book, a part of which came into existence during my brief guest appearance at the University of Odense.

Henning Fenger

Paris
May 1976

1: KIERKEGAARD AS A
FALSIFIER OF HISTORY

A book, you know, has the remarkable property that it can be interpreted any way you please.

We all commit falsifications of history—consciously or unconsciously. Unconsciously, if we misremember or ourselves believe what we write down. Eight out of ten letters dated January plus a certain year are in fact from the next year. Kierkegaard often quotes incorrectly. The many misquotations from the repertoire of the Royal Theater can be blamed, perhaps, on the actors, but even when Kierkegaard has the text on his bookshelf he seldom bothers to verify quotations. His legendary memory is not precise about details. The first dislocations of memory in the *Papers* occur, indeed, in I.B.6, where he twice speaks of a "long passage of time," although it is quite well known that not even a month had passed between the appearance of Kierkegaard's polemic article "To Mr. Orla Lehmann" in *Flyveposten* of April 10, 1836, and the book dealer's delivery of *Humoristiske Intelligensblade* on May 4. If II.A.20 is correctly dated to 1837, then it means that his preoccupation with the motif of the master thief already lay "several years in the past," that is, in 1835.

The conscious falsifications of the journal are more difficult to date. Kierkegaard wrote in random notebooks—from the front and from the back—and on loose sheets of paper. Unlike many other people, he often reread what he had written down, put it in systematic order, and made comments on it in the margin, from the standpoint of later reading or later insight. Are his attempts to erase the traces of his youthful passion of 1837–38 for Bolette Rørdam (see chap. 6) from the period of his engagement

1

(1840–41) or from a later time, when Regine was to be made into one of world literature's great beloveds at all costs? The answer rests in the Assistens cemetery.

Of course, it is most reasonable to think that Kierkegaard began to arrange his facts only after the breaking-off of the engagement in October 1841 and the subsequent leap into a poet's existence. He played the role of the irresistible seducer even in the presence of his best friend, Emil Boesen. The report of December 14, 1841, concerning the Viennese singer Mademoiselle Schulze, who "has such a striking resemblance to a certain young girl, so deceptive that it genuinely affected me to see her in Elvira, of all roles," is just as touchingly naive as are its continuation and its postulate: "When my wild mood comes over me, then I'm almost tempted to approach her, and not exactly with the 'most honest intentions'. . . . It could be a little diversion, when I'm tired of speculation. . . . She lives near me. Well, let's leave it at that." Why not?

With the publication of *Either/Or*, in February 1843, Kierke-gaard definitively established himself as an aesthetician in at least three meanings of the word: (a) as a scholarly analyst of the cate-gories of the beautiful, (b) as a prose-poet in the most varied genres, and (c) as a nihilistic Epicurean. From then on we have rather little cause to depend upon his word; his contemporaries, at any event, took him seriously neither as an ethicist nor as a theologian.

Kierkegaard's Snares for Historical Research

It would be quite unfair to assert that Kierkegaard's contemporar-ies believed that he did not tell the truth, or could not. He simply put out snares for his contemporaries and, in the process, for pos-terity's historical researchers as well. His Socratic irony, his system of Chinese boxes, with editors and pseudonyms, and his indirect form of communication were confusing—then as now. How can we capture Kierkegaard in a statement which corresponds to the facts, or nail him to a standpoint for which he is willing to vouch?

His contemporaries had facts at their disposal which posterity can establish only by means of textual criticism. When Kierkegaard, on June 12, 1842, published an article in *Fædrelandet*, "Public Confession" (*SV*, XIII:397–406), and in it asked "the good people who are interested in me never to regard me as the author of something which does not bear my name" (p. 399), no one in Copenhagen's journalistic world regarded the statement as anything but a joke. To be sure, he had taken great pains with the publication of *Either/Or*, including the copy made by a hand not his own, the negotiations with publisher and printer, the planning of his publicity campaign for the book, and so forth. But it was precisely on this account that the editor of *Berlingske Tidende*, M. L. Nathanson (to whom he evidently promised to offer his next article), P. V. Christensen, who must be the "secretary" named in *SV*, XIII:396 (cf. *Pap*. IV.H.141), his friend H. P. Holst, during whose tenure as editor of *Ny Portefeuille* he published his article "Literary Quicksilver" (February 12, 1843), and his new friend and assistant, J. F. Giødwad, the editor of *Fædrelandet*, knew perfectly well what was going on. Many other members of the literary inner circle, for example the Heiberg coterie—Hertz, Hans Christian Andersen, and P. L. Møller—and Goldschmidt, Israel Levin, and the circle around the *Corsair*, were likewise in on the secret.

It becomes perfectly clear from H. P. Barfod's first volume of the *Posthumous Papers* (1869) that Kierkegaard meant to give *Either/Or* a running start in at least four publications of the day—*Forposten*, *Den Frisindede*, *Fædrelandet*, and *Berlingske Tidende*: there are letters, unmailed, to Giødwad and Nathanson, the editors of the last two. Kierkegaard's desire to assure himself that his name would be connected with that of Victor Eremita, the editor of *Either/Or*, was scarcely for financial reasons but rather resulted from an altogether pardonable author's pride. He wished to be regarded as the originator of the great work—a wholly superfluous wish, since no one else has ever been seriously suspected of having done the deed. The case was diametrically opposed, for example, to that of *Hverdagshistorierne* (*The Everyday Stories*), the authorship of which was ascribed to Heiberg, P. V. Jacobsen, Poul

Møller, and many others—but not, of course, to Fru Gyllembourg, who did write them.

With *Either/Or* Kierkegaard participated in the favorite literary game of the day, playing puss-in-the-corner with anonymity—see Heiberg and "Forf. til 'En Hverdagshistorie' " ("The Author of 'An Everyday Story' "), alias Fru Gyllembourg, see Saint-Aubain and Carl Bernhard, see Hertz and "Forfatteren til 'Gjengangerbreve' " ("The Author of 'Ghost Letters' "), see Overskou and "Forfatteren til Østergade og Vestergade' " ("The Author of 'Østergade and Vestergade' "). The examples are legion. In the 1840s, when Heiberg, Andersen, and Hertz were suddenly exposed to stiff head winds, they also had to conceal both their countenances and their names.

In his capacity as editor, Victor Eremita appeared in *Fædrelandet* on March 5, 1843, with the very ironic "Statement of Gratitude to Professor Heiberg." In the same place, on February 27, he had printed the little essay "Who Is the Author of *Either/Or?*" under the pseudonym "A. F. . . . . ."—a contribution in a conversational vein which, employing both external and internal criteria, makes fun of all the various possibilities concerning the book's authorship, calling attention en passant to the cost of publishing such a large volume.

In the meantime—that is, on March 1, 1843—Heiberg had published a little article in *Intelligensblade*, "Litterær Vintersæd" ("Literary Winter Crop"), where he chats for seven pages about the books published after New Year's—Winther's *Digtninger* (*Poetic Works*), Holst's *Ude og Hjemme* (*Abroad and at Home*), Thiele's *Folkesagn* (*Popular Legends*), mentioned only by name, and *Either/Or*, which—in four pages—is fobbed off with what today would be called a preliminary discussion. There was no question of Heiberg's writing a genuine review of the book's 800 pages—he had had little more than a week at his disposal. He gets around the problem carefully and deliberately by indicating what an imaginary reader, "one," can think about the book after a first hasty skimming. Heiberg's article, reprinted in the last chapter (omitted here) of the Danish edition of this book, is not as bad as Kierkegaard research would like to make it out to be, even though it clearly shows that Heiberg paid no mind to "The Diary of the Seducer" or to the essay about Scribe's *The First Love*. Heiberg was genuinely impressed by the work's second part, which he praises to the skies. However, three facts are decisive for Kierkegaard studies:

In the first place, "Copenhagen's cultural world" had expected an extensive review from Heiberg's hand, treating the book's basic elements. That is apparent from Signe Læssøe's letter of April 7, 1843, to Hans Christian Andersen.

Second, in his thank-you article to Heiberg of March 5, Kierkegaard is so ironic and sarcastic that he cannot for a moment have doubted that he was burning his bridges behind him, as far as the Heiberg circle was concerned. Thereby, in a single leap, Kierkegaard put himself in the camp of the young hotspurs—such as P. L. Møller, Goldschmidt, Carstensen, Brøchner, and Molbech junior—who had long been nipping at the heels of the very Heiberg whom Kierkegaard had particularly wished to please with *Either/Or*. After the "Winter Crop" article, Kierkegaard's *Papers* swarm with sallies against Heiberg, not all equally witty. The sluices had been opened.

In the third place, it becomes obvious that only now, for the first time, does the idea of connecting the aesthetic authorship with a religious one—that is, with the publication of a series of edifying discourses dedicated to the deceased hosier—arise in Kierkegaard's mind. That he was anxious to connect his name as the author of *Either/Or* with the religious production emerges from the article "A Little Explanation," in *Fædrelandet* of May 16, 1843, where he takes pains to point out that "the sermon which concludes a recently published work" (*SV*, XIII:416) is not identical with his sermon in the pastoral seminar of January 12, 1841. The article is signed S. Kierkegaard. *Two Edifying Discourses* also appeared on May 16, 1843. The chronological facts do not support Kierkegaard's later interpretations of the authorship as having been planned from the start in accordance with religious categories. Rather, the facts contradict these interpretations. For further information, see chapter 7.

Kierkegaard also assiduously veiled the story of the origin of *Either/Or* by means of his countless commentaries and explanations. In IV.B.59 (which appears to be an article, ready for the printer, with the title "Postscript to *Either/Or* of Victor Eremita") there is the statement, "For five years I concealed the manuscript which in *Either/Or* I permitted myself to present to the reading public." This note of March 1844 leads us back to the beginning of 1839 and naturally is intended to be taken only as a literary joke on Victor Eremita's part. But should his many efforts to get us to believe that the work was written in eleven months also be regarded as a legitimate kind of joking? In one copy of *Either/Or* there is the following notation (IV.A.215):

> Some people think that *Either/Or* is a collection of occasional papers which I have had lying in my desk. Bravo! As a matter of fact, it is the very opposite. The only thing this work lacks is a narrative, which I began but then decided to omit, just as Aladdin decided to leave one window out. It would have been called "unhappy love." It would form a contrasting picture to the Seducer.

Papers IV.A.221 is also of the same sort: "If, upon publishing *Either/Or*, I had not decided not to use anything old, I'd have found aphorisms, while going through my papers, which could have been put to splendid use." This memorandum of March 15, 1843, is illuminated by an aphorism, found on "a little piece of paper." In *The Point of View for My Work as an Author* Kierkegaard screws up his courage and carries his argument through to the end: "When I began *Either/Or* (of which, speaking *in parenthesi*, there literally existed only about a page, that is, a couple of diapsalmata, while the whole book was written in eleven months, and the second part first), I was *potentialiter* as deeply influenced by the religious element as I have ever been" (*SV*, XIII:526). Now, is one supposed to believe Kierkegaard's latter assertion about his religious seizure when one can prove that his former statement on the genesis of *Either/Or* is—shall we be kind and call it inexact?

Before offering our documentation, we can fairly ask, What does it actually mean—to *write* something? Anyone who is familiar with literary work knows that a thought, a sentence, a paragraph, a chapter, a treatise, or a whole book goes through every imaginable stage from the initial written sketch to the final proof. Kierkegaard is correct only if, by the phrase "was written," he is referring to his own ultimate version, before the secretary—"my little secretary Hr. Christensen" (alias Peter Vilhelm Christensen, born 1819, who became a candidate in theology in 1842 and died in 1863 while pastor in Tønning)—prepared the fair copy of the manuscript. But that the manuscript was prepared in the eleven months before the composition of the preface in November 1842 cannot be correct either—among other reasons, because P. V. Christensen could not have started on the fair copy (necessary to conceal Kierkegaard's own handwriting) until March at the very earliest and must have needed a very considerable time to copy a manuscript of such gigantic proportions.

Amusingly enough, P. A. Heiberg, Kierkegaard's faithful squire, is one of those who have demonstrated most clearly the incorrectness of the information Kierkegaard provides.

P. A. Heiberg's Account of the Genesis of Either/Or

In 1910, the year before the publication of the third volume of the *Papers* (treating the period from June 2, 1840, when Kierkegaard submitted his examination request to the theological faculty, until November 20, 1842, when he finished the preface to *Either/Or*), P. A. Heiberg issued a 36-page pamphlet called *Nogle Bidrag til Enten-Eller's Tilblivelseshistorie* (*Some Contributions to the Story of the Genesis of* Either/Or). Heiberg bases his work in particular on the Berlin letters to Emil Boesen. His analysis of the manuscript and the works preparatory to it is reproduced in the third volume of the *Papers*, first in the chronology on pp. xxiv–xxv and finally in the imposing appendix (pp. 319–27), where Heiberg distinguishes among sketch, versions (preliminary and final), and the printer's manuscript, and also adduces a special column for his own commentaries. By its thoroughness and its penetrating knowledge of Kierkegaard's literary effects, this impressive work commands our respect.

Heiberg's initial conclusions are that "The Equilibrium between the Aesthetic and the Ethical in the Formation of the Personality" was completed in Berlin circa December 7, 1841; that "The First Love" was written in the same city in December 1841 and January 1842; that the manuscript of "The Antique Tragic's Reflection in the Modern Tragic" was concluded in Berlin on January 30, 1842; and that "The Diary of the Seducer" was finished in Copenhagen on April 14. "The Direct Erotic Stages" was finished at the same place on June 12, 1842 (the day after the great cascade of words against the Danish Hegelians—"Public Confession"—had appeared in *Fædrelandet*), while "Shadow Sketch" is from July 25, 1842, more or less contemporaneous with the much briefer "The Unhappiest Man."

What is left of the mammoth book? Save for the preface of November 1842 and the many diapsalmata, there are "The Rotation of Crops," scarcely 20 pages long, among A.'s papers, and among B.'s, "The Aesthetic Validity of Marriage," 137 pages in length. There is also the sermon "Ultimatum," which B. sends to A. under the pretext of having received it from his friend, a pastor (*haud illaudabilis!*) on the Jutland heath, who "means to present it next year and is sure that he will get every peasant to understand it." It is the famous sermon concerning "The Edification Which Lies in the Thought That against God We Are Always Wrong." See page 27.

Certain loose ends remained for Heiberg, who—fair is fair— does not unqualifiedly support the eleven-month theory. On page 6 he offers the information that Kierkegaard himself refers to "The Rotation of Crops" as a "polemic which, as far as essentials are concerned, I have finished in the red book at home," and on page 7 he points out that, "for the sermon concerning the edification which lies in the thought that against God we are always wrong," there exists a first sketch from Kierkegaard's seminary time, 1840–41. At the same time, Heiberg calls attention to the connection between B.'s first large treatise, "The Aesthetic Validity of Marriage," and a manuscript, signed by B., "An Attempt to Save Marriage Aesthetically." This manuscript, which is older than B.'s opus written in Berlin, "Concerning the Equilibrium, etc.," must consequently have been written (in its definitive form?) in Copenhagen before the Berlin trip, which Kierkegaard undertook on October 25, 1841.

It emerges from the original Berlin letters—much more strongly, even, than in P. A. Heiberg's work—that *Either/Or* is a project sketched and begun in Copenhagen and to no small extent discussed with Emil Boesen, Kierkegaard's literary confidant—no doubt his only one. It is not clear when Giødwad enters the picture in earnest; many factors point to the period around 1840–41.

On December 14, 1841, Kierkegaard wrote to Emil Boesen: "I'm writing as though it were a matter of life and death. By this time I've written fourteen printed sheets. Thereby I have completed a part of a treatise which, *volente deo*, I shall submit to you. I have written nothing during the last week, I'm lying fallow and collecting myself, but I notice already that something's stirring within me." The treatise was not necessarily completed around December 7, but the most important part of "The Equilibrium between the Aesthetic and the Ethical, etc." must naturally have been done. The request for Heiberg's translation of Scribe's *The First Love* does not exclude the possibility that Kierkegaard had an earlier treatise at hand—compare P. A. Heiberg's observation (p. 10) that "the first two acts of the manuscript of 'The First Love' are not as even, smooth, and free of corrections as is the rest of the manuscript."

On January 1, 1842: "You ask what I'm working on. Answer: It would take too much time to tell you now—just this much: it is the further work on *Either/Or*." Thus *Either/Or* was already begun in Copenhagen, and Boesen knew what Kierkegaard was talking about. Compare Kierkegaard's letter of January 16, 1842:

I'm working hard. My body can't stand it. So that you can see that I'm my old self, I'll tell you that I've been writing again, a large part of a contribution—*Either/Or*; it hasn't gone very rapidly, but that results from its not being a question of expository writing but rather pure poetic production, something which quite specially requires one to be in the proper mood.

This contrast between "expository writing" and "pure poetic production" explains Kierkegaard's problem as he was working on *Either/Or*. He had various manuscripts with "developments," that is, with aesthetic studies in the Heibergian-Hegelian spirit, but now he wished to transform them or to use them for pure poetic production—very often in order to be able to include his father and Regine in the "scientific" analyses of the various aesthetic categories.

On February 6 to Boesen: "*Either/Or* is quite a splendid title after all; it's piquant and has a speculative meaning at one and the same time." He feels that he absolutely must come to Copenhagen with the manuscript. "Either I'll get through with *Either/Or* this spring or I never shall." And, on February 27, "I'm coming to Copenhagen to complete *Either/Or*. This is my pet thought, and I live in it." An elementary explanation for this ill-timed departure from Berlin was given to Boesen as early as January 16, 1842: "For the rest, I wish I had my papers with me; for I miss them too."

Thus, P. A. Heiberg may well be right, after all: Emil Boesen had been "accustomed to see my works come into being," and the "rolls" which Kierkegaard mentions are manuscripts, folded in the middle and rolled up, so that they could be put into a pocket. Kierkegaard was not a man to use briefcases, and Heiberg's conclusion appears to stand to reason: "that, *before the departure for Berlin*, 'pieces of work' existed, which S. K. took with him to Boesen, in the form of *manuscript rolls*, protruding, for example, from his coattail pocket, in order to read aloud from them to him."

Most likely it was B.'s first treatise on "The Aesthetic Validity of Marriage" which Heiberg, on the basis of the mention of "Magister Kierkegaard," dates between the thesis defense of September 29 and the departure for Berlin of October 25, 1841. Quite apart from the fact that the handsome and freshly acquired academic degree can be stuck in anywhere after September 29, there is something touching in this dating by Heiberg: we are asked to believe that Kierkegaard wrote about the way one saves marriage aesthetically during the last two months of his engagement, months of falseness and double-dealing (documented by means of the original letters to Regine). *Nota bene*, how "one" saves marriage—not how *he* would, for he had long ago decided not to stick his foot into that trap.

The Essay on The First Love

Heiberg touches upon something of essential importance when, on page 9, he mentions that Boesen doubtless had heard of (or seen) "a work," such as the one about *The First Love*, coming into existence. "I recall that you once sent me a little critique of Scribe's *The First Love*; it was written with an almost desperate enthusiasm" (*SV*, II:22)—lines which can be found again, word for word, in the preparatory manuscript to "The Aesthetic Validity of Marriage." Moreover, the essay and the treatise are "written on paper of an identical kind and size." At this point I shall not discuss the hypothesis which lies close at hand—that *Either/Or*'s B. is written with Emil Boesen in mind, that is, as Kierkegaard would have written if he had been able to wield the pen for Boesen; but there are undeniably various elements in the Berlin letters which support such an assumption.

At any event, the sketch for "The First Love" is an old item, perhaps the oldest of the layers in *Either/Or*. One can hardly give too much weight to the ironic introductory remarks. "This article should decidedly have been printed in a journal which Frederik Unsmann had decided to publish at decided times. Alas, what are all the decisions of man?" This remark cannot possibly refer to Heiberg's *Flyveposten*, whose interim editions had no certain dates of publication at all; and the treatise simply did not suit Heiberg's "speculative journal," *Perseus*. Can it refer to P. F. Barfod and P. L. Møller's *Nordisk Ugeskrift*, nos. 1–26, of 1837? In such a case, one has an explanation for an acquaintanceship between Kierkegaard and P. L. Møller as early as the 1830s. Or can it refer to *Søndagsbladet*, which H. P. Holst edited from January through March 1835?

Just the same, it is baffling—not to say suspicious-looking—that Kierkegaard writes, "Now on the other hand, since I have seen it produced again and again, on other stages too [he must refer to Berlin], only now do I grow genuinely thankful toward our stage artists" (*SV*, I:249), those for whose sake he would like to take a foreigner to the theater in order to show him our stage. But who precisely is it that Kierkegaard would like to show to that guest of his?

P. J. Frydendahl, born in 1766, died on February 20, 1836, after having trod the boards for the last time on October 2, 1835, in Holberg's *Barselstue* (*Lying-In Room*); he had acted the role of iron-founder Dervière in Scribe's play for the last time on March 5, 1835. The play was removed from the repertoire for almost a year, after which C. Foersom took up Frydendahl's old part on February 24, 1836. At the same time the part of the manly Rinville was passed along from Gottlob Stage to W. Holst, whom Kierkegaard does not bring up in any connection. In addition, Fru Heiberg is mentioned as Emmeline, but she played that role for the last time on December 18, 1837, and then the piece was allowed to rest until January 3, 1839, when Henriette Andersen took over Emmeline's part, with Fru Heiberg substituting for her on only one occasion, November 2, 1839. Only the indefatigable Phister, whom Kierkegaard also praises to the skies, continued to play Charles until May 29, 1849, when the play was removed from the repertoire for five seasons. Kierkegaard's concluding apotheosis in *Either/Or*, in February 1843, refers in other words to the play's total of twenty-five performances, up to and including that of March 5, 1835.

After that date, the play—starting with its revival on February 24, 1836—was performed a total of twenty-nine times, with a wholly new cast (save for Phister), up to November 1842, when the preface to *Either/Or* was finished. One does not require great mental powers to guess that, in Berlin, Kierkegaard did some embroidery upon an old treatise, an *Urform* of "The First Love." And one does not need to bring a great stylistic sense of language to bear, either, in order to conjecture that the original treatise was almost identical with the essay's introduction, and that it closed with a quotation, by Poul Møller, from his "splendid review of *The Extremes*: herewith the introduction is at an end" (*SV*, I:247). Since this review is mentioned in I.C. 70 under the date "February 1836," and since Poul Møller's review—which is a mighty piece of homage to the grand old lady of the house of Heiberg, Fru Gyllembourg—appeared in the *Maanedsskrift for Litteratur*'s February issue of 1836 (p. 135), one does not need textual-critical genius to see that it was the revival of the play on February 24, 1836, with Foersom replacing the lately deceased Frydendahl, which provided the impetus for Kierkegaard's first article—compare *The Crisis and a Crisis in the Life of an Actress* (1848), again a case where a revival—of *Romeo and Juliet*—enticed Kierkegaard into writing. Whatever performances of *The First Love* he had seen since 1835, partly in Copenhagen with another Danish cast and later on with a French troupe of actors, partly in Berlin—all these performances could not dim the first and unforgettable impression, something which recalls the excitement he felt when he saw *Don Juan* for the first time at the Royal Theater.

The same stylistic deposits from the 1830s can be perceived in the treatise about "The Direct Erotic Stages or the Musical-Erotic," where, after the first enamored and witty pages in the "Insignificant Introduction" (*SV*, I:42), one hears Kierkegaard shift gears—that is, he takes out the old treatise: dry, creaking, overornamented, and aesthetically scientific:

That which this investigation has taken as its primary task is to show the meaning of the musical-erotic, and toward that end once again to point out the various stages which, as they have that in common, that they are all directly erotic, at the same time agree in the fact that they are all essentially musical.

Here reference is made to Heinrich Steffens's *Caricaturen des Heiligsten*, vols. I–II (1819), which Kierkegaard's book dealer had delivered to him on January 13, 1836—a book whose thoughts on music still absorb him on October 9, 1836 (I.A. 260). In addition, attention should be paid to the *Irische Elfenmärchen* of the Brothers Grimm (1826), which occupied him in September and October 1837 (II.A.135 and 169), thus at a time when he long since had been making extensive sketches, following Heiberg's aesthetic scheme (I.C.125), about the three Mozartean figures: the page in *The Marriage of Figaro*, Papageno in *The Magic Flute*, and Don Juan. The two latter roles were done by Cetti, and it is the performance of *The Magic Flute* on January 26, 1837, which inspired the entry in his papers. It is reasonable to believe that in 1837 Kierkegaard was working on an aesthetic treatise for Heiberg's *Perseus* and that he was left with it on his hands (as he was with his Faust treatise, when Martensen got ahead of him) and with his review of Andersen's *Kun en Spillemand* (*Only a Musician*). He got the "review" published as an independent book, but a great part of the remaining material found its way into *Either/Or*.

Whether one says, or does not say, that this book *was* written in 1841–42 will remain a matter of personal taste. We do not know for sure how much Kierkegaard had saved of the papers which he complained to Emil Boesen that he had left in Copenhagen. Many of the pages in "The Antique Tragic's Reflection in the Modern Tragic" bear conceptual and stylistic traces of older sketches and projects. What is new in *Either/Or*, before all else, is the personal element, the many recastings of the relationship to his father and to Regine. Any number of times, P. A. Heiberg employs a metaphor which seems to be particularly clumsy, coming from the pen of a researcher as far removed from the natural sciences as he was—the picture of the fertilized egg in its various stages of development. It must suffice simply to establish that *Either/Or* is a résumé of ten years of contemplations, thoughts, ideas, drafts, sketches, and attempts at writing. It is precisely for this reason that it provides a gateway into the central aesthetic-philosophical oeuvre of 1843–46, the era of the great works.

Concerning the Concept of Irony in Søren Kierkegaard

Among the many land mines which Kierkegaard planted for scholarship, the ironic ones are by no means the least dangerous. There
is a multitude of examples, some wittier than others, beginning
with Kierkegaard's very school days. But it is useful to keep firmly
in mind what the bizarre but by no means unironic Israel Levin
(1810–83)—man of letters, philologist, editor, complainer, booz-
er, and misogynist (and a good deal more)—says in his dictated
"Remarks concerning S. Kierkegaard 1858 and 1869." They have
always been a thorn in the flesh of Kierkegaard fanatics, for, as
Kierkegaard's secretary and, for a time, daily companion, Levin
had an intimate knowledge of his protector, observing him with a
malicious eye for painful details. (Levin exhibited this talent for
ironic and self-ironic surrender of secrets in the strange diary
which, using the third person, he kept concerning his curiously
triangular honeymoon journey to Fanø in August and September
1865, an account known only in an excerpt in *Weekendavisen* of
July 18, 1975.)

> Whoever wishes to treat S. K.'s life should take care not to get
> burned, full as it is of contrasts, difficult as it is to get to the
> bottom of his character. He often refers to twofold reflection;
> all his speech was more than sevenfold reflection. He strug-
> gled to achieve clarity concerning himself, but he was pur-
> sued by every possible mood and was himself such a person
> of moods that he often made untrue statements, persuading
> himself that he spoke the truth. . . . Generally, he lived in a
> world of imagination and empty reflections which seized up-
> on everything and transformed it in every possible way, exam-
> ining it from all sides and reflecting upon it. He never
> understood himself, in his intellectual activity he sought
> nourishment for his infinite yearning. The idea itself was
> enough for him, he "imagined himself into" every sort of exis-
> tence. . . . That is why he sought release in reveries and poetic
> images, and, with his gift for language and his demonic im-

agination, the effect he achieved was astonishing. . . . His imagination was so vital that it seemed he saw pictures before
his very eyes. It was as though he lived in a world of the spirit,
and with a remarkable impropriety and eccentricity he could
depict the most frightful things in a degree of vividness which
was terrifying. . . . Everything about him consisted of inward
emotions. His talk about a wild bachelor's life, about youthful
sins, and so on can refer only to "sinning in the thought."

Levin's remarks are reproduced here in excerpts from Steen Johansen's *Erindringer om Søren Kierkegaard (Recollections of Søren
Kierkegaard*, 1955, pp. 33–38), a book which contains everything
of Levin's preserved in the Kierkegaard archive, together with a
smaller piece by Levin otherwise to be found only in P. A.
Heiberg's *Bidrag til et psykologisk Billede af Søren Kierkegaard i
hans Barndom og Ungdom (Contributions to a Psychological Portrait of Søren Kierkegaard in His Childhood and Youth*, 1895), perhaps *the* work which, despite its merits, was the first to shove
Kierkegaard research down a sidetrack. Are several of Levin's remarks missing? Were they removed by P. A. Heiberg, in whose
eyes Levin was the worst desecrator of his idol? And who corrected
the financial statements?

Levin's assertion that it was impossible to figure Kierkegaard
out agrees with the judgment of other contemporaries. They simply did not know what to make of him. One can sense their reaction in the thank-you letters from Danish poets to whom he had
sent the second edition of *Either/Or* in 1849 with subtly differenti-
ated dedications. H. C. Andersen, who was anything but naive,
could not conceal his joy at having been given the book: "I was
very much surprised, as you well can believe; I didn't at all think
that you had friendly thoughts about me, and now I see that you
do, after all. God bless you for it. Thank you! Thank you!" One
would like to have seen Kierkegaard's face when he received this
honest letter from the hunted animal par excellence of Danish
literature, whom he himself, in *From the Papers of One Still Living*,
had pursued eleven years earlier, with such unrefined means.

Paludan-Müller and Hauch are much more cunning and reserved in their expressions of gratitude.

Certainly, Heiberg was the one who saw through Kierkegaard earliest of all and repaid him—not only with the same coin but with passivity and an unshakable, impeccable politeness. After his "Statement of Gratitude to Professor Heiberg" on March 5, 1843, Kierkegaard did *not* receive the great review he had hoped for; unlike H. P. Holst and Rasmus Nielsen, he did not get to play a role in *Intelligensblade*; and he was no longer invited to the Heiberg home, which from 1844 on was located once and for all in Søkvæsthuset (that handsome classical building on Christianshavn, in which the Heiberg Society is now located). And, finally, he did not succeed—something which plainly irritated him much more than anything else—in getting involved in a polemic with Heiberg after having made a direct attack by means of his sprightly and malicious book, *Prefaces* (1844). In other words, like his honored enemy, P. L. Møller, he was put in his place by Heiberg as one of those writers with whom one simply does not get involved. Heiberg was fully aware of what he was doing as, properly and elegantly, he maintained a distance between Kierkegaard and himself. The master of irony, however, scarcely understood it—he did not realize that he could be outdone at his own game.

Kierkegaard replied with quite primitive forms of irony, partly by playing people off against one another, partly by doing deeds which were the very opposite of what he said. He had made this a practice since his school days. The episode which Brøchner reports concerning Kierkegaard's visit in Sæding, where he was handsomely entertained as the son of the parish's benefactor and finally was to be saluted with a speech of thanks by the parish clerk, ended with his pinching the manuscript of the clerk's speech before the eyes of the flabbergasted schoolchildren. The ironic joke is a piece of student's impudence, or, truth to tell, sheer crudity. His offer of 1840 (III.B.1) to H. C. Andersen to finance the printing of *En Comoedie i det Grønne (A Comedy in the Open)* was of course meant as irony; fortunately, it was not printed until after his death. Beyond question, it was an act of boundless tactlessness toward the impoverished author—Andersen—onto whom he had forced himself. His behavior is wittier when, the next year, he concludes *Concerning the Concept of Irony* with a reference to Martensen's extravagantly flattering review of Heiberg's *Nye Digte (New Poems)* in *Fædrelandet* of January 1841—a reference meant, he said, for the person who "would like to have material for reflection" (*SV*, XIII:393). The irony was not directed at Heiberg but at Martensen, and *he*, of course, could speak for himself.

After his open break with Heiberg, Kierkegaard made a system out of his ironic banter. He did not neglect a single opportunity to poke fun at Dr. Hjortespring and his Hegelian conversion on April Fool's Day, and he made countless jabs at those builders of systems whose works appeared in a "nitid" binding—"nitid" became the catch phrase for referring to Heiberg, just as "matchless" always alluded to Grundtvig. At the same time he praised Fru Gyllembourg to the skies in "A Literary Review" of 1846, just as, in 1848, he wrote with masterful brilliance about Fru Heiberg's performance as Juliet. The house of Heiberg thanked him with a terribly correct sort of courtesy and "warmth," but none of its members gave much attention to these Kierkegaardian intrigues. The situation was not improved by the fact that, both in the *Postscript* and in private, Kierkegaard paid the humblest sort of respects to those deadly enemies of the Heibergs, the famous stage couple Anna and N. P. Nielsen.

All of Kierkegaard's somersaults, and his attempts to play off the members of the Heiberg family against one another and against their clerical friends, Mynster, Paulli, Tryde, and Martensen, failed miserably, with the result that he was the one to be caught in irony's spotlight. For when the master of irony fell prey to the *Corsair*, with his trouser legs of unequal length, one finds him complaining in his diaries about the fact that "distinguished and respected people" did not come to his defense against the literary cads who wrote for the *Corsair*, and against the rabble which now, ironically enough, had suddenly become ironic.

Kierkegaard's Rationalizations-after-the-fact and His Use of Pseudonyms

The importance of the episode with the *Corsair*—a turning point in Kierkegaard's life—cannot be exaggerated. He himself scarcely understood that it turned his relationship to the past upside down. He preferred to live backward, as it were, and to write either about those who were dead, like Poul Møller or his father, or about those who at any event were in no position to reply to him, such as Regine, who had too much tact to make a retort. He had "memorialized" Poul Møller by means of his literary assassination of Andersen in 1838, and by the dedication to *The Concept of Dread* in 1844, richly ornamented with "lion's feet and solderings," as the coppersmith says about the samovar in Hostrup's comedy. He had mythologized his father in *De omnibus dubitandum est*, which however appeared only in the second volume of Barfod's edition in 1872; but, starting in 1843, he had erected the pedestal for the monument to his father with his series of *Edifying Discourses*. He had made Regine Olsen, soon to be a Schlegel, world famous in Copenhagen with his writings of 1843–45, in particular *Either/Or* and " 'Guilty?'/'Not Guilty?' " Now there appeared, with an interval of a few days, the *Postscript*—in which Kierkegaard finally admits the paternity of the pseudonymous writings—and P. L. Møller's yearbook *Gæa*, of which the chief essay, *A Visit in Sorø*, submits the same writings to a penetrating, well-informed, and critical treatment. An enormous literary production by a brilliant poet and thinker, Kierkegaard, is evaluated here by the most exciting critical power of the age. Just then, Heiberg had more than enough to do with battles on external and internal fronts; intellectually speaking, with his unshaken Hegelian-Goethean position, he was at a great remove from Kierkegaard.

At this moment it was only logical that Kierkegaard—who was busily calling down still more of the *Corsair*'s mockery upon his head—should turn toward the past. In any event, he succeeded with surprising speed in persuading himself that he was making a voluntary sacrifice in this case, and that the persecution conducted by the *Corsair* (with 4,000 copies, it was Copenhagen's largest paper) was the logical capstone of a spiritual development. Interpretations and rationalizations-after-the-fact came swarming forth, and industriously employing the Procrustean principle, Kierkegaard now discovered, everywhere, a guidance of his fate and literary activities by Providence itself. He did not have the foggiest notion that H. C. Andersen, whom he held in such little esteem, was simultaneously doing the same thing—in a more talented way—with his *Märchen meines Lebens* (1847), and then with *Mit Livs Eventyr*, 1855 *(The Fairy Tale of My Life)*: see Topsøe-Jensen's dissertation of 1940.

This more—or, indeed, less—voluntary stage of martyrdom, of which Kierkegaad made a religious virtue, caused him to ponder long and persistently about the past. The bygone world became the raw material with which he fed the enormous dialectic machine of his journals. In its turn, the machine ground the material finer and finer. A great deal of effort lay behind the production of the riddles which the future was not meant to be able to solve, and behind the interpretations which it was intended to accept. One is permitted to believe that a large mill often grinds out nothing at all, that molehills are made into mountains, and that mountains once again give birth to ridiculous mice; but, as a literary historian, one must entertain a deep and fundamental distrust of the numerous volumes of the journal after 1846. Unhappily, it is precisely from this arsenal that Kierkegaard research has fetched so much of its material; indeed, the editors of the *Papers* have even used information from this source—for example, reports about the phases of the story of the engagement—as criteria for establishing dates. See, for example, in the third volume the altogether grotesque arrangement of the entries from the journey to Jutland in the summer of 1840 (compare below, p. 163). While Andersen prepared his apotheosis like a true genius, Kierkegaard did not come off nearly as well. Of course, he managed to twist Kierkegaard research until it became dislocated, but the effort provided him with a retinue which he was not always terribly interested in acquiring: among the retinue's members were the ecclesiastical theologians.

The Pseudonyms

It is an accepted tenet of Kierkegaard scholarship that scholars must be required to make up their minds about the pseudonyms, the pseudonyms' relations to one another, and their connection to Kierkegaard himself. Lamentably, I cannot take part in this sport, which has filled hundreds of pages in books about Kierkegaard all over the world. In my view the pseudonyms are roles, and Kierkegaard an author who was also an actor. He acted the parts of his pseudonyms even as he wrote them down, but obviously he was fonder of some than of others. One has to be a Kierkegaard surgeon in order to determine how much of Kierkegaard there is in the various pseudonyms, and when, and how long. There is no answer key for the great men of world drama. How much Shakespeare is there in Richard III, Hamlet, and Lear, how much Molière in Alceste and Argan, how much Ibsen in Brand and Dr. Stockmann? One wonders if the poet himself knew.

Who dares deny that Kierkegaard's relationship to the theater is lifelong, personal, passionate, existential? He spent most of his life's evenings in the Royal Theater, and he was more frequently in the theater than in the church. No one is the same in all circumstances, but Kierkegaard carried the normal process of self-adaptation to extremes. He deliberately—and splendidly—acted roles in the presence of his fellow men, and he had difficulty in determining whether he was in the land of reality or of illusion. What are the autobiographical writings save a confession of a lifelong piece of playacting in the service of a higher cause? Has anyone in world literature done it better than he? If so, it was Chateaubriand and Byron, his predecessors and brothers in conspiracy.

From the very outset the journal teems with projects for plays, sketches for dramatic scenes and characters, and experiments with lines of dialogue. The opera Don Juan and the masterful performances in The First Love had the effect of a religious awakening upon the hosier's son, in whose home theater and dance were worldliness and vanity and sin. Remarkably, he appears not to have been moved at all by the art of the ballet, although he was a contemporary of Bournonville (mentioned by the journals only en passant) and of Denmark's great prima ballerina, Lucile Grahn, who is left in silence.

These theatrical interests must have impelled Kierkegaard to playact in his home at an early age. Here, theatrical performances were carried out in a different way, if one is to believe *De omnibus dubitandum est*, with its accounts of the practice sessions for defending a dissertation, where the father and the two sons often exchanged roles—that is, defended one another's standpoints. After Kierkegaard, upon his father's death, had "had to take up his father's roles" (Brøchner), he could no longer hold the old man off with empty chatter but was forced to take his theological examination.

If Hjalmar Helweg is correct with his theory about the outbreak of the manic-depressive psychosis in the middle of the 1830s, Kierkegaard also playacted outside the home. At the literary cafés and in the student association he acted the role of the merry son of nature, who nonetheless brooded over a melancholy black as night. It was one of the literary attitudes of Romanticism—as were the doubter and the seducer. For many years Faust and Don Juan were Kierkegaard's favorite figures of literature and drama. When in the spring of 1838 his father confided those terrible youthful sins to him, he was also drawn toward Ahasverus and Hamlet. "The truth of the presentiment is verified, that is why Hamlet is so tragic" is what it says in II.A.584, no doubt from 1837. Villads Christensen and Johannes Sløk in particular have had an eye for Shakespeare's enormous importance for Kierkegaard.

Hamlet's role was undeniably tailor-made for Kierkegaard. The curse resting on the family, the father's sins of the flesh, the torments of turning pale thought into action, the melancholy bordering on madness behind a mask of wit—nothing was missing. Not even a Horatio-Boesen and an Ophelia with the poetic family name of Olsen. She is the young, innocent thing whose love the fate of his family keeps him from reciprocating. A father fixation and a father's sin stood in his way. "But break my heart, for I must hold my tongue."

Then, when he discovered what it was he had become involved in: engagement, marriage, even—possibly—children and an official position, he changed, panic-stricken, to villain's roles. Regine would be forced to make the break which he was neither man nor gentleman enough to arrange in a decent way. In the autumn of 1841, in Copenhagen, he acted the role of a cynic in the best Scribe style, without thereby being able to convince the queen of his heart, who was much too healthy and natural not to see through his pretended indifference and his vague loftier considerations. Kierkegaard's later attempt at "getting himself a bad reputation" with respect to his former beloved—in the church, in the city, on the sidewalks, or by means of books, letters, and wills—is amateur theater. The dramatist Kierkegaard was not capable of finishing his play so that the curtain could go down. The actor of the same name spoiled his exit, a sin our Lord is not likely to forgive.

The Dramatic Irony

The dissertation of 1841 dedicates a thorough analysis to "executive, or, as it could also be called, dramatic irony" (*SV*, XIII:329). It is not sufficient to dissemble: the subject must enjoy this irony, which has only itself as a target. Kierkegaard practiced it to excess and thereby acquired an outlet for his indefatigable urge to act. The scenery from his stage still stands on Graabrødretorv, in Magstræde, and on the ramparts beside The Citadel. It was here he established a rapport with his fellow actors (who were wholly strange to him, and quite unsuspecting) by means of that unforgettable sidelong glance of his. He staged the *Corsair* squabble himself through his numerous encounters on the street, reported by Goldschmidt, but he never dreamed that his mise en scène would force him to undertake a role he did not desire, as a religious Erasmus Montanus.

Either/Or can be regarded as the logical result of the playacting of his early years. Now he abandoned himself to literature. Now he spoke behind masks and with many tongues: Victor Eremita, the aesthete A., Johannes the Seducer, the likewise-dead and most unfortunate man, the grandiosely tiresome ethicist B.—through all these roles Kierkegaard (at a safe distance from real life) could give that brilliant role which was, for him, the role of roles, as the great genius in the market town of Copenhagen. Fair is fair: he *was* his role. It was a matchless, a blinding performance, which continues to make posterity catch its breath.

H. C. Andersen improvised and acted his fairy tales. Kierkegaard let the pseudonyms multiply. That allowed him the chance both to write the play and to act it. The pseudonyms sprang out of a poetic spirit with a passionate inclination toward leading astray, and doubling oneself, and concealment. With some justice, Brandes called him "a Protestant Jesuit, who was his own pope" (1877, p. 16). Sadly enough, Kierkegaard's public was quite limited in the years 1843–45, when he gave that series of performances which is unique in world literature. He did not act for mighty Europe itself but for that little, choice inner circle of the Heibergians, of whose theatrical passion he himself was an all too willing sacrifice. When he did not feel satisfied with the applause he got for his performances up to and including the *Postscript*, he changed to other and somewhat more elderly roles—the Socratic peripatetic who instructed his sole disciple in the wisdom of life, the reverent author of edifying tracts, the preacher who seldom appeared in his pulpit, the favorite victim of the *Corsair*, the genius who was not understood and who chose not to cast his pearls before swine, the sinner doing atonement, the pious hermit—and many other roles, all of which are both true and acted.

At last, everything was reduced to a masterly coup, the role of the martyr who stormed the churches and shook a whole nation. Even unto four and five generations after his death. I understand those humanists who, like Brandes and Høffding, excused themselves from Kierkegaard's service after having been blooded by his sword in their youth. They are perhaps not the least among his disciples. No one can accuse Kierkegaard of having ruined his last exit. It was worthy of a Shakespeare, a Pascal.

This writing of literature with his own life is Kierkegaard's true greatness. He is related in the spirit to such supreme dramatists as Shakespeare, Molière, and Strindberg, and—on a lower level—to Pirandello and Anouilh. It goes for them all that, if the world is but a stage, then this stage is truer, more authentic, than real life. Every individual can choose for himself, deciding whether he wants to play the hero or the fool or the commentator standing outside the action. Kierkegaard early distinguished between writing and letting oneself be written: "It is one thing to write oneself, another to let oneself be written. The Christian lets himself be written, and in this respect a simple Christian leads a far more poetic life than many an extremely gifted mind" (the dissertation of 1841, SV, XIII:352). In the treatise on "The Aesthetic Validity of Marriage," presumably written about the same time, there is a depiction of how the very peak of the aesthetic experience is reached when the actor becomes one with his role:

Here I am arrived at the peak of the aesthetic. And in truth, he who has humility and courage enough to let himself be aesthetically transfigured, he who feels himself to be an actor in the play the deity is writing, where the poet and the prompter are not separate persons, where the individual, like the practiced actor who has become one with his character and his lines, is not disturbed by the prompter but feels that whatever is whispered to him is what he himself wishes to say, so that it almost becomes doubtful whether he puts words in the prompter's mouth or the prompter in his, he who in the deepest sense feels himself to write and to be written, who in the moment when he feels himself writing has the line's original pathos, and in the moment when he feels himself written has the erotic ear which captures every sound—he and only he has reached the peak of aesthetics. [SV, II:124]

Only someone for whom the boundary between illusion and reality has been erased can speak thus: an actor-poet, who writes his own role, composes the whole army of pseudonyms with which he has kept other people at a distance from his soul, his passions, his melancholy, his thorn in the flesh, his feeling of loneliness—in brief, everything which elicits that sympathy from which Kierkegaard very much wished to be excused. For, after all, it is not out of pride that Kierkegaard writes of a god who can afford him worthy professional company, acting with and against him, on the stage of life:

> But world history is the royal stage for God, where He—not accidentally but essentially—is the only observer, because He is the only one who can be that. The entrance to this theater does not stand open for any spirit now existing. If he wishes to persuade himself that he is an observer there, then he merely forgets that he himself, after all, is to be an actor on the little stage, leaving it up to that royal observer and poet how *He* wishes to use him in the royal drama, the *Drama Dramatum*. [*SV*, VII:130]

Here the actor and poet of genius speaks with the right his "extraordinary powers" gave him. Only a blockhead can be of the frivolous opinion that this is the truth concerning Kierkegaard as a personality, an aesthetician, and a believer. But even a crumb of "the truth" is worth being taken, of course, from the great master's banquet table.

The Official Interpretations of Kierkegaard's Work as an Author

After all this, it ought to be clear what source value is properly ascribed to Kierkegaard's two autobiographical works, the little pamphlet *Concerning My Work as an Author*, of 1851, and the far more pretentious *The Point of View for My Work as an Author: A Direct Communication, Report to History*, published in 1859 by P. C. Kierkegaard and included in the Collected Works' thirteenth volume, of 1906, where it fills almost a hundred pages. The manuscript has not been preserved, so one can only hope the good bishop has printed the whole of the material. The two works have the same thesis, the official interpretation of the literary production, already stated in 1851 under Kierkegaard's own name:

> The movement which the work as an author describes is: *from* "the poet"—from the aesthetic, from the "philosopher"—from the speculative *to* the suggestion of the most sincere decision for that which is Christian: *from* the *pseudonymous* "Either/Or" *through* the *Concluding Postscript*, with *my name as editor*, to *Discourses concerning Communion on Friday*, of which two were held in Our Lady's Church. This movement is accomplished or described *uno tenore*, in a single breath, if I may say so, so that my work as an author, seen *as a whole*, is religious from start to finish, something which everyone who can see, if he will but see, also must see. [*SV*, XIII:494–95]

The thesis that the literary production is religious from start to finish has been accepted by large segments of Kierkegaard scholarship without reservations and has been performed in every imaginable key and variation. Kierkegaard builds *his* thesis upon three assertions. The first is that the religious element was present from the outset, since the *Two Edifying Discourses*, of May 1843, are contemporaneous with *Either/Or*. The second is that every pseudonymous work up to the *Postscript* was accompanied by *Edifying Discourses*. The third is that the religious production after the *Postscript* was accompanied by the aesthetic treatise concerning *The Crisis and a Crisis in the Life of an Actress* (1848):

> The glimpse of the *Two Edifying Discourses* at the outset meant that *it* was what should really come forth, what should really be arrived at; the glimpse of the little aesthetic article at the end meant, with its faint reflection, that it had come to the surface of consciousness that the aesthetic, from the start, was that which should be left behind, that from which one should go away. [*SV*, XIII:497]

One would certainly like to know what such well-oriented contemporaries as Mynster, Sibbern, Fru Gyllembourg, the Heibergs,
Martensen, Rasmus Nielsen, Brøchner, Goldschmidt, P. L. Møller,
and Frederik Dreier, not to mention such *dii minori* as Lind, Ostermann, Levin, and Boesen, thought when they read this passage.
It is impossible for them to have forgotten what Kierkegaard so
elegantly omits—the campaign against the National Liberals in
the student association and *Flyveposten*, the attack upon H. C. Andersen from ambush, the official theological examination, the dissertation, and the tragicomical story of the engagement—all
pieces which do not easily fit into the puzzle. One wonders if, in
1859, any of the initiates believed that P. L. Møller's notorious article in *Gæa* of December 1845 was the cause for Kierkegaard's having made "in the most appropriate place for such an undertaking,
in an article in a journal, the greatest possible effort to set out in
the direction of the public; and thereby the decisive religious production was begun" (*SV*, XIII:498)? They could not have saved
their lives on the scaffold if the condition for their pardon was a
statement to this effect. On the other hand, such contemporaries
as Brøchner and Holst quite clearly perceived how much it meant
that Kierkegaard was never completely accepted by Heiberg, and
that he wished to compete with him as an aesthetician just on that
account.

Autobiography number one says, with laudable candor, "This is
the way I understand *the whole matter now*; from the beginning, I
was not able to survey what after all has been my whole development" (*SV*, XIII:500). This official interpretation of 1851 raises two
problems at the outset. If Kierkegaard, with *Either/Or*, had wished
to argue for the religious element from the very beginning of his
literary production, why did this fact not emerge from the "Ultimatum," the concluding sermon? Why did he wait until May 1843
with the *Two Edifying Discourses* in memory of the hosier? The
only consistent thing would have been to publish them simultaneously with *Either/Or*.

If, in the same way, Kierkegaard had put his philosophical-aes-
thetic authorship behind him with the *Postscript* in December

1845, why then does he keep silent about the substantial piece of literary writing, *A Literary Review: Two Ages*, of March 1846, and instead put emphasis on the four newspaper articles about Fru Heiberg's performance as Juliet? There are no subtle, religious, authorial-compositional motives hidden here. Kierkegaard could simply not get rid of his Heiberg complex, *he*—not P. L. Møller— was the unhappy lover of the Heiberg dynasty. He felt that, intellectually and socially, he should belong to the circle, and then "one" took the liberty of looking askance at him for his Byzantine style, for his lack of humanism and tact and intellectual humility, for his many cunning, ironic, and unintentionally comical intrigues. Seen from the vantage point of Søkvaesthuset, the son of the hosier was an eccentric pariah who lacked the culture of the heart. Wasn't he a parvenu?

When *The Point of View for My Work as an Author* appeared in 1859, Mynster and Fru Gyllembourg were dead, and P. L. Møller had been sent off to a kind of Parisian exile—to a certain extent, thanks to our hero. The book contained various palpable inaccuracies, but it is especially amusing in its blend of a desire for honesty and its naive self-persuasion. In the third chapter Kierkegaard makes a touching interpretation of "The Part of Providence in My Work as an Author":

> For that I have needed (and how I have constantly needed!) day by day, year by year, the aid of God—to be reminded of it, to be able to announce it punctually, I do not need the help of memory or recollection, or journals and diaries, or the comparing of these with one another; in this very moment I live through it once more in its vividness, in its immediacy. What has my pen not been able to set forth, when it was a question of boldness, enthusiasm, passion almost to the boundary line of madness? [*SV*, XIII:557–58]

Few can employ such big words with greater justification than Kierkegaard did, but they do not make him into any sort of historical witness of the truth; in his whole intellectual type he was as far removed from the historical standpoint as can be imagined. It is his poet's passion which allows a voice to dictate every word he is to write: "For even though it was true that perhaps one glowing expression or another escaped me, the production itself is of a different kind, not of the passion of a thinker or a poet, but of the fear of God, and for me it is an act of worship" (*SV*, XIII:558–59). These are pure words, admirably honest. He speaks of "times when I could not make myself understandable to myself"; he confesses, as "a quite simple human being," that he followed "the urgings of my natural destiny"; and he realizes that

> this, which for me had thus had a purely personal meaning up to the boundary of the accidental, that this then proved itself to have quite another, a pure and ideal meaning, when afterward it was seen as a part of my authorship; that much, which I have done in a purely personal way, that it, strangely enough, was precisely what I should do *qua* author. [*SV*, XIII:561]

In the presence of such an honest confession, how is one to evaluate "Providence," with a pen in its hand, from the standpoint of pure source criticism?

It is less important, after all, that Kierkegaard declares on p. 570 that in a certain sense it was simply not "my intention to become a religious author," but that after he had exhausted his poetic vein he meant to go out to the country as a pastor. What is more important is his declaration, on p. 606, that he has "had too much fantasy and [is] too much of a poet to dare to be called a witness of the truth in a stricter sense," that he is someone who, "far removed from having had a view of the whole matter from the beginning, has learned only step by step to understand himself in having made the right choice."

The Point of View for My Work as an Author, which can readily be regarded as the great solitary's will and testament, ends in the statement that he, Kierkegaard, has been "too much the poet to be a true witness of the truth" (*SV*, XIII:606–07).

Even though theologians and historians use the designation "witness of the truth" in widely disparate meanings, there is perhaps, after all, the possibility of meeting on some common ground: a healthy skepticism toward Kierkegaard's words. It will not detract from him in the slightest. He is and remains one of the world's great Christian *poets*.

That is why Kierkegaard has every right to make literature out of his life. Or to make literature with his life. Or to hold his existence literarily in his hand. Or to let himself be made into literature by Providence or God.

It is neither Kierkegaard's fault nor his responsibility if the learned men, the scribes, docents male and female, have taken him at his word. It is these people who are called to account in this book.

In the presence of acts which can be verified. In the presence of source material of an extremely persuasive nature. And, not least, in the presence of the problem at which this book takes aim in particular, namely, the question of the extent to which the papers of the young Kierkegaard are fiction.

It is obvious, and more than obvious, that the *Papers* of Kierkegaard are different in their nature from such diary material as, for example, that of Georg Brandes. This apprentice of Kierkegaard (an apprentice in reverse, as it were) can literally be followed from day to day; his reading and the impression it made can be checked; his relationship to teachers, protectors, and friends can be pursued, and to the girls who played such a large role, though still a platonic one, in his youth. We can also follow, with great certainty, Brandes's attempts at the literary art and his aesthetic writings from the first sketch to the finished treatise.

None of this is possible with Søren Kierkegaard, whose intellectual life up to *Either/Or*—apart from single articles and a couple of books (*From the Papers of One Still Living* and the dissertation)—has been transmitted to us in a flickering aphoristic form or perhaps, rather, a formlessness which requires the most careful attention from Kierkegaard scholars.

A quotation is not by definition a piece of documentation which can be used according to one's pleasure.

2: KIERKEGAARD'S PAPERS AND LIBRARY

> *To take passion away from poetry and to replace what has been lost with decorations, pleasant regions, applauded woodland scenes, enchanting theater moonshine is a forfeiture like unto the desire to remedy the badness of books by means of the binding's elegance, something, of course, which cannot interest readers but, at the very most, bookbinders.*

It would be generous to assert that Kierkegaard left his literary legacy in the best sort of order. To be sure, he did not hide it in bureaus in secret rooms, bureaus that could be bought from a secondhand dealer later on, nor did he throw it to the bottom of Søborg Lake as a source of subsequent pleasure for frogmen. But, unlike Brandes, he did not keep an elegant catalogue of his reading, month by month, and we have to follow his purchases of books by means of the bills from the book dealers. We can only make our individual guesses at what he read (or borrowed, at any rate) from the libraries of the student association and the Atheneum, which was Copenhagen's most sophisticated reading club, and we know little or nothing about the reading he did at the literary cafés of the time. This café reading must have been extensive, an essential part of his daily existence. The café visits were perhaps more important than the celebrated philosophical strolls.

His literary effects, however, are not as scattered or chaotic as those of a Voltaire or a Diderot, not to mention the wretched fate of the Heiberg papers: I knew a stouthearted native of Vendsyssel who in the 1930s, at Vrejlev Cloister, was ordered to burn Heiberg's letters and manuscripts by the case, and succeeded in saving only a modest part of them for posterity. Kierkegaard, on the other hand, conceived of his journals as reports to history early on. An ingenious means for leading the understanding of his thoughts onto the right track.

The Kierkegaardiana which has been collected, edited, and commented upon since 1855 is impressive, and every Kierkegaard scholar owes a debt of gratitude to Rasmus Nielsen, H. P. Barfod, H. Gottsched, Raphael Meyer, P. A. Heiberg, V. Kuhr, V. Ammundsen, Carl Weltzer, Sejer Kühle, Niels Thulstrup, and H. P. Rohde, and naturally to the first three editors of the *Collected Works* I–XIII (1901–06)—A. B. Drachmann, J. L. Heiberg (the brother of P. A. Heiberg), and H. O. Lange. If there were a tablet honoring the memory of the founders of scholarly Kierkegaard study, the names of these pioneers would have to appear on it, together with those of other editors and commentators. It is not enough for us to read Kierkegaard's writings and papers with his own commentaries, *ad usum delphini kierkegaardiani*. Really, we should also like to see letters, documents, *acta*: in short, primary sources which can be submitted to source criticism.

The Pioneers of Kierkegaard Study

One can read about them at length in the works of Aage Kabell and Aage Henriksen; but, in the present discussion, the subjective Kierkegaard interpreters from the discipline's first phase—Rasmus Nielsen, Brøchner, Martensen, Brandes, Goldschmidt, Rudin, and Vodskov—have been intentionally omitted. It is the collectors of the primary Kierkegaard materials who require our attention. And they naturally require an evaluation in a historical light as well.

Rasmus Nielsen took part in all the movements of his time, from Hegel past Kierkegaard to Grundtvig, but failed nonetheless to leave more than the fragment of a philosophical system behind. He was the first to collect Kierkegaard's newspaper articles, toward the end of the 1850s, and to put them into a historical context. Until the end of the century, there was a great deal of talk about his role as an editor of the *Papers*; but if Kierkegaard did

think of Nielsen as an editor for a while, it was not at any event
what he desired in his last years. Bishop P. C. Kierkegaard's
boundless pangs of conscience in this connection are but one
among the many symptoms of the family's lack of spiritual
equilibrium.

H. P. Barfod's edition of the *Posthumous Papers'* first two
volumes (1869–72) will be thoroughly treated in what follows,
while, on the other hand, the part played by Gottsched, who took
up Barfod's burden in Aalborg in July 1879, will be omitted. Between February 1880 and May 1881 Gottsched published the papers from 1848 to 1855 and thus, in a year and a half, brought
twice as much to the light of day as Barfod had. It is a deed worthy of all respect; but the most difficult problems lie, to be sure,
with Barfod.

The following years saw the publication of a long series of
Kierkegaard letters, of which the most important were the edition
by Carl Koch, in 1901, of thirty-one letters and notes to Emil
Boesen, material partly known from Barfod's work, and then
Raphael Meyer's *Kierkegaardske Papirer, Forlovelsen, udgivne for
Fru Regine Schlegel (Kierkegaard Papers, the Engagement, edited
for Mrs. Regine Schlegel)* in 1904, a work which made *Mit Forhold til Hende (My Relationship to Her)*, issued the same year by
Henriette Lund, utterly superfluous. Meyer's version is the dependable one, authorized by Fru Schlegel. The Lund family,
moreover, through the efforts of Henrik Lund, Henriette Lund,
and the poet-historian Troels-Lund, has demonstrated a strange
attitude toward its renowned relation—romantic, protective,
and possessive. The Lunds are major suppliers of myths to the
Kierkegaard mythology.

Niels Thulstrup, the soul of the Kierkegaard Society, the founder
of the Kierkegaard Institute in Copenhagen, the enterprising spirit
behind the Kierkegaard encyclopedia, for whose first volume we
all wait with such breathless excitement—but oh, what are the
best-laid plans of men?—collected, in 1953, 344 pages worth of
312 *Breve og Aktstykker vedrørende Søren Kierkegaard (Letters and
Documents concerning Søren Kierkegaard)*, plus a modest handful
of the many and carefully chiseled dedications with which Kierke-

gaard provided the gift copies he sent out into the world. Of the volume of notes which appeared the next year, one can safely say that its 140 pages do not offer overmuch material; indeed, in his review Paul V. Rubow called attention to the fact that the most valuable comments were strongly indebted to Sejer Kühle. At the most difficult spots, Thulstrup very elegantly takes the hurdles where they are lowest. Are the letters from the Gilleleje summer of 1835 fiction or not? Or only some of them, and in that case, which ones? Is letter Number 8 of July 17, 1838 (which, according to the commentary, was "certainly written from Hillerød but probably not mailed") to be regarded as a letter in actual fact or a link in Kierkegaard's literary efforts to write an epistolary novella? Is it sensible to accept Emanuel Hirsch's chronological arrangement of the letters to Regine Olsen without further discussion? Could the learned editor not have addressed himself to the problem of deciding which letters and notes are fiction and which have factual and practical information to impart? (See chapter 8.)

The principles of editing and of choice of material in Thulstrup's work become still more mysterious when one notices that letter Number 76 of February 1843 to the wholesaler Nathanson is printed, while the contemporaneous "Epistle to Mag. Kierkegaard" from Victor Eremita (*Papers* IV.B. 20) has not been deemed worthy of being accompanied by the letter to J. F. Giødwad. The letter to Giødwad can be found in Barfod's *Posthumous Papers* (I:366 ff.) but does not differ in principle from the letter to Nathanson. Neither of these letters was mailed. The letter to Nathanson lay among the articles in the *Papers* with a broken seal, the letter to Giødwad was not sealed at all. The letters and the sketches of articles belong together as pieces of incontrovertible documentation for Kierkegaard's wish (altogether justified) to create a sensation in connection with the appearance of *Either/Or*.

Over the years it had become impossible to find the original *Auktionsprotokol over Søren Kierkegaards Bogsamling (Protocol of the Auction of Søren Kierkegaard's Library)* of April 1856 in the used-book stores, and thus Thulstrup did a good, useful, and commendable deed when he republished it in 1957. Kierkegaard's relationship to books, particularly those he owned—for he naturally

read more and other books than those he had in his library—is a
major theme for research. To an eminent extent he was a devourer
of books, a user of books, a collector of books, an aesthetician of
books, a man who had his books bound. Whether or not he may
be called a bibliophile depends on one's definition of the word.

No one has understood this essential side of Kierkegaard's daily
life as well as the Kierkegaard votary H. P. Rohde. It was only fitting that, in 1967, he should issue a work in Danish and English
for the Royal Library with the same theme and title as Thulstrup's
little catalogue. In addition to a sympathetic and understanding
essay about Kierkegaard as a book collector, this splendidly illus-
trated work contains a reproduction, with commentary, of the
main collection in the auction protocol, to which two appendixes
are added. Rohde, who is undeniably right in calling the main collection "a collection stripped of many of its books," has shrewdly
assembled evidence making it still more probable that the two appendixes, about which there has been considerable argument, also
belong (with part or all of their 226 and 325 items) to Kierkegaard's library—which, inevitably, an unbelievable number of
moves had damaged and decimated. The section "Books outside
the Collection" is also of interest. Kierkegaard could have used
these books as gifts, and gift books are an indication of taste and
intellectual orientation.

Kierkegaard research owes H. P. Rohde a great debt of thanks
for an invaluable, indeed an indispensable tool. It also owes him
thanks for the years he spent in tracking down and publishing
Kierkegaard's quotations. Here it is not a question of determining
that Kierkegaard read such and such a book at such and such a
time. He often quoted at second hand and was not particularly
good at reading books to their very end. But the quotation is an
essential matter for Kierkegaard, an existential method of preparation, a kind of primer for his own writings, which so often have
the character of re-creation and pastiche and parody. Kierkegaard
used quotations like a tuning fork by means of which he found the
proper tone. Rohde's careful pursuit of quotations becomes a little
comical only when he parades his booty in *Gaadefulde Stadier paa*

Kierkegaards vej (Mysterious Stages on Kierkegaard's Way, Rosenkilde & Bagger, 1974). Thus he deserves to have the prey which he has shot inspected with the same respect he has shown his colleagues in the field of art history, where he has made corresponding finds and discoveries.

H. P. Rohde's Hunt for Quotations in Kierkegaard's Preserve

These two literary *particuliers* of Copenhagen have much in common. They have time aplenty, loads of it. Neither of them would dream of doing anything hasty, such as saving the poker when the house is afire; of all the ludicrous things in the world, nothing seems more laughable to them than to be in a hurry. One needs good luck to make finds among the second-hand dealers of Copenhagen. If Rohde still has not found a bureau with a secret compartment, he has come, nonetheless, upon books, letters, and drawings among antiquarian book dealers and in private homes. There is no lack of mysterious stages on Kierkegaard's way and on Rohde's. Kierkegaard was particularly interested in Kierkegaard, and so is Rohde (in Kierkegaard, that is). That becomes plain from his many essays, tutti frutti of a lifelong study of Kierkegaard. Some are worth being mentioned individually.

"Gavmild student" ("Generous Student") describes a set of Schiller's collected works from 1830 with Kierkegaard's signature and a paraphrase of Horace's "omne tulit punctum, qui miscuit utile dulci" in Johan Herman Wessel's rendering "At gavne og fornøie. . . ." The book's new owner, a thirteen-year-old boy named Diderik Christian Seidelin, dated the gift (?) June 21, 1833. Is this "spark in the darkness" (I quote from Rohde) a birthday present?

"Troldom" ("Magic") needs only twenty-six pages to depict what happened to a copy of Eichendorff's novel *Dichter und ihre Gesellen* (1834), which Kierkegaard had lent to Hans Brøchner in 1837 and which the latter purchased as a memento at the auction on April 10, 1856, presenting it on the same day to Anna Thomsen, a pretty sixteen-year-old girl, the daughter of the Julie Augus-

ta Thomsen of whom the two half cousins, Kierkegaard and
Brøchner, had so high an opinion. With an intuition almost like
Sainte-Beuve's, Rohde perceives a love story which makes Brøchner
into an instrument of fate in Miss Thomsen's life, something
which was also true of the well-known Swedish museum director
Arthur Hazelius, and to top it all off, at the same time. We get a
feeling of a triangle à la Edvard-Cordelia-Johannes:

> Anna Thomsen simply could not resist the little book with its
> elegant binding of green glazed paper; she took it in her
> hand, leafed through it, reflected upon the memories it con-
> tained, looked at the book and looked at Brøchner, and the
> sight made the cavalier catch fire, inspiring his gallant ges-
> ture. He told her he would be delighted if she kept the book.
> And Anna was beside herself with happiness.

In "The One Still Living" Rohde has succeeded in solving *all* the
riddles connected with Kierkegaard's *From the Papers of One Still
Living* (1838). The method, which neither Brandes nor Vilhelm
Andersen nor Billeskov Jansen thought to employ, is the brilliant
one of determining what authors were *en vogue* in Europe of the
1830s. With the surety of a kestrel, Rohde descends upon Prince
Pückler-Muskau (1785–1871), who he assumes (he does not ask
the H. C. Andersen experts for advice) is "totally forgotten" today.
If one has taken the trouble to read the first volume of the *Papers*,
one will have observed that, under the date of January 22, 1835,
Kierkegaard mentioned his having done some reading in *Tutti
Frutti—Aus den Papieren des Verstorbenen* (1834). Having at his
fingertips what other historians of literature and art have read or
surveyed, Rohde confesses his debt like a perfect gentleman: "I am
indebted to Professor Howard Hong, Northfield, Minnesota, for
the reference to this memorandum."

In the essay "Hjertebogen" ("The Heart's Book") Rohde weaves
romantic thoughts around the fact that Kierkegaard purchased
and dated Christian Winther's collection of poetry, *Haandtegninger
(Drawings)*, on the very day of its publication, January 23, 1840.
After all, that was Regine Olsen's birthday, and we need only

Rohde's documentation in order to be convinced that Kierkegaard
was actually in love with the little lady at this time.

In "Ørkenens sønner" ("The Sons of the Desert") Rohde boldly
enters a field—comparative literature—where he is obviously just
as much at home as he is in art history. Rohde cannot be unaware
of the fact that the so-called field of general and comparative literature passed away long ago, upon the deaths of Professor Paul
Krüger and Professor Paul V. Rubow, and that it is therefore terribly out of date to carry on polemics against a scholar who has
never concealed his debt to these two men. Rohde is enraged to
learn that this *frater taciturnus & comparativus* does not believe
Chateaubriand had any sizable importance for Danish literature;
indeed, he does not even think that this ignorant scribbler has read
the motto of the second part of *Either/Or*.

In return, Rohde himself makes discoveries, belonging to the
category *les plus surprenantes des surprises*, in the field of Denmark's deceased comparative literature. His theory concerning a
"thought-provoking parallel between the fate of Atala and that of
Kierkegaard" is just as remarkable as is the suspicion that P. L.
Møller's interest in Blicher was the product of an influence from
Kierkegaard. His suspicions concerning the extent of the knowledge of Chateaubriand in Denmark are not supported by the com-
paratistic bibliography of foreign authors in Denmark prepared by
Paul Krüger at the Institute for Literary Studies in Aarhus.

"Attisk nattevagt" ("Attic Nightwatch") recounts the torments
Rohde endured in finding the source of a quotation in *Either/Or*, a
problem which neither J. L. Heiberg nor A. B. Drachmann could
surmount. "I had the quotation in my mind for a good many
years, and from time to time I plowed through less familiar authors, but without success." The quotation was in Droysen's translation of Aeschylus, to be found in Kierkegaard's library.

"Paa frierfødder" ("Going Courting") discusses a drawing by
Marstrand, a scene with a suitor, mayhap a new hypothetical portrait of Kierkegaard. One could wallpaper a room with these alleged portraits. Rohde can tell us only that Marstrand was away
from Denmark between 1836 and 1841 and that he perhaps did

not know the young Kierkegaard at all. One understands the conclusion: "Now the drawing is published—the discussion can
begin."

In "Romersk Karneval" ("Roman Carnival") Rohde has found
the drawing by Chodowiecki mentioned in *Repetition*. It adorns
the title page of the parody of Vergil's *Aeneid* by the Austrian poet
Aloys Blumauer, in the third edition. Kierkegaard owned it in an
edition of 1844 *without* the etching. Too bad.

"Drivende skyer" ("Scudding Clouds") talks about the German
quotation in *Repetition* which neither Hirsch nor Thulstrup nor
Peter P. Rohde has been able to deal with. But the last scholar's
namesake can. It is from Wilhelm Müller's poem "Der ewige
Jude," read by Kierkegaard at the latest on August 28, 1837. "How
much simpler it would have been if one had begun by reading
Wilhelm Müller's poem! But scholarship's progress, in this case as
in so many others, has taken the longest way home," Rohde declares with conviction.

"Afbud med komplikationer" ("Excuse with Complications")
prints and offers a comment upon the last known letter from
Kierkegaard's hand, an excuse he sent on May 4, 1855: he cannot
go to an old lady's funeral. Rohde appears to have said just about
all there is to say about the little note. The lady had the poetic
Christian name of Øllegaard (i.e., "beer farm").

Barfod's Edition of the Posthumous Papers, *1865 and Afterward*

H. P. Barfod did not fool anyone—and certainly not himself. When
he moved into the bishop's residence in Aalborg as an assistant in
January 1865, he took control of a literary estate of which a dreadful mess had been made. The fanatic nephew Henrik Lund and
Kierkegaard's brother, who was gnawed by conscience, had seen
to that. Barfod went on board a Flying Dutchman's ship, doomed
to capsize.

In February 1865 Barfod came upon the notorious statement
that Kierkegaard senior, when a shepherd boy, had cursed God
from a hillock in the heather (not on the unpoetic level ground)—

a discovery that made the bishop burst into tears, moved by the suspicion that this was the passkey to all the curses that beset the family.

In March 1865 Barfod sniffed out the document which declared Rasmus Nielsen to be the proper editor of the *Papers*. It was discreetly noted and laid aside, together with a bad conscience; after all, one could afford to have the best conscience in the world.

On November 11, 1865, the sacrosanct tenth anniversary of Kierkegaard's death, Barfod finished his list of 472 items, something which, for lack of anything better, still functions as an altogether conclusive primary source—"The B Catalogue." (For the rest, the bishop had also put various notes and letters to one side, something which did not escape Barfod's sharp glance.)

In the autumn of 1867 Barfod got the power of life and death over papers and manuscripts, the best thing that could happen. He prepared them for printing, often simply by sending the original to the printer. They have not been seen since.

It is easy to be annoyed at such a procedure today. In Barfod's time it was perfectly acceptable. He took a look at his three immediate predecessors: Just Mathias Thiele (1795–1874), who had published Thorvaldsen's papers in two large bundles, *Den danske Billedhugger Bertel Thorvaldsen og hans Værker*, vols. I–IV, 1831–50 (*The Danish Sculptor Bertel Thorvaldsen and His Works*) and *Thorvaldsens Biografi*, vols. I–IV, 1851–56; F. L. Liebenberg's (1810–94) *Samlinger til Schack Staffeldts Levned*, vols. I–II, 1846–51 (*Collections for Schack Staffeldt's Life*); and Peder Hjort's (1793–1871) *Kritiske Bidrag til nyere dansk Tænkemaades Historie*, vols. I–IV, 1852–67 (*Critical Contributions to the History of Recent Danish Thought*), together with Hjort's *Udvalgte Breve fra Mænd og Kvinder til Peder Hjort*, vols. I–II, 1867–69 (*Selected Letters from Men and Women to Peder Hjort*), which had caused even more dispute than did Hjort's previous work. It was Hjort's edition which gave Barfod particular pause, for the age was not inclined to look with friendly eyes upon the publication of correspondence written by persons who were still alive; one also had to think of their descendants. Barfod stuck his hand into a wasp's nest: in

1869 Sibbern, Grundtvig, H. C. Andersen, Overskou, Fru Heiberg,
Monrad, Rasmus Nielsen, Brøchner, and many others were alive,
all of whom could feel themselves touched (painfully) by the first
volume of the *Posthumous Papers*, 1833–43, 506 pages in all,
which appeared on December 13, 1869.

In the introduction to the second volume (1872) Barfod defended himself against the many bitter and far from objective attacks
made upon him. They will not be reviewed here. But Barfod was
actually ahead of his time. He is laudable for having been aware of
the necessity of collecting—while it was still possible—reminis-
cences from people who could remember Kierkegaard. Perhaps
they understood only certain aspects of Kierkegaard's personality,
and perhaps Barfod did not make full use of the material. But he
made a pioneering contribution to Kierkegaard research. Thus he
was ahead of Georg Brandes, who persuaded Brøchner to set down
his important, albeit diffuse memories of Kierkegaard, which
were then published in 1877 in *Det 19de Aarhundrede (The Nineteenth Century)* and later issued in book form by Steen Johansen in
1953.

Kierkegaard scholars have always treated these secondary
sources rather nonchalantly, meanwhile taking whatever they
could use. Nonetheless, these statements are from sources close to
Kierkegaard. One cannot brush aside three separate witnesses,
such as Sibbern, Holst, and Brøchner, when they assert that
Kierkegaard was intellectually dependent upon Hegel and Heiberg
in his youth. They knew what they were talking about. They had
been on a personal footing with Kierkegaard, yet they regarded
him, it is self-evident, in his natural proportions. Even though he
was a gifted man, a talent, a genius in their eyes, he could still be
easily compared to Grundtvig, Mynster, Heiberg, Andersen, and P.
L. Møller. It remained for posterity to discover Mont Blanc on the
Danish island of Lolland.

Nor did Barfod, despite his admiration for the genius that was
Kierkegaard, lose his healthy sense of proportion. He knew well
that he had entered upon a difficult (read: hopeless) undertaking,
but with true modesty he regarded his edition as a set of "contri-

butions to the understanding of [Kierkegaard] and of his life among us," as "contributions preceding the depiction of his life which will no doubt appear some day" (*Posthumous Papers* I:vi). His foreword, fifty-five pages long, makes no bones about these editorial problems, which Heiberg and Kuhr swathe in an impenetrable fog of circumlocutions, guesses, and surmises.

Using a Danish spoken by mortal man, Barfod establishes that the "largish assembly of handwritten papers" found after Kierkegaard's death had been "collected and partially arranged in groups with a care which indicated the author's eagerness to guard them against dispersion and destruction"; that Kierkegaard "had thought of the possibility of their eventual publication"; and that this was especially true "as far as their most overwhelmingly significant part, 'The Journals,' was concerned." Barfod's description of the preserved material is so complete and precise, in contrast to what Heiberg and Kuhr have to say, that it deserves to be repeated here:

Apart from a number of larger and smaller folders, notebooks, loose sheets and single scraps of the most various sizes, strips and snippets, sketches and aphorisms, excerpts from works he had read, lists of books he had read or planned to read, etc., etc.—apart from all this there was also, and this appeared to be the main material, a fairly long series of diaries, or as their author called them himself, "Journals," thirty-six in number, kept from March 1846 until (the spring of?) 1855, all bound in quarto and marked NB, NB2, NB3, etc., up to NB36, containing 7,600 pages in all but written as a rule with a rather large hand and on lines which were quite widely separated. As a sort of introduction to this collection, there are twelve larger and smaller items (diaries would probably be the best word for them) of altogether disparate dimensions, which—with partly longish and empty intervals—more or less fill in the time from 1833 (but actually getting under way only in July 1835) until February 1846. Some of them, however, were only memorandum books, kept

to an extent in pencil, most of them undated, now and again
containing, however, a helpful notation of the year. Ten of
them were found marked thus: AA (June 1835–October 11,
1837), BB (March 24, 1836–March 19, 1837), CC (1833), DD
(May 24, 1837–January 28, 1839), EE, "ad se ipsum" (February 1, 1839–September 23, 1839), FF (September 13, 1836–August 18, 1838), GG (only fragments are preserved, August 6,
1838–April 3, 1839), HH (June 14, 1840–1841?), JJ (May
1842–February 1846), and KK (July 23, 1838–December 6,
1838); it can easily be seen that the alphabetical order does
not indicate the chronology. Several of these little books were
used alternately at one and the same time. Two of the books
bore no markings: one of them, a little pocket notebook
bound in leather, can be proved to come from 1840, while the
other has no special mark or indication of time whatsoever
but lacks any special sort of contents. In addition, there were
some small remains of a diary, marked L, which may come
from 1839 or 1840. These books, like the later, far more complete and more carefully linked "Journals," soon proved, however, to have been something different in the author's eye
from what diaries are generally wont to be. They contain,
in fact (together with some but not terribly many notes concerning external matters, and side by side with isolated
emotional outbursts), investigations of themes which had
occupied the diary keeper at a given time, plans for treatises
and speeches, texts for sermons, and finally a multitude of
occasional ideas, small notes, quotations, and more of the
same. In brief, the "Journals" give the impression of having
been a main channel—partly coordinated with the principal literary activity—for the late recluse's urge toward
intellectual release.

As far as I know, there is no better description of what Kierkegaard's "Papers" actually are. Therefore, Barfod, whose edition
vanished from the secondhand bookshops years ago, needs and
deserves to be heard. After having completed the catalogue on No-

vember 11, 1865, he made a clear statement of *his* thoughts concerning *his* plan for a publication of Kierkegaard's papers:

> Immediately, from the very outset, it was my intention to collect everything from these papers which could be regarded as belonging, even in the broadest sense, to the biographical category, and which could serve to illuminate or explain Søren Kierkegaard's life and development, his relationship to other people, his view of moods and conditions. The limit I thus set myself was and is quite vague, to be sure, in that almost every statement, every aphorism, can be called—and to a certain extent is—a glimmer, a beam, often perhaps only a broken beam of the light in which this remarkable personality can at last be fully understood. And yet I believe that I have proceeded deliberately when, in accordance with my plan, I have also included what perhaps are a good many small matters, although I surely did not wish to dilute the memory of the mighty spirit with trifles; I not only collected sheaves and blossoms, I also reached out for single straws and small seedlings. I have also proceeded deliberately even in those isolated instances in this book where—and it has naturally not escaped my attention that it can be done—one is able to point out as much as half a page which has already appeared in other printed works. But even this has its great importance, in my opinion. For that which functions elsewhere as only a part of a work, as a mood expressed poetically or otherwise, proves itself here to be taken straight out of Søren Kierkegaard's own life, to be one of the shining facets of that rich intellectual existence, polished in the school of suffering. [*Posthumous Papers* I:x]

After mentioning certain diapsalmata which "grew out of the author's most secret emotions," Barfod continues (I:xi):

> A draft, a hint, a plan, even a quotation which seems to betray that Søren Kierkegaard found a personal application for it—I have included almost all such things, to the extent that I

was aware of them: such fragments can be the first isolated sketches of later works, or they contain seeds which the author perhaps has forgotten and abandoned and which he has included in his rich literary activity in some other way. But on this account the book may also create the impression, in many places, of being a collection of materials, something which I have already recognized that it in fact is, in certain ways, an archive set into as good an order as possible, comprising separate and often not even mutually connected *contributions to the future depiction of Søren Kierkegaard's history*. I repeat myself here on purpose, for I wish to emphasize as strongly as possible the importance which I attribute to my book, or at least to *this* part of it. After all, it lay in the very nature of the undertaking that the collected and serviceable material ought to be arranged—and then, of course, to be published?—*according to its chronology*.

Here Barfod wisely calls attention to the fact that with his first volume he wishes only to provide an introduction to the thirty-six connected journals from 1846 to 1855:

For the reader of this must keep in mind that *the present volume falls completely outside the period of time treated in those "Journals"* and so can only have taken its material from the series of *smaller* diaries, notebooks, and pocket memorandum books, which were found marked AA–KK and L (see above), as well as from the unbound papers. It would hardly have been proper to ignore all or several of these years (1833–43) altogether, in order to let the public draw immediately upon the source of the more connected entries, for then the whole work would lack a purpose; the edifice would lack an entrance. [*Posthumous Papers* I:xi]

It is quite unlikely that Barfod guessed that he, with these sober words of his, followed the line of Sainte-Beuve, whose obituary Brandes had written at about the same time for the *Illustreret Tidende* of October 31, 1869. Nor that, with these words, he had provided the plan according to which Kierkegaard's *Papers* (1833–46) themselves ought to have been presented. And according to which plan—in my opinion—they still ought to be published. Every other editorial plan will treat the source material cavalierly. But the material *was* treated cavalierly; and the result is what we have to deal with today.

Heiberg and Kuhr's Edition of Kierkegaard's Papers, 1909–1948

The edition of Kierkegaard's *Papers* by P. A. Heiberg and Victor Kuhr (1909–48) is nothing to joke about. The twenty monumental octavo volumes fill their user with fear and trembling. The editors' achievement itself has the same effect, for the two learned gentlemen carried out their work alone, even though Einer Torsting is named as coeditor from 1926 on. Naturally enough, they could draw upon the enormous sum of knowledge which the three editors of the *Collected Works* (1901–06), A. B. Drachmann, J. L. Heiberg, and H. O. Lange, represented. But the Sisyphean task bears signs of having been given a farfetched sort of solution by these scholars, who possessed pronouncedly theological, philosophical, and philological qualifications. The same is true of the photographic reproduction which Professor Niels Thulstrup issued in 1970 for the Danish Language and Literature Society and the Søren Kierkegaard Society. To Thulstrup belongs the honor of seeing to it that volumes XII and XIII provide the complete excerpts from Kierkegaard's reading, together with his notes from lectures, plus his notes for 1831–39. The urgently needed index volume was entrusted to *stud. theol.* Niels-Jørgen Cappelørn. It is fearfully difficult to be a theologian.

It is good to have all of this laid out before us. If it concerns Kierkegaard, nothing is too small. But one misses the historians who could have undertaken a responsible edition of the early papers. Heiberg and Kuhr's bombastic preface of September 1909 identifies the object of the edition as nothing less than a Søren Kierkegaard *diplomatorium*, including:

(1) Everything which exists in the public domain or in *private* possession, or can be proved to have existed, of *literary* Søren Kierkegaard manuscripts.

(2) Everything which exists in the public domain or in private possession of documents and materials concerning S. K., his parents, and forebears. . . . The edition will present first of all a series of volumes with the *literary manuscripts, the letters excepted, to the extent that these are not included in S. K.'s journals, then letters from, to, and about S. K.,* and finally *documents and materials.*[*Papers* I:vii]

Such an all-embracing ambition creates a muddle by definition. What are *literary* manuscripts? Those that have been printed, those ready for printing but not printed, those merely in draft, or simple sketches and isolated thoughts? What are documents and materials concerning Kierkegaard and his family? Here, to be sure, there is something tangible, if one scrapes the bottom of the barrel, and Barfod provides more than do Heiberg and Kuhr. What are letters *from* Kierkegaard? Until this very day, no one has been able to distinguish between "genuine" letters (that is, letters that have been mailed) and fictive letters, which never left the writing desk, because they—like certain letters to P. W. Lund and Emil Boesen— were intended for incorporation in literary (belletristic) works. And what are letters *about* Kierkegaard save the night in which all cats are gray? Do the report letters of the Rudelbach sisters from the 1830s fit the bill, or the testimonials collected in letter form by Barfod in the 1860s? Israel Levin's notes about Kierkegaard, dictated to Lieutenant Wolf, are not less valuable, are they, because they are not in letter form? In brief: the edition of Hieberg and Kuhr, its plan and its division into parts, is unclear and imprecise from the very start.

The collection and classification of the material in the first volume is limited to the literary effects which the university library received from P. C. Kierkegaard in 1875, and thus *after* Barfod's publication of the first two volumes of *Posthumous Papers* in 1869 and 1872, covering the years 1833–43 and 1844–46; the third volume, with the papers from 1847, came out in 1877. The commentary of Heiberg and Kuhr, formal and urbane, is not however very good-natured:

> With constantly shifting standpoints concerning the arrangement of the material and editorial policy, amidst cutting-out, pasting-together, providing-with-a-key, adding-notes-for-the-typesetter and much else, amidst crossing-out and correcting, etc., the oldest section of the manuscripts was prepared to be sent to the printer as part of a manuscript for Barfod's edition of the *Posthumous Papers*. [*Papers* I:ix]

After the condescending observation that the general attitude toward the value of manuscripts was different in Barfod's time from what "it is in our days," that is, 1909, they conclude with a lament that they have been compelled to a great extent to use the *Posthumous Papers*, Barfod's catalogue, and his copies of the original manuscripts as sources for the new printing. At the same time, they make a great show of having abandoned the chronological order for the sake of *objective* reasons and principles of arrangement, boldly asserting that "the very nature of the material has caused it" (*Papers* I:x). And now there follows the brilliant passage about those principles of publication from which Kierkegaard research has suffered for generations:

> Considering the first main division's manuscripts from S. K.'s own hand, they fall into three groups almost automatically: a group with the character of diary entries (from isolated exclamations to notes for connected descriptions in travel diaries), a group connected with the development of the authorial activity of one sort or another (from brief essays and newspaper articles to large works), and a group connected with study and reading (from small aphoristic sketches to whole *sets* of lecture notes and extensive excerpts). Corresponding to these three groups the present volume will be found to be divided into three sections, which for the sake of convenience are des-

ignated merely with A, B, and C; in doubtful transitional
cases the place which the piece was given in the original manuscripts has provided guidance for its location here.

To top it all off, there has been carried out, furthermore, within
Group C and "also partly within Group A, an objective division
between Theologica, Philosophica, and Aesthetica" (I:x). By means
of these three groupings within the three groups the editors have
succeeded in creating a perfect and absolute chaos, concerning
which—without malice—one can use Kierkegaard's own words:
"discursive discussions and incomprehensible commentaries concerning the category of higher lunacy" (II.A.808, given the date of
1839—on what grounds?).

Barfod put his cards on the table, openly confessing his own
helplessness and lack of consistency. More or less consciously,
Heiberg and Kuhr lead their readers down the wrong track, so that
no mother's son can see how disconnected and problematical
Kierkegaard's notebooks in fact are. Never mind the many serial
numbers and chronological registers; but it is really quite dangerous "to let consideration for affinity or an accidental connection
outweigh respect for the chronological order" (I:xi), as Heiberg
and Kuhr say they have done.

Anyone who is willing to spend a couple of hours at the Royal
Library looking at Kierkegaard's early papers will see how hopeless
it is to try to bring order into their ranks. That is why it surely
would have been more honest if one had chosen *either* to publish
the twelve books, or folders, from before the time of the journals—
the twelve items described by Barfod, with the addition of the random papers—*or* to have opted for the following principle: dated
entries in one section, undated ones in another. The most important passage in Heiberg and Kuhr's long preface ought to be
printed in heavy letters at the beginning of every edition of the
Papers:

But although we thus are of the opinion that, as far as the
majority of the undated entries are concerned at any rate, we
have given them the place in the chronological progression

where they approximately belong, or can have belonged, it still must be expressly emphasized that the chronological arrangement tacitly employed in the edition—whenever the importance of the chronological factor is to be accentuated—cannot be accepted as something accomplished for good and all but as something temporary and hypothetical, which it stands to reason can be improved in many cases. [*Papers* I:xiii]

Translated into everyday language, this means that they stuck in the numerous undated slips where they believed they could aptly be used to support the concept of Kierkegaard they already had! It is astonishing, putting it mildly, that in the *Papers'* second edition (a photographic reproduction, of course) no attention was paid to the editors' own express opinion concerning the chronology's altogether doubtful value. It is high time that a team of experts be given the task of identifying, that is, dating and placing, the papers of the young Kierkegaard. In Annelise Garde, Denmark possesses a skillful graphologist, and the Royal Library has at its disposal both experts and technical equipment to aid in the identification of paper, watermarks, types of ink, and so forth. Of course, we shall never attain absolute accuracy in determining when Kierkegaard wrote what, but we can certainly not afford the reputation of putting up with the results of Heiberg and Kuhr.

Let Kierkegaard smile, in his heaven, at these mechanical and practical concerns, but allow me to ask, Is it only for Kierkegaard's sake that we read him? That's a compliment he would have refused to accept.

I closed my eyes and chose a packet of Kierkegaard's papers— it didn't matter to me which one—in the Royal Library. It turned out to be A, Package 41, Folder 2, which, according to Heiberg's index of the Kierkegaard papers, elegantly written by hand (there is a photographic copy of it in the catalogue room at the Royal Library), contains notes from Journal FF with the dates September 13, 1836, to August 18, 1838, although enclosures 5–6, 25–26, 29–30, 38–40, 51–54, 69–70, and 97 are missing. After untying the ribbon, one finds a whole stack of identical transparent envelopes, each containing small slips of paper, usually with handwriting on both sides. On each envelope there is a notation in India ink as to where these pieces are located in the edition of Heiberg and Kuhr. It is difficult to determine how much of the work of these editors is owed to Barfod, including the pagination in pencil, the crossings-out, and the pastings-over (I hope the word exists in Danish). If one compares one's own immediate impression with the information given in the "Sources, Description of Manuscripts, and Text-Critical Information" at the very end of the *Papers'* first volume, one is undeniably given "material for thought," as Kierkegaard says.

It is not apparent from the text of Heiberg and Kuhr that I.A. 241 and I.X.248 of, respectively, "September 13, 1836" and "September 25" are the front and the back of the same strip of paper, and only the initiate can figure it out from the "Manuscript Description." In both cases the handwriting is indeed "meticulous," but can the graphologists assure us that one writes the same way before and after an interval of eleven days? The only reasonable thing would have been to print the front and back of the piece of paper together, without taking the eleven-day interval into account.

The same is true of I.A.249 of "September 26, 1836," the reverse of which is I.A.253 of "October 6," whose fifth word, "first," is crossed out and whose parenthesis is not completed. One must figure out all of this for oneself from the description of the manuscript. Here one can also read that "The Coincidence" [Sammentræffet] in I.A.276, which is the reverse of I.A.275, originally was "The Meeting" [Sammenkomsten], while one has to take great pains to discover that Kierkegaard has confused *Don Juan's* second, third, and fourth acts.

I.A.277, which is the front of I.A.278, does not get any commentary save a description of its handwriting, which is once again: meticulous. It is a dog-eared piece of paper, and the text begins, "Concerning the Vaudevillelike in the Bouffo-Aria. Figaro." There follows a lacuna of about half a line, whose opening parenthesis is not included. Then there follows, "Address to the Public." This is rather different from *Papers* I.A.277: "Concerning the Vaudeville-like in the Bouffo-Aria in Figaro (Address to the Public)." What is missing in actual fact is what Kierkegaard thinks Figaro is or says in his address to the public.

One can continue in the same pedantic way, but when one publishes Kierkegaard's papers, pedantry is not only a virtue but a necessity. A scholarly edition ought to have photographic copies, on its left-hand page, of the many and various loose scraps of paper, and on the right a description and commentaries. We must be able to afford it, after all. We have only one Kierkegaard.

Did P. A. Heiberg Act in Good Faith as the Editor of the Papers?

Naturally, Heiberg acted in good faith in the sense that he himself believed he had as much right and authority as a lifelong occupation with Kierkegaard can give the editor of such difficult material. He believed that his editorial principles were more correct, more scholarly, than Barfod's. I do not have sufficient knowledge about Kuhr's part in the edition to be able to distribute the responsibility between him and Heiberg, but the involved, careful, veiled form of the language reminds one a great deal of Heiberg's own writings. Not of Kuhr's books, which people in my university days used in their cramming for the philosophical examination.

As far as I can see, there is no doubt that Heiberg's view of the Kierkegaard home, particularly the relationships between the father and the sons, played a role in influencing his treatment of the *Papers*, in both his dating and his arrangement of them. Few—if any—Kierkegaard scholars have fallen victim to the same extent to Kierkegaard's own attempts at mythologizing. The main source for this assertion is P. A. Heiberg's *Søren Kierkegaard i Barndom og Ungdom: Efter trykte og utrykte Kilder*, 1895 (*Søren Kierkegaard in Childhood and Youth: Based on Published and Unpublished Sources*), which has the modest introductory title *Bidrag til et psykologisk Billede (Contributions to a Psychological Portrait)*. Its

opening confession will leave no one in doubt about the author's
existential involvement:

> And so, for my part, I must confess that I have felt a stronger
> urge to hearken to "the great accuser" than to defend myself
> against him, and that I have found more "happiness" in sit-
> ting alone than in "sitting together," and that until this very
> day I have not got past the standpoint that, for me, S. K.'s
> journals are still "The Book of the Judge."

This foreword, without pagination, containing its ironic quotations from Grundtvig's silver-wedding psalm about the pleasures
of conjugal life, would have thoroughly pleased Kierkegaard, dead
for forty years:

> There can hardly be any well-founded doubt that scholarship
> can only profit from presenting itself, as it were, to S. K. for
> examination—yes, it even seems to me that a Danish scholar
> can justifiably be reproached if his scholarly work reveals that
> he has skipped this examination, no matter how it may have
> happened.

This might well be regarded as a demand for an existential involvement as a *conditio sine qua non* for scholarly work with
Kierkegaard. Heiberg himself never recovered from his reading of
Either/Or in his student years: "It is in this light that S. K. has
constantly remained standing before me." And, in fact, on a pedestal, so that "the book's content is actually made up of quotations
for the most part, but it is also connected with my concept of S. K.
as a personality which, on account of its dimensions in a psychological sense, in height, depth, and breadth, is an inexhaustible
source of instruction for me—and of refreshment." Thus we have
in P. A. Heiberg an editor, and a critic of his sources, who lies in
prostrate admiration before his statue of Kierkegaard, whose
Christianity he seems never to have doubted.

Seen in the light of its time, *Søren Kierkegaard in Childhood and
Youth* is not without its merits. Kierkegaard's father and the rector
of the Borgerdydsskole, Michael Nielsen, are made into the two

dominant forces in Kierkegaard's childhood, but two other teachers, Frederik Olaus Lange and Ernst Boiesen, also come to the fore.
Although Heiberg bases his work on primary sources here, he
must take recourse to *The Point of View for My Work as an Author*
(1859) in order to demonstrate the early and all-pervasive melancholy of Kierkegaard's childhood. Resolutely eliminating the candor and the cheerfulness to which contemporaries bear witness,
he produces the portrait he desires, painted in somber, opaque,
demonic colors. The secret note and the thorn in the flesh become
carefully guarded taboos, which only the initiate dare approach.
His "concretions" concerning the relationship of melancholy to
Kierkegaard's physical being and his demonic reserve are taken by
Heiberg principally from the journals, a matter he mentions in the
following settling of accounts with Barfod (pp. 129–30):

"At this point, I wish to settle my main account" with H. P.
Barfod directly, Barfod whose general shortcomings as the editor of the papers have been correctly pointed out, in my opinion, by the reviewer in *Dagbladet* [February 23, 1870: Heiberg
thought it was C. F. Molbech]. As for Barfod in his capacity as
a collector of biographical materials, I must call attention to
the fact that all his so-called "comments" about S. K. (what
he lays claim to is a "heading that makes no claims") are
excerpts from letters he has received, excerpts partly emended
and partly badly mixed up, quite undependable in their en-
tirety. His modesty in the claims he makes concerning his
scholarly reputation may, at this point, be satisfied with the
recognition of the fact that: (1) in the course of a doubtless
very extensive correspondence, which may have occasioned
him considerable inconvenience, he had caused these letters
to be written, and that (2) he did not destroy them. On the
whole, his work with the papers bears only all too obvious
signs of not having been carried out with the "first fruits" of
his intellect (see his own admission in the *Posthumous Papers*, III:xv). Barfod's primary and genuinely commendable
merit in this matter is that he, in the year 1865, put together a

full, precise, and detailed catalogue of the manuscripts then available to him in a well-arranged, complete, and intact condition. Now this catalogue can be used, among other things, for determining what Barfod threw into disorder later on, to a great extent rendering the material incomplete, spoiling and damaging it in a most shameful fashion.

And there is much more along the same line about Barfod's "indefensible thoughtlessness in his stewardship of the property entrusted to him," and a sarcastic compliment to him for not having destroyed still more, despite everything, "so that what now is missing [among the manuscript materials] *almost* without exception coincides with what has been printed" (p. 130). P. A. Heiberg's final sigh:

> As far as the editorial work itself is concerned—apart from the purely subjective differences of opinion, which can be argued *pro et contra* in every editorial matter —Barfod's part in the process, as well as his editorial activity in general, suffers from the fault that it is basically planless and characterized everywhere by a high-handedness which is anything but brilliant. Dixi, et animam meam liberavi.

Naturally, it is nice to learn that the great Kierkegaard psychologist, P. A. Heiberg, has liberated his soul with respect to the bishop's assistant, H. P. Barfod, who had the misfortune of being the first to publish the canonical writings. But the statement does not inspire confidence in Heiberg's having set about *his* task with an unbiased mind. We have already seen that, in 1910, Heiberg had no very remarkable understanding of the way *Either/Or* came into being; the famous (or infamous) piece of writing from 1912, *En Episode i Søren Kierkegaards Ungdomsliv (An Episode in Søren Kierkegaard's Youthful Life)*, does not need to have been a deduction from the *Papers'* first volume of 1909. Rather, it *can* have played a role in influencing the arrangement of the *Papers* in such a way as to allow for the visit to a bordello in the spring of 1836.

Even though such an allegation is unpleasant, it cannot be put aside without further ado. On his page 7, P. A. Heiberg asserts with an impressive frankness that Kierkegaard's archive for 1834–55 is like the face of a clock, "from which we can directly read his movements: as a rule from week to week, and sometimes even from day to day," and that is precisely the fact which makes the "blank from April 22 until June 6 [1836] . . . as it was found to exist according to Barfod's catalogue in 1868" highly suspicious (*An Episode*, pp. 6–7).

What we know (or Heiberg knows) about Kierkegaard in this lacuna is undoubtedly impressive: (1) he received three copies of the *Humoristiske Intelligensblade* from Reitzel, (2) he got a pair of black trousers repaired, (3) he had a new cloth coat made for 36 rigsdaler, 4 marks, and 8 shillings, and (4) he helped his father in making out the list of householders in the latter's property, Nytorv No. 2. All this took place in May 1836, but "on *this* clockface a thirty days' blank in the direct readability of the clock's movement, such as the one we have come upon here, is a striking matter, and one which requires an explanation" (*An Episode*, p. 7).

Danish Kierkegaard research in the year of our Lord 1912.

The Blank in the Spring of 1836

The explanation of the blank cannot be found in the *Papers'* first volume, which had nothing between I.A.166, where Kierkegaard holds a conversation on April 18, 1836, with Head Police Clerk Jørgen Jørgensen from the Police-and-Criminal Court, who was drunk that day (Jørgensen, that is), and I.A.167 of June 6, where Kierkegaard indicates that it is necessary for a person to have God's assistance in order to improve. In that vile black hole of seven to eight weeks, however, Kierkegaard did have the time to make extensive excerpts from *Die Poesie der Troubadours* of Friedrich Diez, Zwickau, 1826 (I.C.89), and to complete a good-sized statement against the *Humoristiske Intelligensblade*, nos. 1 and 2, for *Flyveposten* (I.B.6).

Strictly speaking, other things also took place in Copenhagen during those weeks.

On April 16 the Royal Theater gave the premiere of H. C. Andersen's *Skilles og mødes (Parting and Meeting)*, a double vaudeville which after a great deal of discussion was presented as a drama in two parts, *Spanierne i Odense (The Spaniards in Odense)* and *Fem og tyve Aar derefter (Twenty-five Years Later)*. It was accompanied by a ballet the three times it was given—*Amor og Balletmesterens Luner (Cupid and the Ballet Master's Moods)* at the premiere, *Afguden paa Ceylon (The Idol on Ceylon)* on April 20, and *Bjergbøndernes Børn (The Mountain Peasants' Children)* on May 3, all three ballets by Galeotti; Lucile Grahn did not appear in any of them. On April 30, Casimir Delavigne's five-act play *Don Juan af Østrig (Don Juan of Austria)* had its premiere. It was given four times that season with W. Holst as Don Juan; it naturally interested Kierkegaard, who was consumed by thoughts of the Don Juan figure just then. We do not know if he saw the romantic opera *Hans Heiling*— with music by Heinrich Marschner and text by Eduard Devrient—which attained five performances before the end of the season; but at any event he later revealed his acquaintanceship with Henrik Hertz's imperishable *Sparekassen (The Savings Bank)*, performed on May 26 and May 31 with great success, although the theater's biggest names did not perform in it. Kierkegaard need not have been assailed by boredom before he, on June 6, together with Hertz, Poul Møller, and several others, took leave of the Heibergs on the eve of their departure for Paris. Nothing indicates that the farewell party at Brogade 3 had anything to do with the banquet in *In vino veritas* or the phrase discussed in the soap-cellar drama, "I-came-recently-from-a-party." And still less indicates that Kierkegaard went to a house of ill fame afterward. And with P. L. Møller into the bargain.

P. A. Heiberg's matchless theory about Kierkegaard's fall does not deserve an extensive refutation. It is comical—especially because it has gone around the world and has been taken in profound earnest. Its basis in the sources comprises undated and undatable notes (I.A.174, 179, 164, 177, and 178), and most important, I.A.175, an entry to which Knud Jensenius has devoted a large essay. One can say only that it was written after the premiere of *Guldkorset (The Golden Cross)* at the Royal Theater on March 4, 1836. Heiberg's theories about Kierkegaard's having heard *Don Juan* and *The Marriage of Figaro* "probably . . . for the first time" may well be of no interest; but he is right in his statement on page 11: "For the time being, theology has altogether vanished from the tale."

As far as Kierkegaard was concerned. The story about the bordello, which is completely unprovable, has to depend upon the *Papers'* mention of "the excesses of my youthful life" (II.A.520), of "my aberration, lusts, and excesses" (IV.A.107), and in particular, in IV.A.65, of the young and high-strung person who, letting himself be carried away by his emotions, visited a whore. With unshakable gravity, P. A. Heiberg's hypothesis follows on page 17:

> All of this appears to me to make it extremely likely that, in his consciousness, S. K. constantly manipulates the memory of a simple fact, a fact which at any event had such clear external contours that he could imagine the possibility of others being able to make use of it as an accusation against him.

Even for Puritans of 1912 there was very little one could get one's teeth into here. If Kierkegaard, alone or with his drinking companions, did at last go to a house of prostitution, the fact has no greater interest than the serious problems arising from the possibility that Kamma Rahbek spent the night with J. P. Mynster at Spjellerup parsonage, or from the bliss which Constance Leth perhaps bestowed on Grundtvig at Egeløkke. As far as I know, only one personality of the Danish Golden Age had his career gravely damaged by moral accusations: P. L. Møller. Charges made by Kierkegaard.

The sketch mentioned by Heiberg turned into the well-known midnight scene, "A Possibility," from " 'Guilty?' /'Not Guilty?' " of 1845, but Heiberg, with his "Investigation of Our Title Deeds," something worthy of a local customs officer, did not succeed in

confiscating any forms with interesting personal details. Heiberg
could fittingly have called his pamphlet "Pages from the Notebook
of a Keeper of Public Order" (III.A.245). One could almost believe
that he had tagged along to the bordello, he is so sure that it was
only after "the unusually splendid evening meal" (p. 32) and the
subsequent fall from grace that Kierkegaard became prey to "the
melancholy and sadness, which, as a matter of fact, began to
show themselves only toward 1837 in the extant notebooks from
his early years" (p. 39). Nevertheless, this observation does not
keep Heiberg from asserting that, "for a time after the evening of
May 1836, café life still [seems] to have retained its attraction for
him." And worse still: II.A.562 reveals that Kierkegaard played bil-
liards as late as 1839.

This magnificent tissue of guesses, conjectures, postulates, hypotheses, and distortions concludes with the thought that worry
about his "loss of purity" towed Kierkegaard back, two years later,
into the cozy harbor of the Christian faith. That Kierkegaard never
accepted the call to a pastorate resulted from "the guilt which he
carried with him as a secret, but which he imagined that others
could possibly use as an accusation against him" (p. 54). *Dixit* P.
A. Heiberg, who thereby denies that *de occultis non judicat eccle-
sia.* If Heiberg is not rendering a judgment, what else is he doing?

Thoughts and ideas from the tractate on the bordello are further developed in the psychological study of 254 pages which
Heiberg published under the troublesome title *Et Segment af Søren
Kierkegaards religiøse Udvikling,* 1918, *(A Segment of Søren Kierkegaard's Religious Development),* with the spotlight pointed at the
period from June 1, 1835, to May 19, 1838. This is the crown of P.
A. Heiberg's lifelong Kierkegaard research, which often had the air
of being a kind of hagiolatry. "The treatment is detailed to the
point of being long-winded, and conscientious to the point of being pedantic," Aage Kabell says (p. 245) in *Kierkegaardstudiet i
Norden,* 1948 *(The Study of Kierkegaard in the North),* perhaps the
most skillful, most learned, and wittiest guide one can desire in
the jungle of Kierkegaard research.

Heiberg's main thesis, taking Kierkegaard's religious development as a story of recovery, is profound and interesting. It leads us quite naturally to another kind of Kierkegaard research, the kind cultivated by physicians, psychiatrists, and psychoanalysts.

Here the historian will land in considerable difficulties, as the next chapter demonstrates.

3: KIERKEGAARD IN THE
DOCTOR'S OFFICE

*After my death, no one will find in my
papers (and that is a consolation for me)
a single piece of information about what
has really filled my life; find the writing in
my innermost self which explains
everything, and which often turns what
the world would call trifles into
enormously important events for me, and
which I regard as unimportant, when I
take away the secret note which explains
it.*

Few geniuses have had the life they led in their youth as thoroughly combed over as has Kierkegaard. Detectives in the fields of psychology, psychiatry, law, medicine, and theology have turned every scrap of paper upside down and carried on extensive excavations in the family's history. To make a résumé of the "conclusions" of P. A. Heiberg, V. Ammundsen, Troels-Lund, Frithjof Brandt, J. D. Landmark, Knud Jensenius, Hjalmar Helweg, Carl Weltzer, Sejer Kühle, Hohlenberg, K. Bruun Andersen, Carl Saggau, Ib Ostenfeld, and Sigurd Næsgaard (to name only a handful of the important Northern scholars) is a well-nigh impossible undertaking. One has to *choose* among hypotheses. I acknowledge my debt to Helweg, Bruun Andersen, and Saggau, but I confess my insecurity when confronted by the many and often contradictory statements that specialists have made. Was Kierkegaard healthy or ill? Normal or insane? Straightbacked or hunchbacked? The truth must certainly lie somewhere between these uncomfortably impertinent questions. But where?

Kierkegaard's Appearance

Let us begin at the beginning—the man's appearance, both his
physique and his manner of dress. He could not escape the way he
looked. His appearance followed him like the shadow in Chamisso
and H. C. Andersen. His unfortunate back, like his uneven trouser
legs, became a part of his fate.

When Kierkegaard speaks of his youth in his *Papers*, he always
stresses how frail, slender, weak, and sickly he was. His schoolfellows bear unanimous witness to this, and they were never in any
doubt that he made up for his physical inferiority with sarcasm
and banter. Barfod strongly emphasizes (I:xliv) the comical element in Kierkegaard's dress, even though his father was in the
clothing business.

> It was always the same, made of an unusual sort of rough
> blackish cloth and tailored in a very strange fashion; his jack-
> et had a pair of short tails, and he always wore shoes and
> woolen socks, never—as far as anyone could remember—
> boots. This quickly got him the nickname of "The Choirboy,"
> because his clothes so much resembled or at least were remi-
> niscent of those of choirboys from the church schools. (His
> dress retained this unusual, somewhat eccentric and awk-
> ward appearance almost the whole time until he became a
> university student.)

Kierkegaard's other nicknames, Søren Sock and "The Fork," referred in part to his father's former métier and in part to his ability to stick a fork into people, especially his teachers, whom he
assiduously teased—not least his big brother, when the latter
tutored him. Kierkegaard was small. In preparatory school he suffered from not growing the way his comrades did. That explains
his special position as the "latecomer" in the family, allowed a
greater freedom of speech than were his six older siblings.

On a visit to the Agerskov family in Buddinge, in 1825 or 1829,
Kierkegaard is supposed to have fallen out of a tree, but no one

knows if it was the fall that caused the deformity of his back. In his books from 1942, *Søren Kierkegaard set udefra (Søren Kierkegaard Seen from Without)* and *Det særlige Kors (The Special Cross)*, Rikard Magnussen adduced a series of statements and pictures which seem to confirm the notion of Kierkegaard as a hunchback. Since the medical record from Frederiks Hospital in 1855 says nothing about this, it is no doubt safest to think of a deformity of the back whick took the form of a rather pronounced crookedness, a so-called scoliosis. It depended upon the observer whether one wanted to characterize Kierkegaard as "somewhat misshapen or, at any event, hunched" (Hertz), or "with shoulders which jutted out somewhat" (Goldschmidt), or "somewhat irregular throughout his whole form" (Brøchner), or "with a crookedness, as if a touch of hunchbackedness were just on the verge of appearing" (Sibbern), or "high-shouldered" (Regine Schlegel), or "bent-backed" (Otto Zinck), or frankly "hunchbacked" (Carl Brosbøll and Troels-Lund).

This defect, which was quite mercilessly revealed in the cartoons of the time, was naturally felt by Kierkegaard to be a cross he had to bear, a source of suffering, a thorn in the flesh. There is something pathetic about the statements of his last years, in which Kierkegaard agonized over never having been young, never having been like others, never having been able to run with the crowd, never having been able to play or to enjoy himself. After only four days' service in the King's Life Guard, a student group, he received the chief surgeon's "Statement of Physical Unfitness," and it was only later that he found it amusing thus to have immediately put aside the "demand of the time." In general, his physical appearance had something involuntarily comic about it. He did not dare to show himself on a dance floor (cf. Goldschmidt's statement below, p. 156), and his strange crablike progress along the sidewalks demanded great maneuverability from his fellow strollers. Even as a young and aesthetic dandy on horseback he fell—not from the horse's back but, what is still worse, into the category of the comical:

He did not cut a particularly good figure on horseback. It could be told from his manner that he had no great confidence in his ability to control the horse if it should take it into its head to misbehave. He sat stiffly on the horse's back, and one got the impression that he was constantly remembering the instructions of his riding teacher.

This is what Brøchner has to say; the cartoonist of the *Corsair*, Peter Klæstrup, immortalized Kierkegaard in a cruel drawing in which Kierkegaard is the rider and Regine is the horse. Therefore it is particularly amusing that in the Heiberg book *Prefaces*, of June 17, 1844, Kierkegaard tries to play the part of the experienced rider (*SV*, V:7):

To write a foreword is, as it were, to have done something which justifies demanding a certain attention; as it were to have something on your conscience which breeds familiarity; as it were to make a bow in the dance although you don't move; as it were to press your left thigh tight against the horse, to tighten the rein on the right, to hear the charger say Pst! and to tell the whole world you don't give a hang.

But it was not Kierkegaard who behaved with such authority; it was Heiberg himself. He was an excellent rider and had his own horse. Whether or not it was the dandified Heiberg and his beautiful wife who in 1836 got Kierkegaard to change to an elegant way of dress, and to spend a fortune at the tailor's, need not be discussed here. But there is something pathetic in the attraction the Heiberg circle exerted upon him, the sick man's longing for health and naturalness, the cripple's longing for straightness and good looks. Yet Kierkegaard never fitted neatly into the circle of people who, like the Heibergs, knew how to solve their problems discreetly—and they undeniably had a great many problems in the 1840s. With the years, Kierkegaard's admiration and longing were transformed into neurotic hatred and bitterness.

Kierkegaard's Physical and Mental Illnesses

Kierkegaard was not only small, feeble, and misshapen, he was also ill: indeed, no infirmity exists which Helweg, Ostenfeld, Saggau, and Carl Jørgensen, as well as many other *doctores*, do not pin on him. The diaries contain many testimonials to indispositions, headaches, insomnia, nervous tension, and nervous pain, which were not merely the results of intense intellectual work coupled with a lack of exercise and fresh air. Perhaps there was a specific ailment, tuberculosis of the lungs, which can be traced back to 1835 (I.A.75). Troels-Lund's theory has been taken up in our days by Carl Jørgensen, who finds particular support for it in the letter of April 2, 1841, from H. F. Lund to his brother in Brazil: "The one who is rather ill is Uncle Søren. . . . His chest has been affected and he has begun to spit blood again." This is the source, according to Carl Jørgensen (whose five volumes, *Søren Kierkegaard: En biografi med særligt henblik paa hans personlige etik* [*Søren Kierkegaard: A Biography with Special Attention to His Personal Ethics*], are distinguished by an eminent ignorance of even the most elementary principles of source criticism), of Kierkegaard's migratory arthritis, fits of euphoria, nocturnal perspiration, and many and various moods. Kierkegaard's tuberculosis explains both his fear of intense sunlight and his feats of boozing. His heliophobia is also connected with his conjunctivitis. That Kierkegaard has intestinal colic around 1851 goes almost without saying. We lack only podagra and degenerative arthritis.

The learned men cannot agree about the cause of Kierkegaard's death. Helweg hesitates between compression of the spinal cord as a result of an affliction of the spinal column (a tubercular bone disease) and genuine inflammation of the spinal cord—myelitis. The latter view is supported by the physician J. O. Jacobsen, while Carl Jørgensen goes in for abscesses on the lungs. Myelitis, which begins at a fairly early age, would explain many of the symptoms in the diaries: lameness in the legs, difficulties in walking, disturbances of the sense of touch, and pains when urinating. The last problem was a source of particular and growing embarrassment to Kierkegaard, which would explain both the infrequency of his sermons and the hermitlike existence of his last years. He barricaded himself in his many apartments, he restlessly moved from one address to another, and saw only the people who, like Giødwad and Levin, helped in publishing his articles and books. Levin's account of a visit during which Kierkegaard fell to the floor and stammered has nourished the suspicion that he was an epileptic. Even as H. C. Andersen was, according to chief physician Mogens Lund (*Berlingske Tidende*, September 21, 1975).

Two such outstanding psychiatrists as Hjalmar Helweg and Ib Ostenfeld have concerned themselves with Kierkegaard's mental constitution. Proceeding from the Kierkegaard family's notorious mental illness, the former diagnoses Kierkegaard as a manic-depressive, since he regards him as having been healthy and normal in his childhood and youth; he holds the opinion that the depressions began in earnest only in 1835. Kierkegaard never recovered from this psychosis, and his life is a long conflict between the urge toward public activity and the isolating effect of his depression, something which goes directly against P. A. Heiberg's conception of Kierkegaard's religious crisis as the story of a cure. A literary observation falls quite easily into line with Helweg's sober and impartial book. Kierkegaard's urge to participate in active life was, in fact, a need to take part in the world of poetry and the theater. It was unfortunate that his psychosomatic sufferings made it impossible for him to find a suitable niche for himself in Copenhagen's intellectual circles, in particular that of the Heibergs, whom he had approached in humble admiration during the years when he was estranged from his home. Later he assailed the Heibergs with a passion which can lead one's thoughts to the misshapen and psychopathic figures which attracted Kierkegaard: Richard III or Høgne of the fairy tale, whose mother had conceived him with a troll.

Ib Ostenfeld, whose proud humanism and empathetic powers make him an ornament of the Danish medical profession, does not share Helweg's opinion; engaging in dignified polemics, he has expressed his disagreement in his writings about Kierkegaard and his family, most recently in the little pamphlet *Søren Kierkegaards Psykologi*, 1972 (*Søren Kierkegaard's Psychology*). Ostenfeld's lifelong intellectual companionship with Søren Kierkegaard gives this work its warmth and humanity. I must flatly admit that I simply do not understand why Ib Ostenfeld—who after all, in *Poul Kierkegaard: En Skæbne*, 1957 (*Poul Kierkegaard: A Fate*), has demonstrated that the father, the brother, and the latter's son had all inherited manic-depressive tendencies—is so hesitant to regard Søren Kierkegaard as a manic-depressive too, at any event, from the second half of the 1830s on. "It is impossible to find any manic-depressive tendencies in his publications or diaries, or in his biography" (p. 68).

A nonspecialist in pathography naturally cannot dare to make diagnoses, but if one reads Kierkegaard's papers from the 1830s everything seems to support Helweg's hypothesis, and nothing seems to refute it (not even proceeding from the assumption that a great part of these notes is fictive in nature). One does not feel drawn magically to that which is divided and disturbed if one does not have something of these qualities within one's self. Shouting into the forest (as Hoffmann, Heine, and Börne did), one gets an answer from Echo, a main character in that tiresome but psychologically fascinating "Strife between the Old and the New Soap Cellar," Kierkegaard's play from his student days. No one on earth, not even a psychiatrist with Ib Ostenfeld's authority, can persuade me that the drama is written by a "normal" person—whatever that is. Let us be allowed to keep our geniuses who are not normal—a Rousseau, a Strindberg, a Nietzsche, a Munch, a Céline. The world would be poorer if it did not have them. Perhaps it is just such geniuses who can advance the world a little by the very force of their inconceivable naiveté. Let us realize our youthful dreams in our old age and, as Swift himself did, enter the madhouse we built in our youth. Unlike children, let us hope that we shall never become reasonable creatures!

It will take more than pathographic arguments to invalidate Helweg's book of 1933, which in a layman's eyes is built on a granite foundation. But perhaps the phallocratic psychoanalysts can manage it.

Kierkegaard Undergoes Psychoanalysis

Among Danish psychoanalysts, Sigurd Næsgaard put Kierkegaard on his couch in 1950, in *En Psychoanalyse af Søren Kierkegaard (A Psychoanalysis of Søren Kierkegaard)*. Kierkegaard's love for his father is an unconscious hatred which, suppressed, fights its way to the surface everywhere. The disciplinarian's curbing of the child's natural instincts made the boy into an impotent adult, feminine in his tendencies and hopelessly depressed. Therefore Kierkegaard hates his father without knowing it, the father who forced him to renounce, to surrender, and to abandon life. This hatred, composed of impotence and despair, makes him aggressive, and when his aggressions are checked he sets out to commit murder by means of his irony, without realizing that it is the father's super-ego he wishes to attack.

There is a paucity of material concerning the second component of the Oedipus complex, the child's love for his mother and his sexual attachment to her, something with which the Norwegian J. D. Landmark has worked. Næsgaard overlooked a couple of historical sources of some interest, on the one hand Brøchner's statement that he was warned by his cousins against the fifteen-year-old Kierkegaard, "a terribly spoiled and naughty boy, who was always clinging to his mother's skirts," and on the other hand Martensen's lines in *Af mit Levned*, 1882 (*From My Life*), thus a late source, and from a time when Martensen certainly could not have had reason to say anything nice whatsoever about Kierkegaard:

Once he came to us in a state of deep depression and told us that his mother was dead. My mother repeatedly declared that, although she had experienced a good many things in her

life, she had never seen a human being as deeply sorrowful as
S. Kierkegaard was at his mother's passing, something which
caused her to conclude that he must have had an unusually
profound sort of spirit. [p. 79]

Næsgaard goes on to regard Kierkegaard's love for Regine as an
unconscious extension of the supposed infatuation with his mother, and he conjectures that this natural erotic feeling, as it is ema-
nated, is transformed into a love for his father. Kierkegaard
developed his femininity so consistently that it required male objects in order to release and absorb its energies. On this account
Kierkegaard identifies his father with God, letting both of them
function simultaneously as the male object, intruding from without. The feminine Kierkegaard felt a strong urge in this direction,
although God's intrusion into man takes the form of a rising
stream of suffering. The result is that infatuation with religious
passion which, particularly in Kierkegaard's last phase, is expressed in *Training in Christianity*. During the final years of his
life an enormously strong masochism recurs: his aggression is now
not only directed outward but is self-destructive.

Although I have strong reservations concerning many details, I
believe that Næsgaard has hit upon some essential features of
Kierkegaard's makeup, for example, the fact that the martyrdom,
beginning with an envy of Heiberg, continuing in the *Corsair* feud,
and ending in the battle with the church, had a therapeutic effect:
it freed Kierkegaard from a tremendous inner pressure and as it
were diverted his attention from the private theater of his soul and
that theater's problems. An outward-directed aggressivity runs
like a red thread through Kierkegaard's life: his teasing of his
schoolmates; his revolt against his older brother; his conflict with
his home and his father's melancholy; his sallies against members
of the National Liberal Party; his assault upon H. C. Andersen; his
mocking of the first brood of Danish Heibergians, with Martensen
bearing the brunt; his offensive against Heiberg and Heiberg's two
idols, Hegel and Goethe; his hysteria in the question of P. L.
Møller, Goldschmidt, and the *Corsair*; his attack upon Mynster,
Martensen, and the whole of the Danish state church. Kierkegaard

could survive only if he let off steam at proper intervals. Otherwise the boiler would explode.

At this point, let us leave the physicians for the time being, after arriving at a kind of conclusion about Kierkegaard's childhood and adolescence until 1830, when he took the arts examination. Those many and gloomy depictions of the oppressive atmosphere do not apply to the years before the series of deaths began to rain down on the family: his mother, two sisters, a brother, and a sister-in-law die between 1832 and 1837. All the same, Kierkegaard's childhood was not a bed of roses, despite the home's freedom from financial care. A home to which he could not take his schoolfellows, a mother on whom he seems to have looked down despite her spoiling of him, a domineering elder brother, a stern old father, and for his own part, a half-comical role as the eccentrically dressed son of the rich hosier.

Life in the open air, hunting, riding, sailing, skating, balls, visits to the theater, and trips (apart from the summer vacations in northern Zealand)—Kierkegaard was as unfamiliar with these things as he was with playing games and with any sort of social life outside the family and the merchant circles of Copenhagen. That joie de vivre and cultivated upbringing which Heiberg, the child of divorced parents, had enjoyed in his childhood and youth in the Gyllembourg home on Bredgade was a closed world for Kierkegaard.

Kierkegaard's Sexual Anxiety

There is plenty of evidence in the works and the papers that Kierkegaard (again in contrast to Heiberg) was sexually warped, thanks to his upbringing. If his father (as we shall directly see) had his reasons for regarding sex as the sin par excellence, it was not by accident that he kept Søren isolated from his comrades. We know that the father, in the 1820s at any rate, shared a bedroom for a time with his two sons, obviously in an effort to keep them from the ugly vice of "self-pollution." According to the view of the time, that vice was the root of all evil, in particular of melancholy and insanity; as a matter of fact, the family was convinced that

Uncle Peter had gone mad because he had "laid hands upon himself." An entry such as VI.A.105 gives us more than just a vague notion of the old man's methods:

> Granted that it was impossible for him to overcome the impressions of childhood. And such a "leading astray," with respect to what sin is, can very well be caused at times, perhaps, by good intentions. As if a man, having led a very dissolute life, regarded the sexual drive as sin itself, with the precise intention of frightening his son away from what he himself had done, and forgot that there was a difference between himself and the child—that the child was innocent, and therefore must of necessity misunderstand.

The Concept of Dread, June 17, 1844, submits the problem to a penetrating analysis, but even the most generous interpretation will show that Kierkegaard had difficulty in not identifying sex with sin. He describes his own situation here: "Many a young life was ruined because rigorism made it melancholy and turned sex into sinfulness." Expressions such as "secret guilt" and "sin" often appear in the *Papers*, and it may be permissible to go still further than to Levin's "sinning in the thought," quoted above on page 16. After all, Levin provides examples:

> It was as though he lived in a world of the spirit, and with a remarkable impropriety and eccentricity he could depict the most frightful things in a degree of vividness which was terrifying. Thus in "The Attic Nights" he described a Greek who indulged in pederasty, and his opposite, an anchorite who lived in a forest, assailed by temptations of the spirit, all with an attention to detail which was indecent and demonic . . . . Lust burned in his soul, even though his body was quiet. His feeling about his accounts of such things was that only the obscene thoughts should be avoided, not the bold words; his opinion was that "poetry is not for children with a pacifier in their mouths or for half-grown girls, but for mature persons." [quoted in Steen Johansen, pp. 34–35]

Scholars determined long ago that masturbation was a reality of Kierkegaard's existence, something which can readily be connected with sinning in the thought. In *Haandbogen i Therapien*, 1852 (*The Manual of Therapy*), Oluf Lundt Bang, Kierkegaard's physician, says that "one of the worst cases is the melancholy of the patient who, awakened to a recognition of his sins, has been shattered by books depicting their fearful results, a melancholy which can be combated only with great difficulty and which can lead to suicide." Not to mention other fearful results: hypochondria, spermatorrhea, paralysis, and impotence. II.A.20 shows that the hosier had his suspicions about his son:

> I still remember the impression it made on me when, a number of years ago, in youthful enthusiasm for a master thief, I had occasion to state that it was only a misuse of one's strength, after all, and that such a person could no doubt force himself to change, and my father said with great earnestness; "There are crimes which one can combat only with God's constant aid." Hurrying down to my room, I looked at myself in the mirror (cf. Friedrich Schlegel, *Sämtliche Werke*, vol. VII, B, p. 15, bottom of the page). Or when Father often stated that it was a good thing, after all, that one had "such an old and venerable father confessor, to whom one could open one's heart."

In translation: keep away from sex, my boy, and if you have committed the sin which is worse than a crime, then confess it to Mynster. When Kierkegaard ran downstairs to look at himself in the mirror, it was because masturbation was supposed to show up in a bad color, black rings around tired eyes, and so forth. The reference to Schlegel's fairy-tale novel about the wizard Merlin, who had been begotten by the devil on a young girl (the reason that the devil had no power over him), concerns the passage where Merlin cannot resist a beautiful virgin. The girl wished to learn his magical arts, and from now on she held him forever captive with her sensual power:

Als das Mädchen nun allein geblieben war, überlegte sie
unaufhörlich die Rede des Weibes und sprach immer mit sich
selbst davon. Dadurch wuchs in ihr die Lüsternheit immer
mehr, die der Teufel durch jene Reden in ihr entzündete, so
dass als sie des Abends ihre Kleider abgelegt hatte, be-
trachtete sie ihren schönen Leib und freuete sich dessen. In
Wahrheit, sagte sie, die kluge Frau hat Recht, ich wäre ohne
den Genuss eines Mannes ganz verloren.

The story about Merlin is also mentioned in *The Concept of
Dread* (*SV*, IV:338), where Kierkegaard plainly expresses his dread
of and longing for sin: "Besides, life offers phenomena aplenty
where the individual in his dread stares at guilt almost longingly,
and yet fears it." Therefore he compares dread to dizziness. "He
who becomes guilty through dread is innocent after all; for it was
not he himself but dread, a foreign power, which seized him, a
power he did not love but was afraid of; and yet he is guilty all the
same, for he sank into dread, which he indeed loved, in that he
feared it" (*SV*, IV:134). The same joy, mixed with terror, in the
pleasures of sensuality attracted him demonically to Mozart's
overture to *Don Juan:* "Does not one have in the overture what one
in general has said without knowing what one says—despair; Don
Juan's life is not despair, but it is the whole power of sensuality
which is born in dread, and Don Juan himself is this dread, but
this dread is nothing but the demonic lust for life" (*SV*, I:126).

Kierkegaard's sensuality, constantly repressed, drove him inevitably into the arms of those works of literature in which the sensual element was most openly displayed, from Goethe's classical
sensuality to Schlegel's, Byron's, and Heine's sophisticated and
melancholy cult of woman. His sympathies in Danish literature
were for an (intellectual) eroticist such as Baggesen, a vigorous
celebrator of woman such as Oehlenschläger, especially in his
Aladdin, and Christian Winther, who appeared to the youth of the
1830s as the boldest prophet of free love. On the other hand, he
possessed too much of the Heiberg orientation to have any taste
for Aarestrup, and he was too much the snob to tolerate the rather

unostentatious eroticism of Carl Bagger and P. L. Møller, both of whom (as was well known) converted theory into practice.

Since Kierkegaard had to subdue his erotic drive so brutally, he wrote literature about it. The letters to Regine are shot through with eroticism, and the dissertation is noticeably interested in the German Romantics' morality or lack of the same; "The Diary of the Seducer," *Repetition*, and *The Stages* are filled with erotic moods of an intellectual sort, and with a sadistic element which is by no means small. Love has seldom had an unhappier lover than Kierkegaard; he was its platonic admirer. Kierkegaard became a poet on the strength of his repressed sexual drive, and quite unironically, he regarded himself as a great eroticist.

If Kierkegaard *was* actually a masturbator—when, how often, in what way—that ought to be a matter of some indifference. His constant circling around narcissistic themes and mirror motifs, such as the interest in the Merlin story, leads the thoughts in a certain direction. We know that H. C. Andersen kept a careful account by means of a secret sign language, as is now evident from his published diaries. In our days, when nothing pertaining to this area is concealed in the press or in sex manuals, the French-Spanish poet Arrabal has glorified masturbation as a sophisticated erotic art. K. Bruun Andersen, who has analyzed Kierkegaard's sexual life and sexual dread more thoroughly than anyone else has, is of the opinion that he continued the practice until 1849 (X, pt. I, A.637), despite all his resolves, and that he was able to find a full sublimation for his sexual urge only in the last years of his life.

That his private form of eroticism might have made him impotent is an academic question, since Kierkegaard was hardly ever in a situation in which he could demonstrate his potency or lack of it.

The Syphilis Theory

The scribes can interpret the sacrosanct entries about the secret note, the thorn in the flesh, and the great earthquake as they will. But the little pamphlet published by the Danish physician Carl Saggau in 1958 under the title *Skyldig—ikke Skyldig?* (*Guilty—*

Not Guilty?) seems to me the most plausible attempt to answer the many unsolved riddles. I opt for this thesis without following it in all its details. It has the advantage that, in connection with certain pieces of historical knowledge and a literary familiarity with Kierkegaard's mode of work as a man of letters, it causes a good many bits of the puzzle to fall into place. Even for those people who give Kierkegaard a primarily religious interpretation.

For the time being we shall ignore the entry about the curse hurled at God when Kierkegaard's father was a shepherd boy. It did not prevent Kierkegaard senior from making a rapid and impressive career for himself in Copenhagen at a time when, rumor has it, he lived a mildly profligate life and was a patron of taverns. If the celebrated bordello theory is valid, it is possible that the father naturally fell prey to the obsession that he, in a state of drunkenness perhaps, had fathered a child. See "Solomon's Dream" and "A Possibility" in " 'Guilty?'/'Not Guilty?' " But is it likely that something as ordinary, according to the moral standards of the day, as a visit to a whore could have prevented a young man from getting married?

This is the nub of the matter: why did he wait until he was thirty-eight to get married? For a man with a normal sexual life and an outstanding place in the congregation of the Moravian Brethren, it meant that he must either continue patronizing houses of prostitution or hire a housekeeper. A liaison or a kept mistress was hardly in the merchant's style. Thus Saggau proposes the theory that the father had contracted syphilis in his youth and that the inserted section, "A Leper's Self-Observation," is Kierkegaard's poetic circumlocution of what the father had let fall concerning this youthful sin of his. When Simon leprosus discovers at dawn that Manasse is gone, he wanders lamenting among the graves in the desert. (*SV*, VI:220):

> Thus he has gone away to the city. Yes, I know it. I have discovered a salve, the application of which causes everything that has been effaced to turn inward, so that no one can see it, and the priest must declare that we are healthy. I taught

him to use it, I told him that the sickness did not end on that account, that it turned inward, and that one's very breath could infect another, so that the latter would become visibly leprous. Then he cried out in jubilation—he hates existence, he curses men, he wishes to take revenge, he will run to the city, he will breathe poison upon them all. Manasse, Manasse, why did you give the devil a place in your soul, was it not sufficient that your body was afflicted with leprosy?

Here the initials M and S (Manasse/Mikael; Simon/Søren) have been reversed. Manasse is Søren, who walks abroad among men without guessing that he, as a leper, can spread infection. Simon is Mikael Kierkegaard, who had syphilis in his youth but who was given a clean bill of health by a physician after having used the salve. In reality, the illness has taken root, has gone into his blood, so that he can still infect others, or has already infected them.

At that time physicians were unable to decide whether or not the treatment of syphilis with the newly discovered mercury salve was effective in the long run. The infectious material could enter the bloodstream, so that it all ended with paralysis of the brain— progressive paresis—or it could attack the spinal marrow as Parkinson's disease, *tabes dorsalis*. The fact that fifteen to twenty years were regarded as necessary for determining whether a patient was healed or not—this can explain why Kierkegaard senior waited so long to get married. He wished to be sure that he was healthy, all the more because he appears to have married for the sake of love. His happiness lasted only two years: on March 23, 1796, his first wife died suddenly, having borne him no children.

On March 10, 1797, he applied for royal confirmation of a marriage contract with his housekeeper, Anne Lund. The wedding took place on April 26, and on September 7, 1797, their daughter Maren Kirstine was born. A false step of this sort must have been a source of great embarrassment for the rich hosier, who had enjoyed the respect of the Moravian Brethren. The application for a marriage contract was aimed so obviously at an early divorce that the authorities had to deal Kierkegaard a reprimand: he must, if you please, accord wife number two the normal rights of inheritance.

After these difficulties at the outset, the marriage seems to have taken a normal course. Despite the war, the couple's finances were excellent, and up to 1813 seven bright and healthy children were born, four boys and three girls. On September 14, 1819, the twelve-year-old Søren Mikael died after having run into another boy in the schoolyard, and on March 15, 1822, Maren Kirstine died—twenty-four years old and unmarried. Nothing indicates that the hosier devised a personal, religious interpretation of the two deaths. The relationship with the Lunds, begun in 1824, made the home brighter, friendlier, and more sociable, and the extremely valuable source material which Carl Weltzer presented in 1937 shows a harmonious, happy middle-class family with two daughters nicely married and two quite gifted sons, destined for learned callings. The third son would take over the business.

In the 1830s, sickness, sorrows, and deaths were showered upon the family. P. C. Kierkegaard returned home in 1830 from his great trip abroad and immediately got into difficulty with the authorities on account of his Grundtvigian sympathies. Nicoline Lund died on September 10, 1832, in childbed, thirty-three years old, leaving her husband and four children. In October 1833 the family learned that Niels Kierkegaard, who had been unwilling to enter a mercantile career and so had emigrated to America, had died in Paterson, New Jersey, on September 21 of that year.

The winter of 1833–34 saw a quiet but definite break between Peter and Søren Kierkegaard. In May 1834 the mother, Anne Kierkegaard, fell seriously ill, and died on July 31, 1834, without, as far as we know, Kierkegaard's having arrived at her bedside from northern Zealand. On December 29, 1834, Petrea Severine Lund died, thirty-three years old, after having given birth to a son. Following these deaths, stillness fell over the home on Nytorv. The hosier and the elder brother sat brooding over their depressions and problems, while Søren Kierkegaard began to raise a kind of aesthetic cain with exciting visits to the theater and sensational appearances in the student association (1835) and in Heiberg's

Kjøbenhavns Flyvende Post (1836). P. C. Kierkegaard's marriage to
Elise Marie Boisen, the bishop's daughter, on October 21, 1836,
lasted less than a year: she died on July 18, 1837.

Søren Kierkegaard, who after a more or less complete break
with his family had moved away from home, appears to have returned to his father's bosom on or around his twenty-fifth birthday, May 5, 1838.

It is humanly understandable that the hosier would examine his
own soul in this situation and seek to find an explanation for the
tragedies of the last six years. After all, there was enough material
for self-accusation and reproach, even though our only means of
finding out what was going on within him are those the son has
provided in his works and in the *Papers*. The childhood curse
hurled at God, the visit to a house of ill fame in his youth, syphilis,
the possibility of an unknown illegitimate child, the many years
without a wife, the loss of his beloved helpmeet after a brief period of happiness, the sexual fall from grace with the housekeeper,
the disgrace in the eyes of the Moravian Brethren and the authorities, the wife who was beneath him, the loss of five children, the
worries about Peter, who got into difficulties with Mynster and
with the university, about Niels, who did not wish to take over the
family business, about Søren, who was dedicating himself to
drink. Perhaps the two surviving sons had syphilis after all. Who
could be sure that he, Mikael, had been cured by the salve which
the doctor had given him? All that remained was to expect that
the last two sons would die before they reached the age of Christ,
that is, Peter before 1839 and Søren before 1847. Only after he had
followed them to their final resting place would he himself be
ready to receive the judgment of God.

A modern reader will perhaps find this web of thoughts cruel
and barbarous in all its grimness. But for the hosier, reared in the
beliefs of the Moravian Brethren, it made tragically good sense: the
Lord was a jealous God who visited the sins of the father upon the
children. It was a matter, no doubt, not of clearly formulated
ideas but of perpetual self-accusations, of guesses, reproaches, and
obsessions; he constantly wrestled with them, brooding over them

without being able to achieve a definite view of what had happened.

Nor do we know what the old man, either directly or by implication, had confided to his youngest son, and whether the latter believed in a horrible disease as a divine punishment for his father's repeated falls from grace. Everything points to such a belief, and nothing appears to contradict the idea. The dating of the composition of "The Great Earthquake," a little earlier or a little later—the scribes have squabbled valiantly about this point—is a matter of small importance. The decisive factor is that one must imagine that a confession in one form or another had been made by the father, a last, almost desperate attempt to lure Søren—who had for some years walked the paths of sin—back to his home and the Christian fold.

Whatever happened, the father at any event provided Søren Kierkegaard with a matchless piece of raw material, about which he could write for years to come. Most clearly, most openly in " 'Guilty?'/'Not Guilty?' " where he surrendered the secret key. It is quite natural that the book should be signed *frater taciturnus*. Kierkegaard's brother, who wept for both his father and his late wife, did not understand what it was all about. He believed that it was the old story about his father's cursing of God on the heath, in his childhood.

4: THE EPISTOLARY
NOVELLA, "LETTERS"

> *Therefore I have given this piece of writing such a general title (it was intended to be called "Letters"), in order to make my contribution toward preventing what is often a loss for the author and sometimes for the reader—misunderstanding.*

In March 1835 Kierkegaard abandoned his attempt at a drama, *The Master Thief*, after having busied himself with the noble robber for several months. Perhaps he realized himself that his powers were not sufficient to create figures for the stage, or perhaps other literary figures got the upper hand. Among them, first and foremost, Don Juan and Faust. Everything else had to make way for the Faust figure, in which he also found a ready home for the seducer. Kierkegaard became infected with the Goethe fever which gripped Copenhagen after Goethe's death in March 1832; in the Goethe cult, Oehlenschläger and his group and Heiberg and his school were united.

The Goethe Fever of the 1830s

In 1827 and 1828 *Flyveposten* constantly mentions Goethe as the poet of the age, the literary equivalent to Hegel, the age's thinker. On September 17, 1830, J. L. Heiberg began a long series of articles, reprinted in *Prosaiske Skrifter*, V:215–326, in which, by means of liberal quotations, he made capital out of the Goethe-Schiller correspondence for his own aesthetic theories. Like Heiberg, Goethe and Schiller struggle against dilettantism, like Heiberg they are spokesmen for "the perfectibility which separates the artist from the dilettante" (V:221), like him, they find in the unity of material and form the most essential condition for a poetic work of art.

Bournonville's three-act ballet, *Faust* (which never became a part of the Bournonville tradition despite its being reduced to two acts in 1855), had its premiere on April 25, 1832, thus one month and three days after Goethe's death; it was not planned as a memorial performance. Kierkegaard mentions it on various occasions, but it is obvious that he was impressed only by those performances in which Bournonville himself danced the role of Mephistopheles, in other words, the performances from June 10, 1842, to March 10, 1848. Bournonville's entrance through a window, during which he actually hung in the air, "this surge within the leap itself, which is reminiscent of the leap of the bird of prey and the beast of prey" (*SV*, IV:398), made an indelible mark upon Kierkegaard, who knew nothing about the ballet and could not guess that this method of a leaping entrance was a good French tradition, perhaps executed from a table behind the scenes. In 1832 and on the twenty-four occasions the ballet was given before June 10, 1842, Bournonville danced the rather tamely romantic part of Faust, while A. Stramboe was Mephistopheles, and Madam Kretzschmer, just released from the Royal Prison, was Margaretha. Lucile Grahn substituted for her only once, on September 29, 1835. The ballet enchanted the public with its clever invention of dances, its picturesque scenery, and its romantic medieval atmosphere.

On June 19, 1832, a fragment of Goethe's *Faust* was presented in a translation by Heiberg and Hertz. It was the scene where the student (played by Overskou) visits Faust (W. Holst) and Mephistopheles (C. Winsløw). On June 30 Oehlenschläger, who was resigning his post as rector of the university, held a commemorative address about Goethe. His journal, *Prometheus*, made a great Goethean display, and in the winter of 1834–35 he lectured about Goethe's best-known works. The selected writings appeared in six volumes in 1832–35 in a translation by Simon Meisling and F. Schaldemose; volumes 3–5 contained *Wilhelm Meisters Lehrjahre* and *Wanderjahre.*

Furthermore, the Royal Theater offered *Egmont*, in Schorn's translation and with Beethoven's music, on June 2, 1834; it was subsequently made a part of the repertoire and presented on September 5, November 5, and December 20 in the 1834–35 season. Kierkegaard mentions it in I.A. 33 and I.A. 34 (November 22, 1834, and January 19, 1835); he probably saw the last two performances. Clara's fate, in particular, in the first scene of the fifth act, appears to have stirred him powerfully by its demonstration of how near the comic lies to the tragic. Clara was played by Madam Holst, while N. P. Nielsen's interpretation of the self-assuredly cheerful Egmont was forceful and passionate.

In March 1833 Heiberg published his Hegelian manifesto, *Om Philosophiens Betydning for den nuværende Tid (Concerning the Meaning of Philosophy for the Present Time)*, which places Goethe above Shakespeare as the poet who, combining poetry and philosophy, brings the age's own thoughts to conscious life. Heiberg's salute to Goethe and Hegel, but lately deceased, made a deep impression on the youth of the time:

Goethe and Hegel are doubtless the two greatest men which recent ages have produced; no other men deserve to be called the representatives of our time to the same extent, for in their works the whole intellectual life of our time is concentrated, as both existing and present, that is, including the future in a unity with the past. Therefore, although the two have now been called away from their earthly existence . . . they by no means belong to the past, to that which is dead; on the contrary, as the most present of all spirits, they will be fully understood and comprehended only by the coming generation (Pr. Skr., I:417). . . . That which distinguishes Goethe from all contemporary poets is the same thing which distinguishes Dante and Calderón from their contemporaries, the fact that they set forth the poetry of their age, insofar as poetry can do that without denying its peculiar nature. . . . Since the rebirth of the sciences, these three poets are perhaps the only ones of whom this is true, and so they are the only ones who can

> justly be called *speculative poets* (pp. 418–19). . . . Hegel's sys-
> tem is the same as Goethe's. . . . To characterize Hegelian
> philosophy in a few words, one can say that it, like Goethe's
> poetry, reconciles the ideal with reality, our demands with
> what we possess, our wishes with what we have attained. [p.
> 430]

In the summer semester of 1833 Kierkegaard attended Sibbern's
lectures on aesthetics and philosophy, no doubt identical with the
first volume of Sibbern's aesthetic work, *Om Poesie og Konst*, 1834
(Concerning Poetry and Art), the third and last volume of which
came out only in 1869. In 1833 Sibbern takes a very peevish attitude toward the formation of concepts, systematics, and terminol-
ogies, and mixes life and art in a fashion quite unacceptable to a
Hegelian. At that time Kierkegaard was in his Heibergian stage, it
is true, but hardly a Hegelian as yet; his relationship to Hegel will
be taken up in this book's next section, concerning Niels Thulstrup's dissertation. We do not know for sure what he got from
Sibbern, but the first volume of the poetics, with Goethe and
Oehlenschläger as its chief figures, is a collective expression of the
taste and the ideals which the first Romantic generation possessed:
"The Men of 1803." We know that Kierkegaard admired
Oehlenschläger, Mynster, Ørsted, Steffens, and Poul Møller. Poetry is life, and only the poetry which comes from life is true. All
good art is an individual unfolding of a view of life. This is what
they said. And this is what Goethe said.
  Neither Kierkegaard's relationship to Goethe nor his relationship
to the Faust figure in its countless versions, from the popular tale
of the Middle Ages to Grabbe's and Lenau's Faust poems, will be
described here. His relationship to Goethe has been excellently, if
not exhaustively, treated in Carl Roos's book of 1955, *Kierkegaard
og Goethe.* Instead, some examples of the Goethe fever of the 1830s
will be provided, in an effort to point to a historical criterion
which Kierkegaard scholarship has too often overlooked. For lack
of a better term, one could call it the criterion of improbability. It
is improbable that certain events in the political and literary histo-

ry of the time can have escaped Kierkegaard's attention, even though he does not touch on them directly, or does so only peripherally.

Thus it is improbable that he could have been unaware of the Goethe fever, even though the passages in the sources now available offer very little that is concrete. Without any doubt, the excerpt (I.C. 46) from F. M. Klinger's *Faust's Leben, Thaten und Höllenfahrt* (1799) was made in March 1835, as was, of course, the excerpt from the same author's *Der Faust der Morgenländer oder Wanderungen Ben Hafis* (1797), dated March 7, 1835. Judging by the size of the books, then, Kierkegaard must have read 600 pages of Klinger's two Faust novels in a short time. It is worth noting that Klinger, Rousseau's most warmhearted disciple among the poets of the Sturm and Drang, equips Faust with a social indignation which was in keeping with Kierkegaard's dramatic sketch *The Master Thief.* But we have solid ground beneath our feet: even if I.C. 51 is undated, it is from before March 16, 1835, and its account of the contents of C. Ludwig Stieglitz's *Die Sage vom Doctor Faust* (which Kierkegaard found in the *Historisches Taschenbuch,* Leipzig, 1834, edited by F. von Raumer) provided no fewer than 107 titles of a Faust bibliography.

Through Raumer, Kierkegaard found his way to F. A. Rauch's *Vorlesungen über Goethes Faust* (Catalogue 1800), Falk's *Goethe aus näherem Umgang dargestellt,* Harro Harring's *Faust im Gewande der Zeit* (Leipzig, 1831), Grabbe's tragedy *Faust und Don Juan* (Frankfurt, 1829), Lessing's treatment of the Faust story, and Schreiber's *Szenen aus Fausts Leben* (Offenbach, 1792). When Kierkegaard read each of these works cannot be determined with any certainty, but by the spring of 1835 he must have clearly perceived that it was possible to write about definite literary types, that these types often had their roots in the Middle Ages, and that they represented something universal, something common to all mankind. As early as January 29, 1835, he had compared the master thief with Till Eulenspiegel, who on March 16 seems "to represent the satyr element in the North." On March 28 the Wandering Jew, Faust, and Don Juan are mentioned in two notes, I.C.

65 and 66, something which has caused certain scholars to believe
that the three stages were already taking shape in Kierkegaard's
mind. From these and other notations made at the same time, the
two editors of the *Papers* have drawn a conclusion which sins by
ignoring an essential fact—Kierkegaard's relationship to the contemporary Danish novella, a new genre which was then blooming
in both theory and practice:

> Within the subgroup Aesthetica of Group C the vast majority
> of the material is composed of a series of excerpts, which are
> partly connected to S. K.'s intensive concern with Goethe's
> works and personality, partly with what he himself calls his
> "project" in this period (I.C. 83, p. 236), a project which
> seems to have been that of collecting material for a character-
> ization of the spirit of the Middle Ages through a general his-
> torical study of the phenomena peculiar to the age in all the
> fields of intellectual life, in literature, art, religion, science,
> and social conditions, concentrating itself *on a more intensive
> and concrete study* of the expression of the popular spirit of
> the Middle Ages in poetry, legend, fairy story, and tales, espe-
> cially in the representations of ideas which emerged from the
> realm of popular consciousness in the Middle Ages (compare
> *SV*, I:69 ff. [an altogether irrelevant reference]): Don Juan,
> Faust, the Wandering Jew—all of it illuminated by *a parallel
> and more abstract Hegelian philosophical interest* through the
> definition of such concepts as the Antique, the Romantic ("Di-
> alectic"), the Modern—the Comic, the Tragic, Irony, humor,
> resignation, etc., etc., in determining the stages in the devel-
> opment of the intellect, taken generally, both within "world
> history" itself and within the "microcosms" of the particular
> individual. [*Papers* I: xv–xvi]

Out of gratitude to my old philosophy teacher Victor Kuhr, I
shall ascribe this hideous sentence, a parody of Kierkegaard's style
at its worst, to P. A. Heiberg, lock, stock, and barrel; but why
didn't Kuhr's well-known sense of humor make him intercede?

What are the facts behind this unfortunate tirade concerning Kierkegaard's "project"?

Simply that the *Papers*, after Barfod, were in such disorder (a condition for which Kierkegaard himself was ultimately responsible) that they could not be published under any single standpoint. Notations, outbursts, commentaries, idle thoughts, excerpts, and literary sketches are scattered helter-skelter. There is no purpose in trying to enforce some plan or model upon such an incoherent body of material. It shows us Kierkegaard in his Sturm und Drang period, when his genius seeks to find itself in many different ways, via religion, philosophy, aesthetics, and, last but not least, literature.

Heiberg and Kuhr do not have the same excuse for their Byzantine hypothesis as does the scholar who, for example, wishing to depict Kierkegaard and the Royal Theater, must take recourse in the criterion of improbability: it is inconceivable that Kierkegaard, who attended the theater almost daily, would have been unaware that an art of the dance, meeting international standards, had been created in Copenhagen by Bournonville and Lucile Grahn—whose piquant private relationships were the talk of the whole town—although there is not enough source material to give us Kierkegaard's opinion about it. As already stated, Heiberg and Kuhr have no such excuse. Anyone able to read cannot help perceiving that the aesthetician Kierkegaard is in a Heibergian stage from the beginning. Anything else would be improbable! But P. A. Heiberg could not abide his namesake, J. L. Heiberg, because his pet, Kierkegaard, was never accepted by the Heibergians. That this relationship is something which influenced the arrangement of the papers cannot be proved, but it can be regarded as probable.

It is not my intention to depict the "breakthrough" of the modern prose tale in the 1820s, but I may be permitted to take issue with the myth which asserts that the modern novella and novel, replacing the verse narration and the saga pastiche of High Romanticism, arose around 1825. To be sure, the myth is based on historical data: Blicher's *En Landsbydegns Dagbog,* 1824 *(The Journal of a Parish Clerk)* and Poul Møller's *En dansk Students*

Eventyr, 1824 *(A Danish Student's Adventure)*, Oehlenschläger's
Øen i Sydhavet, 1824–25 *(The Island in the South Seas)*, Sibbern's
Gabrielis Breve (Gabrielis's Letters) and Ingemann's *Valdemar Sejr*,
both 1826, Fru Gyllembourg's *Familien Polonius*, 1827 *(The Polonius Family)*, and Carl Bernhard's *Nummer Syv*, 1828 *(Number
Seven)*. But it is incorrect to conclude from these premises that we
are confronting a "breakthrough" of prose here, involving both
Oehlenschläger's followers and the Heibergians. The literary facts
tell a different story.

Poul Møller's *En dansk Students Eventyr*, originally planned as a
historical novel à la Walter Scott, turned out to be an incomplete
tale with a contemporary setting, read in the spring of 1824 before
an audience at the student association. It had no importance for
Danish literature before its publication in 1843 in the third volume
of the *Efterladte Skrifter (Posthumous Writings)*. *En Landsbydegns
Dagbog* became well known only after it was printed in Blicher's
Samlede Noveller (Collected Novellas), vol. 1, of 1833.
Oehlenschläger's *Øen i Sydhavet*, with its broad, old-fashioned
form, pointed backward to the novels written in the wake of
Robinson Crusoe, just as Sibbern's *Gabrielis Breve* harks back to
Werther. Ingemann's *Valdemar Sejr* owed a debt to Walter Scott,
but Scott never became a favorite of the Heiberg school, whose
ideals in historical fiction were Mérimée and Vitet (cf. P. V. Jacobsen's letters and diaries and Carl Bernhard's later chronicles). The
same Carl Bernhard became seriously productive only from the
middle of the 1830s on, and Heiberg's and Christian Winther's
contributions to the first three years of *Flyveposten* consisted of
only a contemporary novella by each of them.

Fru Gyllembourg, on the other hand, contributed no fewer than
five stories, among them "En Hverdagshistorie" ("An Everyday
Story"), which gave the genre its name. This is the explanation for
the omnipotent place she had in Kierkegaard's literary conscious-
ness during these decades, and for the devoted homage he paid
her in both the book about H. C. Andersen (1838) and "A Literary
Review" (1846).

The Summer of 1835 in Gilleleje: The Fictive Letters and Notes

Fru Gyllembourg is not Kierkegaard's only model. He sought still others, lying further away in time. Not the garrulous Jean Paul, whose works he owned and knew, but Sibbern, Goethe, and Blicher. His close friend P. E. Lind had taken Jean Paul as a model for his novel *Johan Gordon*, which Heiberg had issued in two installments in *Flyveposten*, in March and April 1835, thus a short time after H. P. Holst had got his first novellas published; they followed French models (Jules Janin). *Johan Gordon* was praised to the skies in an anonymous review, signed T. G., in *Søndagsbladet* (June 14, 1835), immediately before Kierkegaard's departure for Gilleleje. Kierkegaard no doubt wished to rival his two friends, but under no circumstances did he want to employ their style. Above all, he meant to offer proof of a more profound view of life. Unfortunately for him, he was at the time in the midst of a disharmonious and tentative relationship to Christianity, with whose Grundtvigian form, the theory of the church, he settles accounts in a series of diary entries from April and May 1835. "Søren, it seems, is simply not preparing for his examination just now, God help him to overcome this inner ferment in a good way and for the deliverance of his soul," P. C. Kierkegaard noted in March 1835. It was the family's intention that the long stay in Gilleleje would keep him away from the baleful influence of Copenhagen.

Even before his departure from Copenhagen on June 17, 1835, Kierkegaard appears to have decided to write a modern philosophical novel in epistolary form. There are a good many indications that it, like *Gabrielis Breve*, was going to depict a youth, at odds with himself and in search of a goal, who finds peace and tranquillity during a journey from the capital to the country. I.C. 66, from March 28, brings the three mythical figures together.

> One often hears people say that someone is a Don Juan or a Faust, but they don't readily call a person the Wandering Jew.

But why shouldn't there be individuals of this sort, after all, who have simply absorbed too much of the Wandering Jew's nature?

The letter, which bears the date "Copenhagen, June 1, 1835" has given Kierkegaard scholarship gray hairs. They have been come by honestly. The letter was printed for the first time in the *Posthumous Papers*, I:38–45, with this introductory note by Barfod: "No doubt a copy of or a sketch for a letter—as it appears—to the zoologist P. W. Lund in Brazil." Barfod also gave a commentary on page 186 to the effect that the famous zoologist P. W. Lund, "a son of S. K.'s maternal uncle, stayed in Brazil from 1825 to 1829, and then was back in Denmark for a while in 1829 and in 1831–32, whereupon he returned once again to Rio and Lagoa Santa." This does not prove that the letter *is* to P. W. Lund, probably the person who, during his stay in Copenhagen, imbued his nephew early with an interest in the natural sciences, something to which both the *Papers* and the works bear witness aplenty. Kierkegaard appears to have been an assiduous reader of the popularizing *Dansk Ugeskrift*, published (from 1831 on) by the botanist J. F. Schouw, a journal whose second volume included his uncle's paper with the amusing title "Om de brasilianske Myrers Levemaade" ("Concerning the Mode of Life of Brazilian Ants," *SV*, XIII:64).

Kuhr and Heiberg reprint the letter in question as I.A. 72, putting it after the latest datable entry, I.C. 69, a nonfiction description of a visit to Pastor Lyngby on August 4 and a boating excursion with him on Søborg Lake. The "you" who is addressed in the letter of "June 1, 1835" is identified without hesitation as Peter Wilhelm Lund (1801–80).

Niels Thulstrup includes the letter in his edition of *Breve og Aktstykker* under the date June 1, 1835, as if it were a matter of a real letter to P. W. Lund: "The letter, of which only the rough draft is known, is directed to the natural scientist P. W. Lund." He also gives the usual information about Lund's stay in Copenhagen, his kinship to Kierkegaard, and the surmise that "S. K. no doubt met him at the home of H. F. Lund," Kierkegaard's brother-in-law. Thulstrup's authorities are just as dependable as are Henriette Lund's book *Naturforskeren P. W. Lund*, 1885 *(The Natural Scientist P. W. Lund)* and Troels-Lund's *Et Liv*, 1924 *(A Life)*—in fact, these *are* his authorities. Indeed, one has to admire the faith of theologians in the printed word, for beyond the letter's first lines about "your description of your stay in Brazil" and "your first entrance into the marvels of nature," nothing justifies an interpretation of the letter as an "actual" one.

Now, it may seem unreasonable that Kierkegaard would write a fictitious letter to an uncle in Brazil, in which, in his effort to make his status clear—"I'd like to try to show how my affairs stand"—he mentions three professors of the natural sciences by name, H. C. Ørsted, J. F. Schouw, and J. W. Hornemann, as well as one from the field of theology, oddly enough the nontheologian Heiberg. There is nothing strange in this if one can accept the theory of a sketch for a Faustian novella whose hero is a student of theology intellectually related to Kierkegaard, a hero who has been plunged into religious doubts by a natural scientist intellectually related to P. W. Lund:

> Now it is quite in order, for the rest, that wine ferments before it turns clear; but this condition is often unpleasant, all the same, in its single moments, though it naturally, taken as a whole, has its pleasure, to the extent that it nonetheless attains its relative results within all the general doubting. In particular, it has a great importance for the person who, by means of it, has come to a clear understanding of his destiny, not only for the sake of the peace which follows in contrast to the storm which has preceded, but because one in this case possesses life itself in quite a different sense than before. This is the Faustian element, which, to a certain extent, comes more or less into its own in every intellectual development, and on this account it has always seemed to me that one ought to grant the idea of *Faust* a universal importance. Just

as our forefathers had a goddess who represented longing, just so, in my opinion, Faust is doubt personified. And he is not supposed to be anything more, and it is, I suppose, a sin against the idea when Goethe lets his Faust be converted, just as when Mérimée let his Don Juan be converted. Do not make the objection that Faust, in the moment when he turned to the devil, undertook a positive step after all, for precisely in this, it seems to me, there lies one of the most profound elements in the story. He gave himself over to the devil; for Mephisto, to be sure, let him gaze through his spectacles into the interior of man and into the secret hiding places of the earth, but Faust must constantly doubt Mephisto because the latter could never enlighten him about that which is most profound in an intellectual respect. As a result of his idea, he could never turn to God, insofar as he, in the moment when he did it, would have to tell himself that, in truth, enlightenment was to be found here; but in the same moment he would have denied his character of being a doubter.

After this, Kierkegaard undertakes a demonstration of the same doubt in other spheres; for example, when a person who wishes to develop his powers in a certain direction does not know what suits his personality best. The two-part attempt to make his status clear, which now follows, cannot—according to the interpretation we have applied here—have any absolute source value attributed to it as an illustration of Kierkegaard's relationship to the natural sciences and theology. It is striking that the author of the letter makes remarks of such profundity about the natural sciences and provides characteristics of Ørsted, Schouw, and Hornemann while failing to mention a single theological representative of orthodoxy and rationalism. Neither H. N. Clausen, his most important theological teacher, nor Grundtvig, with whom he had just settled accounts, nor Mynster, whose romantically individual Christianity can surely not be said to represent the orthodoxy in which the letter writer asserts that he grew up, nor

Schleiermacher, whose works Kierkegaard had studied and discussed the year before with Martensen.

In passing, it should be observed that Schleiermacher is another fine example for the employment of criteria of improbability in Kierkegaard scholarship. In 1833 Schleiermacher visited Copenhagen, where he was lionized on September 27 at Skydebanen and feted in the student association the next evening, and where he preached at the morning service in St. Peter's Church on Sunday the 29th. It was a reception with a grandeur seldom vouchsafed a foreign intellectual personality in Denmark before or since. It was the autumn's great event, and so it is inconceivable that Kierkegaard should not have partaken of it.

None of the authors or works named in the letter make a definitive dating possible, but it is worth noting that Mérimée's novella about Don Juan, *Les âmes du Purgatoire,* could be read in the *Revue des Deux Mondes*, III:377–434, thus in the issue of October 1834, and that the letter's allusion to those "natural sounds from Ceylon" comes from the work *Die Symbolik des Traumes* (1814), of the German natural philosopher Gotthilf Heinrich von Schubert, the second edition of which Kierkegaard got from Reitzel on February 22, 1836 (Catalogue 776, not 777 as Thulstrup says). Schubert's *Die Geschichte der Seele* was obtained from Reitzel on January 12, 1836 (Catalogue U, 97). Of course, Kierkegaard *can* have read about these "natural sounds" before February 1836; they made a strong impression on him as an expression of nature's irony and are cited in the dissertation (*SV*, XIII:329). But if the letter is fictive, then this allusion to Schubert may justify dating it after Feburary 22, 1836. At any event, in their commentary on the proposition of I.A. 72, "For the learned theological world seems to me to resemble Strandveien on a Sunday afternoon in the season when Dyrehaugen [the royal park north of Copenhagen] is open," Heiberg and Kuhr referred to I.A. 73, which follows the letter: "There is something particularly ironic in the Dyrehaugen excursions of the Copenhageners; they seek to shake off the petty bourgeois dust of the city, to escape themselves—and they find themselves once again at Bakken [a popular amusement park, which still exists]." This note, added later by Kierkegaard, is dated January 14, 1837, and it is to be connected, as the editors correctly point out, with the beginning of I.A. 328:

> In a strange illusion, the one person cries out constantly that he has got past the other, just as when the Copenhageners set out for Dyrehaugen with a philosophical mien "in order to see," without recollecting that they themselves thereby become an object for the others, who of course have also made the excursion in order to see.

Amusingly enough, I.A. 328 begins a series of entries which Heiberg and Kuhr themselves date in the years 1836–37 and which Kierkegaard has introduced in reverse order in Journal CC, on pages 1–46. These entries had already caused Barfod exquisite pain; he presents them as a special group for the first time in *Posthumous Papers*, I:10–23, but gives them the quite arbitrary date of 1833. His successors protest against this in their introduction with the observation that, "according to the chronological clues the content provides, they must certainly be placed toward the end of 1836 and the beginning of 1837." One can agree with Heiberg and Kuhr here, but only with the addition that, in this case, the letter to P. W. Lund (?) of "June 1, 1835," can also perfectly well be from the same period, that is, if it is a fictive letter with a fictive date.

In the letter to Lund (I.A.72) one line stands by itself after Kierkegaard's great attempt to make his status clear: "Nonnulla desunt," which Thulstrup translates, "a good part missing." Nobody would write this in a letter or a draft of a letter, but one certainly could in a literary manuscript or a sketch for one. If the letter to Lund is compared with the real letter to P. E. Lind of July 6, 1835, the difference is unmistakable. The reply to the letter of June 27 from his friend Lind depicts Kierkegaard's torments in finding his way into the future, but it is concerned mostly with real milieus, with his friends and fellow students, and with real

events—Tage Algreen-Ussing's speech during the festival at
Skydebanen on May 28, the genuine and the false opposition to it,
and Lind's polemic against Algreen-Ussing in *Kjøbenhavnsposten*
of June 16 and 19, 1835. Until he got Lind's letter Kierkegaard
knew nothing about the second article, since he left Copenhagen
on June 17 and did not read newspapers in Gilleleje.

The letter to Lund (I.A.72) has a clear continuation, however—
I.A.75, dated Gilleleje, August 1, 1835, and beginning, "In reality,
my affairs stood just as I have tried to show in the previous pages."
Thulstrup has wisely omitted it from his *Breve og Aktstykker*—is
that because it does not seem addressed to anyone in particular?
Or ought it to be regarded as literature? It is the celebrated notation with, "it is a matter of finding a truth which is truth for me,
of finding the idea for which I wish to live and die," immortalized
on the monument of Gilbjerghoved in northern Zealand. The existentialists are glad to have the passage, the theologians less so.
(Immediately preceding it, Kierkegaard talks about the deity but
not about God, an unfortunate circumstance, of course, if we are
dealing here with a real letter or diary entry.) Extending his earlier
attempt to determine his status with respect to the natural sciences and theology, he now touches upon the field of jurispru-
dence and furthermore expresses a wish to become an actor, "so
that, by putting myself into another's role, I could obtain, so to
speak, a surrogate for my own life"—compare the interest in the
master thief, to whom indirect reference is made. The letter writer
continues by depicting his efforts to find "a focus in which all the
rays are collected." Only those who suffer from literary color
blindness can fail to see that the following passage is imaginative
literature:

> I have sought such a focus too. I have sought an anchorage
> both in the bottomless sea of pleasures and in the depths of
> knowledge. I have felt the almost irresistible power with
> which one pleasure offers its hand to another; I have felt that
> sort of false enthusiasm which it is able to elicit; I have also

felt the boredom, the sense of being torn, which follows upon it. I have tasted the fruits of the tree of knowledge and, early and often, have found happiness in their goodly taste. But this happiness lay only in the moment of recognition, and afterward left no deeper mark within me. It seems to me that I have not drunk from the cup of wisdom but have fallen into it.

This could well be called a terribly exaggerated statement, judging by all we know about Kierkegaard up to the summer of 1835. Nor does the resigned air of the conclusion jibe with the facts: the youngest son who, after the deaths of his sisters and his mother, casts himself into an aesthetic mode of life in open defiance of his Grundtvigian big brother and of his father, the latter utterly abandoned to his depressions. The letter by no means has to have been written at Gilleleje on August 1, 1835. Rather, like the preceding one, it was written in Copenhagen in 1836. Of the notations which accompany it, I.A.76–80, only one, I.A.78 (which in its turn is a note added to I.A.77), has been given a date, September 20, 1836. There are many indications that Kierkegaard used the summer vacation of 1836 for reexperiencing the journey to Gilleleje of the previous year. Perhaps it was a sort of compensation for his staying in the city that second summer for financial reasons; his father would not pay for his vacation.

The main entry, I.A.75, provides no clues beyond the mention of Socrates and Socratic irony. The accompanying marginal notes point to 1836: Kierkegaard got Novalis's *Schriften* (Berlin, 1826) from Reitzel on January 4, 1836 (Catalogue 1776, I.A.80). "Morad der Buckelige." an Arabian tale, which could be found in *Bilder Magazin*, no. 40, 1835, appears to have been read in March 1836 (I.A.144) either in German or in a Danish translation in *Riises Bibliothek for Ungdommen* vol. II, sixth issue, 1836 (I.A.79). The entry I.A.145, which consists of a continuation of the note about the Arabian tale and its *sens moral* (that there is always a little catch in the fulfillment of all wishes) perhaps can lead the trail still further.

The Gilleleje Summer of 1835 Recalled

I.A.145 refers to C. C. Rafn's edition, *Nordiske Kæmpe-Historier efter islandske Haandskrifter*, vols. I–III, Copenhagen, 1821–26 (*Stories of Nordic Warriors according to Icelandic Manuscripts*) (Catalogue 1993–1995), employing *Ketil Hængs Saga* and *Buesvingers Saga* as examples of the strange, Hamlet-like comedy which sometimes "is played out with the world, in that the most unlikely person suddenly emerges with a power and might which is not particularly pleasant for those who made his apparent foolishness a butt of their jokes." A still more remarkable example—of how the individual who pretends to be mad can exceed all others in wisdom—is found by Kierkegaard in Gustav Schwab's *Buch der schönsten Geschichten und Sagen.* vols. I–II (Stuttgart, 1836), which he bought from Reitzel on January 10, 1836—the story of Robert der Teufel, who was compelled to play the part of a fool and a mute. Here Kierkegaard finds a natural transition to an "investigation of the role of fools in the Middle Ages" and mentions as examples "Wagner's, Leporello's, and Sancho Panza's relations to their respective masters, in order to attack, from a different side, the selfsame idea we mentioned in a different connection." Since Kierkegaard does not normally call himself "we," but prefers the "I" form, it is natural to ask whether I.A.145 is also a fragment or a sketch for a letter.

C. C. Rafn's *Nordiske Kæmpe-Historier* also lies behind I.A.333, with a date which is presumably fictive, December 2. It belongs to I.A.328–41, which are connected, and which the editors date to 1836–37. In reality they may be regarded as having been written very late in 1836 and early in 1837; the entry of December 2, 1836, which can be interpreted as a letter or a notation, in accordance with one's taste, has the following text, in extenso:

> I do not wish to speak with the world ever again; I wish to forget that I have ever done so at all. I have read about a man who spent fifty years in bed, never spoke to anyone, and, like Queen Gudrun after having quarreled with O . . ., I wish to

take to my bed after having quarreled with the world. Or I
wish to flee to a place where no one knows my language or
can understand it, and I cannot understand theirs, where I,
like a Casper Hauser number two, can stand—not really
knowing how it happened—in the middle of a street in
Nürnberg.

Queen Gudrun is mentioned in Rafn's first volume, of 1821, and
Casper Hauser plays an outstanding role in *Flyveposten* of 1828 (a
run of the journal with which Kierkegaard occupied himself in
1835: compare I.C.46 [Andersen's *Journey on Foot*]); Kierkegaard
made excerpts from the journal's dramatic-aesthetic proposals
(1828 again) on January 16, 1837, in I. C. 124.

If we look at the connected group I.A.328–41 (1836–37) we find
that Barfod does not give us much help; he merely says, concerning I.A.328, "The beginning of what follows seems to be missing.
As far as one can tell, it is the copy of a letter—it is not known to
whom." The whole group bears the stamp of the epistolary form.
It cannot be dated with any certainty, but all the mentions of authors, quotations, and allusions, taken together, will provide a basis for a placing and a defining of the suite's connections with the
rest of the papers.

With its six pages, I.A.328 is by far the longest. It fits neatly with
Kierkegaard's two attempts to determine his status, from Gilleleje
(I.A.68 and I.A.72); perhaps it belonged to page 51 of I.A.72: *Nonnulla desunt*. The metaphor about the Dyrehaugen excursions of
the Copenhageners brings us to I.A.73, dated January 14, 1837.
The observation concerning elderly critics, who always look for
elderly models with which to assault their contemporary world,
corresponds to the thought of I.A.223, with reference to Heine's
Die romantische Schule (Hamburg, 1836), supplied by Reitzel on
February 16, 1836 (Catalogue U, 63), and read on August 12,
1836—compare I.C.95. The allusion to Martensen's article in the
Maanedsskrift for Litteratur, vol. XVI (p. 516), refers to the issue
of 1836. The joke about the application of the Hegelian trinity to
boots turns up in I.A.317 from January 5, 1837. The polemic

against the modern politicians, the National Liberals, corresponds in spirit and tone to the articles in *Flyveposten* from the spring of 1836. The ridiculing of the demands for thrift of "our men of finance" quite certainly arises from Kierkegaard's reading of *Kjøbenhavnsposten* of December 1836. The marginal note, I.A.329, refers to Görres's *Die christliche Mystik*, of 1836, which Kierkegaard got from Reitzel on November 11, 1836; only the preface appears to have been read (Catalogue 528–32).

I.A.331 is certainly not a letter in actual fact. After having dutifully told us where in the United States N. A. Kierkegaard died, even Heiberg and Kuhr add, "Presumably the whole is to be regarded as a fiction, after all." It is the wittiest, most exaggerated, and best written of the "Letters":

> I have been in mourning since I last wrote to you. You will detect it from (among other things) the black sealing wax which—although generally I detest such external signs—I have had to use, for I could get my hands on nothing else in our grief-stricken family. Yes, my brother is dead; but strangely enough I do not really mourn for *him*, yet my grief for my brother who died several years ago, on the other hand, is quite overwhelming. On the whole, I have noticed that my grief is not of a nature which grasps something immediately, but increases with time, and I am sure that, should I grow old someday, I shall really begin to think about the departed, not—as it is said in the formulas of consolation—in order to rejoice at the thought of meeting them on the other side but in order truly to feel that I have lost them. Now, as far as my late brother is concerned, I am sure that my grief will awaken only after much time has fled.

The passage calls for reflection. Assuming that both the two letters to P. W. Lund and the "letters" cited here are fictive, and assuming that they were written down in any case *after* the rash of deaths in 1832–34, but *before* the father's passing, how could Kierkegaard imagine that his epistolary novella was publishable? Even beneath the pseudonyms, the originals of the figures in the

"Letters" are easily discerned: the famous natural scientist in Brazil, the pitiful family, the brother who had just died (N. A. Kierkegaard), for whom he did not mourn nearly as much as for the brother who had passed away several years before (Søren Mikael Kierkegaard, who died in 1819.)

The whole of Copenhagen could see through this story, which, if it had appeared, would have been regarded as a scandal, an insult to his family—that is, his father, his brother, and the two Lund brothers-in-law.

Matters do not improve when, in the following passage, heavy-handed fun is made of mourning, funeral parlors, and all the traditional and external ceremonies which accompany death:

In the first moment so many ludicrous circumstances turn up that I can't help laughing. Let me give you one example. To-day my brother-in-law the commission agent—I've mentioned him earlier, and I'll give a closer description of him when the occasion arises—entered in order to console his sister; in his delicate and oddly laughing voice, which so excellently parodies that gentlemanly quality he strives to achieve in his outward appearance, he burst out: Ja! Was ist der Mensch? A clarinet, I answered, whereupon he abandoned his role altogether and tried to explain to me that the true gentleman did not have a voice like a bear's but a sonorous and euphonic one. . . . Now the undertaker entered in order to find out if—in addition to ham, salami, and Dutch cheese—anything else should be served; he offered to make all the necessary arrangements, an offer which my brother-in-law the commission agent opposed, because, as he said, it would be good for his sister, her heart so deeply laden with pain and woe, to have something to think about, so that she would forget the desolation and the stillness which surrounded her after the loss of her "late husband." . . . Now I shall skip over the intervening days. At last the day of the funeral came. Huge quantities of the cheese, sausages, and ham mentioned above were served, various wines and cakes were not lacking—one cannot spy anyone enjoying it—oh, how great the grief is! Here, the rule from the book *How to Behave in Polite Society*—that no one may begin to eat before his neighbor does—is genuinely fulfilled at every meal. On such occasions, in the old days, a natural association of ideas reminded one of the true proposition that a hero is nothing without beer and food, and therefore funeral feasts were held, but see what has become of the funeral feast now; for the undertakers, pall-bearers, grave diggers, etc., are the ones who do the eating for all of us. On such occasions I, too, am assailed by a terrible appetite and start before anyone else, despite the rules of behavior in polite society, and nevertheless no one wishes to follow my example.

This is as malicious as it is witty. It comes as no surprise that young Kierkegaard's eye—an X ray for everything superficial, stilted, hollow, false, and pompous, not least within the church—has seen the ridiculous element in official middle-class obsequies, even when the admired Mynster himself gave the funeral sermon. Is the brother-in-law a caricature of one of the two Lunds? Is the caricature even more malicious than appears from the quoted passage? A description of the commission agent at his dressing table has been omitted here, a passage in which he uses the appropriate instrument, a pair of tweezers, to pull out one or another of those hairs of his which "had become a little gray or which recalled the original color—red—a little too much."

And now another letter writer. Her brother. A captain in Brazilian service. Characterized by his military brevity. The letter of condolence arrives on the wedding day:

Dear sister! I shall not mention what he was for you, you no doubt feel it all too well yourself. I only want to say that, despite the fact that I see a hundred cases of it every day here, I feel in truth, nonetheless, that I have had only one brother-in-law, just as you doubtless feel that he was your first and last love.

                                        Your brother

Of "December 2," I.A.333, only the beginning has been adduced above. The continuation fits with the two letters to Lund:

> The misfortune lies precisely in the fact that, if someone has developed something beforehand, as it were, it turns out to be oneself. The other day I told you about an idea for a Faust, and only now do I perceive that I was describing myself; I can hardly read about an illness or think of it before I get it myself.

The letter dissolves into random thoughts and Kierkegaardian ornamentations, familiar from other passages: the book dealer Soldin, who asks his wife if he is the one who is speaking; Echo as the grand master of irony—compare the character in the Soap Cellar drama; Caligula, who wished that the heads of all the Romans could be attached to a single neck (I.A.246, from September 20, 1836). As for I.A.334 about the bridge of sighs, and I.A.335 about the gadfly on the great man's nose, compare the Soap Cellar drama, and I.A.337, with its reference to Brentano: *Die mehreren Wehmüller und ungarischen Nationalgesichter*, which Kierkegaard owned in an edition of 1833, also contained Eichendorff's *Viel Lärmen um Nichts*. An extensive résumé of the first of these novellas is given in I.C.86, lacking a date, but from 1836.

In this presentation quotations have been used extensively, even pedantically, although it has been impossible to provide a firm dating of the material and to give it an appropriate location in the whole, let alone to determine what plan it was that Kierkegaard originally had in mind. The absolutely central entry, the "matchless discovery" and the "secret note," was the undated one of II.A.46, which has a clear connection with all the entries previously mentioned. In my opinion it explains Kierkegaard's "my project" (I.C.83). As its title it has "An Introduction":

> Most people generally begin reading a book with a notion about how they themselves would have written, and how another person has written or would have written, and, as it were, a similar prejudice sets in when they are about to see a

person for the first time, and as a result thereof, then, very few people really know how the other person looks. This is the point at which the first possibility of not being able to read a book begins, proceeding thereafter through a countless throng of nuances up to the highest step—misunderstanding. The two most directly opposed sorts of reader meet—the most stupid and the most brilliant, both of them having the quality in common that they cannot read a book, the former because of a lack of ideas, the latter because of a plenitude of them; therefore I have given this piece of writing such a general title (it was intended to be called "Letters"), in order to make my contribution toward preventing what is often a loss for the author and sometimes for the reader— misunderstanding.

Thus, at some time or other, Kierkegaard wrote the preface to a book, "this piece of writing," which was intended to be called "Letters." It can scarcely be determined with any certainty, or even probability, what sort of plan it was that Kierkegaard had made. But one can attack the problem from another side, namely, by sorting out the entries from the Gilleleje summer which are "factual," not literary.

The Gilleleje Summer of 1835: The Actual Events

Kierkegaard scholarship is agreed (with itself) that Kierkegaard was in Gilleleje from June 17 to August 24, 1835, staying at the inn owned by Christopher Mentz. That Kierkegaard wrote letters, now lost, to his father is clear from the latter's reply of July 4, 1835, which also reports that the old man has had the older brother, Peter, answer Søren's letters—perhaps because he himself was suffering from colic. Of letters to his friends in Copenhagen, only the one to P. E. Lind, of July 6, 1835, has been preserved, a reply to a letter of June 27 from Lind, evidently the first and only one which Kierkegaard, to his ill-concealed irritation, had received from the acquaintances in Copenhagen who had promised to write to him—something which "makes a mixed impression on me."

Lind's letter, which is not extant, doubtless told about his controversy with Chancellery Secretary Tage Algreen-Ussing (1797–1872), an elderly man in the eyes of these youngsters and palpably one of the two friends' pet aversions. P. E. Lind took his stand in a more or less anonymous fashion, that is, under the signature "r". Having presented long and detailed accounts of the banquet given by the Society for the Freedom of the Press on May 28, the newspaper *Kjøbenhavnsposten* on June 6, 1835, printed a toast offered on this occasion by Algreen-Ussing, in which he distinguished between genuine and bogus opposition, comparing them respectively to genuine and bogus eau de cologne, of which the latter was the Danish brand, produced by a certain Mr. Brøndum—who may be the same man who immortalized his name by means of Brøndums Snaps. The eau de cologne of Denmark, and Mr. Brøndum, were defended on June 7 by an unsigned article in *Kjøbenhavnsposten* which asserted that Algreen-Ussing himself had abused the freedom of the press. Algreen-Ussing, an indefatigable writer of letters to the editor, struck back with three columns of "Opposition to the Opposition," and on June 16, the day before Kierkegaard's departure, Lind seems to have involved himself in the debate with a contribution one column long, signed "r," in which he, using an amusing expression, censured Algreen-Ussing for having committed "an act of violence out of lack of tact." He got a brief reply the next day, in which the Chancellery Secretary referred to his right to have his speeches and toasts printed verbatim, rejecting "hateful and, I dare add, ludicrous insinuations of this sort." On June 19, 1835, still protected by his "r," Lind backed out of the controversy with a tame account of its history. There followed, on June 21, 1835, a concluding statement of four lines from the pen of Algreen-Ussing. Kierkegaard's interest in this feud against one of the bigwigs of the National Liberals, and his sense of involvement in it, appear with utter clarity in his letter to P. E. Lind of July 6, 1835. It is impossible to find out who his "acquaintances" were. But the letter contains a salvo heralding the autumn's campaign against the National Liberals:

As far as your quarrel with Ussing is concerned, it is impossible for me to understand exactly what has happened, since I haven't seen a newspaper since I've been here. However I am delighted that you've caught hold of him; for I was annoyed at the manner in which he defended the original defender of Brøndum [the short, unsigned article in Kjøbenhavnsposten of June 7, 1835, not by Lind]. Whoever it was certainly deserved a little smack on the fingers for his melodramatic defense, but Ussing merited being thoroughly hauled over the coals for his crafty method of interpreting the matter. Thus it was my intention to write something against him, and one of my acquaintances, whom I urged to write what I wished to have written, has no doubt failed to do so. I wanted to show him, you see, that the whole secret lies in a suppression of a part of his previous speech. Now this has become academic, of course, since you have got him to the point of confessing that he was wrong. It's no doubt best to let his subsequent behavior pass without comment.

The final observation most likely had to do with the campaign which the ever-busy pen of Algreen-Ussing mounted against the Thaarup family, *père et fils*, in connection with a political pamphlet that had been translated from Danish to German.

On the whole, the author of the best-seller *Johan Gordon*, P. E. Lind, was the man of the hour during these summer months, when friend Kierkegaard engaged in lonely fantasies in northern Zealand. Even though the letters are not preserved, it would be unreasonable to think that Lind failed to keep Kierkegaard oriented about the summer war between the "Soranians" (the literary group associated with Sorø Academy, which rallied around Oehlenschläger) and the Heibergians. Poul Møller started it off on July 7 and 8, 1835, with a protest of mighty breadth in *Kjøbenhavnsposten* against the review which Christian Winther's *Digte (Poems)* had received in *Litteraturtidende*, no. 16. It was a correction ex cathedra, which, apart from aesthetic questions, established that Winther had never enjoyed official favor, for he had received neither fellowships nor calls to a pastorate nor travel money. The reviewer in *Litteraturtidende* turned out to be Professor Christian Wilster, at Sorø Academy, whose anonymity was unhesitatingly stripped from him by Møller, and after a statement by D. G. Monrad and an ironic final furbelow by Wilster, the controversy came to an end on August 11, 1835. The public must have felt that Poul Møller and Monrad were the victors.

The debate concerning Carl Bagger's *Min Broders Levned (My Brother's Life)* was more complicated. It was begun on July 18, 1835, with an anonymous review by Peder Hjort, who demonstrated a surprising amount of goodwill toward Bagger (a product of Sorø Academy) and an implacable hatred of European romanticizing as represented, above all, by Byron: Byron's Danish disciple Paludan-Müller had the riot act read to him. This flood of words caused Lind, employing the readily decipherable letters "r. l–d," to come to the aid of Paludan-Müller with an altogether warm and positive statement. This in turn prompted a contribution on August 19 with the signature "P. g.," which disassociated itself from Paludan-Müller, and a concluding reply on August 26 from Lind, an urbane closing-off of the debate, in which Hjort himself had refrained from joining.

Thus it was Kierkegaard's friends and fellow students P. E. Lind and D. G. Monrad who had risked their skins in the press while Kierkegaard himself had cultivated his soul and the writing of literature in northern Zealand. Of course, Kierkegaard followed it all as closely as he could, directly and indirectly. Lind himself departed for Bornholm the same autumn, so he cannot have had anything whatsoever to do with Kierkegaard's carefully prepared assault on the National Liberals in the student association (1835), and the next year in *Flyveposten*.

While all this was taking place in Copenhagen, Kierkegaard sat making literature at Gilleleje Inn—or, at any event, making notes and sketches for his epistolary novella. The first, I.A.63, fills almost four pages in the *Papers*. Kierkegaard had been at the inn for some time, perhaps a couple of weeks, and had made excursions to Esrum, Fredensborg, Frederiksværk, and Tisvilde. In his trunk he had brought along J. G. Burman-Becker's *Efterretninger om de gamle Borge i Danmark og Hertugdømmerne*, Copenhagen, 1830–31 (*Information about the Old Castles in Denmark and the Duchies*), with a preface by Johan Gottfridsen; in its first volume he could find extensive material about Søborg Castle, which lay on a point of land extending into the lake, itself described as being partly dried up and partly grown over. During his visit he could read a detailed account in the same source about the imprisonment of Archbishop Jakob Grand and his escape to Bornholm, even as he could find out about King Valdemar's hunt, Queen Hedvig, and Tovelil. He did not see Saint James's chapel, of which only the granite foundations now remain: it was not excavated until 1839.

Kierkegaard's main source for legendary material was, by the way, J. M. Thiele's *Danske Folkesagn*, vols. I–II, 1818–23 (*Danish Popular Legends*) (Catalogue 1591–92); the first collection, of 1818, was particularly rich in material that would interest him. Here he found not only the legends about Søborg Castle and Gurre Lake, recounted by Burman-Becker, but also the three different versions of the legends concerning the origin of the springs of Saint Helena. Kierkegaard arrived shortly before Midsummer, and his description of the havoc wrought by drifting sand has nothing to do with Thiele. He himself must also have seen the miraculous springs, to which the population made pilgrimages at Midsummer, and he calls attention to the circumstances, as though it were a strange piece of fiction: "Just in this region, where health is sought, many have found their graves. Seen in the evening sun, the whole seems to be a legend brought to life before one's eyes, a version of the Job story in which Tibirke Church plays the main role." Amidst the tents, tables, German peddler-women, orators, and the inspector of the springs, the poet introduces his own portrait by coquettishly underlining the contrast between himself and the superstitious local population, "a person with modern clothes, glasses, and a cigar in his mouth." Compare the famous aesthetic portrait from 1838.

Concrete descriptions are given only of the land around Helena's grave, the inscriptions on the "placards" of the people who have been healed, the plank shed containing the three springs, and the account by C. Wilhelm Schrøder, the "inspector of the drifting sand," concerning the visit of Crown Prince Frederik on June 18, 1774. Kierkegaard made a copy of this account in extenso. A marginal note indicates that Kierkegaard was particularly interested, during his visit at Fredensborg, in the pillars in Nordmandsdalen, a valley in the park of the royal castle. He apparently spent Midsummer Night at the springs of Saint Helena, so the notes about this are clearly from June 24.

With Thiele as his romantic guide, he visited Gurre Castle, "where they are currently engaged in excavating the ruins" (I.A.64, undated). The visit provides an opportunity for a recapitulation of the legends about King Volmer, Gurre, and the king's wild ride, together with a grand romantic comparison between Gurre and Søborg Lake itself:

> Gurre Lake is also a part of this; rather long and not very broad in relation to its length, it has flourishing beech forests on its one side, and on the other forests with smaller, more stunted trees. Along a good part of its shores, the lake is bordered with reeds. When one sees this landscape in an afternoon light, when the sun is still sufficiently high to give the friendly landscape its necessary sharp contours, like a melodic voice which is accentuated sharply enough not to be lisping, all of our surroundings seem to whisper to us: this is a good place to be. It is secret, intimate impressions of this sort that a lake surrounded by forests (large enough both to separate and to unite at one and the same time) can elicit; it is something the sea cannot do. The rushes that wave in the wind along the shores are a quite special part of the view. While the soughing of the trees lets us hear King Valdemar's hunt, the sound of the horns, and the barking of the dogs,

those rushes seem to be breathing their approval—the blond maidens who admire the knight's bold ride and noble bearing. How different the view is in this respect from that of Søborg Lake. The great rushes also bend before the wind, but their soughing proclaims battle and power. And then the sea, which is forever in movement like a mighty spirit, and even in its greatest quiet is a harbinger of violent passions. A quiet melancholy rests upon the surroundings of Gurre Lake: it lives, so to speak, more in the past. And that is why it is overgrown, too; the sea on the other hand conquers parts of the land—they stand opposed to one another like two hostile forces. The stretch of coast is barren and sandy; the land lifts itself up in order, as it were, to do battle with all its might. The sea has its greatest force when the storm joins in with its bass voice, and when its own deep roaring vies with the thunder of the heavens and the whole world is illuminated by the lightning. Gurre Lake is most beautiful when a gentle breeze curls its blue surface, and bird song accompanies the whisper of the rushes; the sea is accompanied by only the hoarse cry of the lonely gull. The former (the sea) is like a recitative of Mozart, the latter like a melody of Weber.

The following depiction of the way to Hellebæk, with a visit at Odinshøj and the trip home via Gilleleje, is by a romantic portrayer of nature, who does not forget to note his impressions of the forest, its animals, the birds, and the multitude of ponds (Kobberdammen, Bondedammen?) with their white water lilies, *nymphæa alba.* The lighting is carefully noted: "The beams of the midday sun," Tibirke Church "seen in the evening light," the springs of Helena and their burial mound in "the dawn light with its strangely living movement," and Gurre Castle "in afternoon light." The *Papers* often touch on the problematical nature of light.

After answering P. E. Lind's letter on July 6, Kierkegaard sets out on an excursion to Esrum on July 8, 1835, appearing to have gone on foot from there over Nøddebo to Fredensborg. Astonishingly enough, Kierkegaard makes observations worthy of a forester: "On the right hand one constantly has the woods, variously beech and fir. At single spots one finds delightful plantations of firs, three to four years old." On the way, a thunderstorm overtakes him, but it turns out to be a mere shower. He offers a romantic description of what was a new experience for him—in contrast to the coming of a thunderstorm over the sea, with which he was familiar. The rain is so heavy that Kierkegaard has to look for shelter and, having forgotten by this time that he is on foot, he puts his carriage under cover at a peasant's house, loaned from the novellas of Blicher:

> Now I myself, clad in my huge chenille, entered the main room, where I found a company, composed of three people, in the process of eating dinner. As for furniture, there was naturally the large, long table, at which our peasants are wont to eat; and furthermore a four-poster bed, a fine example of the species . . . . The next room, to which the door stood open, was a storage space for fine and coarse linens, and other woven stuffs, and so forth, in such topsy-turvy quantities that one could have readily believed one had landed in a little robber's colony, for which both the location of the place (with Esrum Lake on the one side, and Grib Forest on the other, and not another house for a mile around) and the appearance of the inhabitants themselves seemed suitable. Let us now take a little closer look at them. At the far end of the aforementioned long table, the man of the house sat with his sandwich and a bottle of brandy before him. He listened quite calmly to my story about my unfortunate fate, merely sipping from his glass now and then, something he seems to have done rather often, to judge by the cubic content of his nose. However, the frequency of this enjoyment had not in any way weakened its agreeableness, and I am sure that he drank his schnapps with the same zest as someone who had just resigned from an abstinence society. The woman was not terribly tall, with a broad face and a nose turned up in a rath-

er ugly fashion, and a pair of crafty eyes; describing their manner of making a living (by doing bleaching), she assured me that people had to earn their keep somehow. In addition, there was a little round-shouldered girl, the same creature that had shown itself at the window and that I had first taken to be a child.

One can detect a tyro narrator here, still unsure of himself; nothing in the depiction of the three persons, the drunken man of the house, the ugly wife, and the round-shouldered girl, actually indicates "a little robber's colony." That is the result, rather, of having read Blicher. After describing the continuation of the ride through Grib Forest amidst thunder, lightning, and rain, Kierkegaard and the twelve-year-old Rudolph Mentz, the innkeeper's son, take refuge in a second house:

Wretched and tumbledown. The people poverty-stricken. The wife a homebody. She sat weaving. The husband talked through his nose. The first thing to catch my eye when I entered was a sort of door to an alcove which was made of an old plank; a girl in simple country dress was painted in it, and it bore the following text: "My field, it does feed me, my sheep gives me clothes, my house gives me shelter, the best way it knows." I asked for a little bread for my horses, which they were not very willing to give, since they had only half a loaf. Yet they let themselves be persuaded, and since I paid them rather generously, the woman answered that she didn't want to take *so* much; but she let herself be persuaded to take it when I observed that I could do without it and she might well have need of it.

Thus, despite the fiction about a walking tour at the outset, Kierkegaard has been driving a coach pulled by two horses; the innkeeper's son Rudolph is with him. What about the driver? It is the first and last time we ever hear that Kierkegaard could drive a coach himself, with all that entails of hitching up the horses and unhitching them again, not to mention keeping control of them in thundery weather. If Kierkegaard was really able to do such things, there is something edifying in the thought that against Kierkegaard we are always wrong.

The next sketch, I.A.66, starts off with its date on a line by itself, "Hillerød, July 25, 1835," and its underlining of the place leads our thoughts to I.A.75, often mentioned above, "Gilleleje, August 1, 1835," which—likewise standing in a line all by itself—likewise has the name of the place underlined. Consequently it *can* be a fictive entry, written like the others toward the end of 1836 as a part of the novella "Letters." If it is not fictive, it presupposes "a considerable march through the forest" and an "acquaintanceship with several little lakes of the sort I like so much" (see above), details which would then bring Kierkegaard to Hestehaven and Carls-Sø. A romantic description is given of "one of the most beautiful views I have ever seen," but the time is expressly indicated as being in the morning: "On the other side the land rises, a large beech forest, and the morning light puts the individual illuminated points in strange contrast to the shaded ones." Either Kierkegaard has made the journey on foot at night from Gilleleje to Hillerød—a distance of twenty kilometers—or he has gone from Gilleleje to Hillerød to spend the night there and then to undertake a morning excursion on foot, or the whole is part of the novella "Letters":

> And the church bells called one to worship, but not in a temple built by human hands. If the bird does not need to be reminded to praise God, should not the human being also feel reverence, albeit without a church, in the true house of God, where the vault of heaven forms the church's loft, where the roar of the storm and the gentle zephyr replace the bass and descant of the organ, where the trills of the birds compose the joyous song of the congregation, and where the echo of the stone church's arch does not repeat the voice of the pastor, but where everything is resolved in eternal antiphony?

I opt for the third of the three possibilities: there is nothing concrete in the letter save the two geographic points which Kierkegaard had seen, of course, at some time or another in the summer of 1835; but the pantheism at the conclusion, so very much like that of Goethe or Oehlenschläger, fits the moods of the "Letters" perfectly—a Werther performance à la Sibbern's Gabrielis.

The brief, undated I.A.67, on the other hand, is very precise in its mention of an excursion to Sweden on July 27 and 28 in the company of a cousin of Pastor Hans Christian Lyngbye (1782–1837), minister of the parish of Søborg and Gilleleje and a botanist into the bargain. The trip took them to Mölle, where they visited Baron Nils Kristoffer Gyllenstierna (1789–1865) at Krapperup Manor; it may be assumed that they spent the night there. The next day they climbed Östra Högkull and Västra Högkull and undertook a botanical excursion to Kullen in order to collect plants, which Lyngbye later "was kind enough to send to me dried and wrapped in paper." No attempt was made at a literary description of this first of Kierkegaard's trips abroad.

I.A.68 is dated "July 29," but the date does not stand in a line by itself, nor is the place, Gilleleje, given. The entry, three pages long, nonetheless has the same literary character as the two mentioned above and depicts Kierkegaard's favorite route: from the inn over Sortebro along the waterside fields to *Gilbjerget*. "This point has always been one of my favorite places." The italicization of Gilbjerget comes five lines down in the text, which, moreover, with its character of a reckoning with "my past life" and its handsome, melancholy picture of the sea's calm and its agitated power, has a pronouncedly literary character and a clearly religious element. If it had not been a piece of fiction, Kierkegaard, who in less than three years had lost a brother, two sisters, and a mother, would scarcely have talked about "the few dear departed," who it seems to him are not dead but hovering in the air together with him. Nor can it be himself that he mentions as "the constitutive principle in the little circle," the one who "has found that Archimedean point from which he can lift the whole world"; if there was anything which Kierkegaard, the Faustian doubter, *lacked*, it was just that. To be sure, Christ is named a couple of times, but not as a divine being. Instead, there is talk of "the power which directs the whole," but neither can this vague concept be interpreted, I believe, as an expression of *stud. theol.* Søren Kierkegaard, unless he was actually at a great remove from Christianity.

I.A.69 is undated but, making no literary pretensions at all, depicts an excursion with Pastor Lyngbye on Søborg Lake. Lyngbye was collecting algae for the sake of the molluscs, and Kierkegaard was impressed by the luxuriant vegetation and the many wild ducks, sea gulls, and crows. Together they examined "the ruins of the castle" described—as Kierkegaard says—in J. G. Burman-Becker's *Efterretninger om de gamle Borge*, Søborg Church, of whose interior an account is given, and the so-called Søborg Stone with its runes. Nothing but facts—as in I.A.70, which gives a brief account of the "Gable Congregations" of the inhabitants of Gilleleje and of the terror of the fisherman when a boat, "during my stay out here," stayed away too long on a trip to Hesselø in stormy weather. The peasant mentioned in I.A.71, Jens Andersen in Fjellenstrup, no doubt actually existed; he captured Kierkegaard's attention because, apart from being very well read in the Bible, he was quite familiar with Saxo Grammaticus, Snorri, and the Icelandic sagas which the pastor had lent him. Kierkegaard talked with him and noted with distaste that his speech, whether he was drunk or sober, was equally loathsome.

This is the end of the factual information concerning Kierkegaard's stay in Gilleleje, and it is only a matter of curious interest to determine, with Sejer Kühle's aid, that several letters were received and sent here: on June 29 a letter from his brother and Søren's reply to his father; two small letters of July 18 from Søren and one from his brother, together with money and cigars, etc.; on July 11 a further letter from his brother with letters from Henrik and Mikael Lund enclosed; and the letters from home—his father—of August 17 and 21, the latter containing eighty rigsdaler. It was expensive to keep the young gentleman going in Gilleleje.

Rumors about his stay are reflected in the comments of Levin, who was always glad to gossip: "In Gilleleje, where he was called 'the crazy student,' he confused and frightened the girls by the way he looked at them when they came into his room" (Steen Johansen, p. 35). On August 24 he was in Copenhagen again, and if he immediately began work on his very extensive review of the National Liberal press, in preparation for his lecture of November 28, 1835, before the student association, we have a quite plausible explanation for the fact that the Gilleleje sketches were composed later, that is, in 1836, probably at the end of the year.

Kierkegaard and the Novella Literature of His Time

Naturally, it is humiliating to have to confess that one cannot solve the riddle of the Sphinx, but I am consoled by the thought that other scholars will be just as incapable as I am of reconstructing the novella "Letters" in the way that Kierkegaard planned it, drafted it, sketched it, and thought it out. A finished artwork, *the* finished work of art, cannot be re-created from a shattered torso. The Gilleleje sketches, both the actual ones of 1835 and the fictive ones, written a year later in Copenhagen, must be regarded as Kierkegaard's first attempt to acquire his own style and individual content. The attempt succeeded. The best passages stand up very well against the superb nature description in " 'Guilty?'/'Not Guilty?' "; as a matter of fact, one may well prefer the first sketch, "Søborg Lake," to the later, completely polished one in the *Collected Works*. It has an impressionistic freedom about it which is lacking in the more elaborate version of 1845.

If one can accept the hypothesis about an epistolary novella, one must also be receptive to the thought that many of the entries in the *Papers*' first volume (and, in my opinion, not a few in the second) belong in this category. The title "Letters" does not necessarily mean that the whole novella would have consisted of letters. Kierkegaard wishes to renounce neither the use of a narrator, that is, a narrator in the first person, nor the possibility of including random thoughts, brief essays, and sketches in his work. I.A.340, with its title "Something about Hamann" written in bold letters, shows how he had originally conceived his, that is, the narrator's and letter writer's, observations about his reading encapsulated within the fictive text. The references to Hamann, Simon Stylita, and the book dealer Soldin make it seem reasonable to place its composition in September-October 1836. The suite of entries I.A.94–99, with the title "Philosophy and Christianity Can Never Be United," also appear to be intended for the "Letters"; at any rate, they seem almost to presuppose a recipient: "Now, I have tried to show, . . . Now, as further confirmation I shall provide the following outline . . ." No one writes that way in a diary.

The Hegelian enthusiasm for great men, which Kierkegaard demonstrates here, continues the Goethe-and-Hegel cult of Heiberg in *Om Philosophiens Betydning (Concerning the Meaning of Philosophy)* and harmonizes perfectly with the fictive letter from Gilleleje, I.A.75: "Therefore, it is with joy and inner edification that I regard the great men who thus have found the precious stone for which they will sell everything, even their own life." The first entries, I.A.94 and 95, are dated, respectively, October 17 and October 19, 1835, which seems to fit the criteria for dating contained in the text, and the attached notes, I.A.100 and 101, are dated, respectively, September 10, 1836, and January 14, 1837, something which fits perfectly with Kierkegaard's work on the "Letters" during the autumn of 1836 and the beginning of 1837. The many references to Hamann's writings are based upon F. Roth's edition (Berlin, 1821–43), nine volumes altogether, of which the last, vol. VIII, pt. 2, was supplied on December 12, 1843, by the book dealer Philipsen (Catalogue 536–44). The thought about the incompatibility of philosophy and Christianity can very well have been born during the composition of the "Letters."

It makes sense to imagine a longish pause in Kierkegaard's "project" between the homecoming from Gilleleje on August 24, 1835, and the beginning of June 1836, when the Heibergs left for Paris. There was his first appearance in the student association (November 28, 1835) with the lecture "Our Latest Periodical Literature," which must have required a through preparation; there was the whole debate with the National Liberals, that is, Hage and Lehmann, in four issues of Heiberg's *Flyveposten*; there was that attack made on Kierkegaard in *Humoristiske Intelligensblade* (May 1836), a direct attempt to ridicule him; and last but not least, there was his personal acquaintanceship with the Heibergs and Fru Gyllembourg. Thus Kierkegaard could hardly have had time to devote himself to his novella, neglected and more or less forgotten, before the summer of 1836, when every thought of the official theological examination seems to have disappeared into the mists. It is possible, of course, that he went through the religious crisis postulated by P. A. Heiberg, but, as we have seen above (chapter 2), it is by no means obvious that such a crisis took place.

It cannot be denied that his own inner life was a dance on the edge of a volcano, just as one cannot put aside the psychiatrists' assertion that the manic-depressive psychosis now emerged in full bloom. But even if one has read Lichtenberg, one does not compose brilliant diapsalmata without having oneself been a part of the emotions which are their secret signature. And there are many seeds of the "Diapsalmata" of *Either/Or* here, so Kierkegaard is absolutely right in maintaining that he could have found several more such items in his old material and used them. For connoisseurs in the field a prompter's cues, as it were, will suffice: "No, I do not wish to leave the world—I will go into a madhouse, and I will see if the profundity of madness does not reveal itself as the mystery of life." "I grieve, on the other hand, when a child is born, and I wish, Would God that it at least might never have to undergo confirmation." . . . "I wish—no, I do not wish for anything at all. Amen!"

The dry references following are to please the pedants. Here one finds an anticipation of "Diapsalma" Number 12; "Age realizes the dreams of youth, etc. . . ," Number 83, "Why was I not born in Nyboder, etc.," and Number 6, "I simply do not feel inclined . . . ," a longer but more easily comprehensible form of which is in II.A.637. One may dare to assert that many of the Kierkegaardian diapsalmata were originally conceived as inlays for the epistolary novella; in fact, Number 3 is taken directly from I.A.331, which was quoted extensively above, on page 99:

I have always noticed how quickly people begin to say "my late husband, my late wife." Just as there is an analogous phenomenon: the more quickly a woman talks about discipline—the less modesty there is. In addition, one will certainly have observed that at the beginning, in response to one of the questions which is directed to every child in that brief résumé of knowledge which is vouchsafed them: "What does the child want?", one allows the children to answer: "A spanking," and with such melancholy reflections what is the child's first and no doubt most innocent period begins—and nevertheless one denies original sin.

"Diapsalma" Number 67, "I have only one friend, and that is Echo" comes from the letter of "December 2," which also offers a sketch for Number 36: "When I get up in the morning, I go right back to bed again." "Diapsalma" Number 87 is the one which can be traced furthest back into the past, to I.A.169, of June 10, 1836:

A wandering musician, playing a sort of reed pipe or something like it (I couldn't see what it was, since he was in the courtyard of the next house), performed the minuet from Don Juan, and the apothecary pounded his pills and the maid was scrubbing in the courtyard and the stable boy curried his horse, knocking the hair out of the comb onto the stones, and from another corner of the city, far away, the voice of a prawn seller resounded, etc., and they noticed nothing and perhaps the flute player noticed nothing either and I felt very well.

Even if Kierkegaard actually had an apothecary as his neighbor in Nytorv, the above passage is surely a mood picture for inclusion in the epistolary novella. At any event, this diapsalma plays an essential role in the "Postscript to *Either/Or* of Victor Eremita," mentioned on page 6 above, which Barfod explains is "probably from March 1844." The article is dated by Kierkegaard himself: why, then, is Barfod in doubt about it?

In this article, which was made ready for printing, Kierkegaard makes fun of *cand. theol.* J. F. Hagen's review in *Fædrelandet* of May 7 and 21, 1843, and of Hagen's attempt to identify the aesthetician A. on the basis of his "having lived here in the city side by side with an apothecary." Hagen thus accuses Kierkegaard of being identical with A. "It occurred to me that this track could lead to something. Perhaps, using this bit of information, one could provide some help for the secondhand dealer's memory, perhaps one could come across some clue among the apothecaries and especially among their neighbors, etc." And Kierkegaard continues sarcastically in IV.B.59:

> According to the facts to which Mr. Hagen himself has called attention, A. has been a public school teacher, and later a member of a traveling theatrical troupe; I myself am reminded that he has also traveled abroad (cf. the article about *The First Love*). The diapsalma he refers to has no year, no date, no indication of the place other than the one given there. Since the matter is of extreme importance for me, I'd prefer not to engage in idle chatter about it.

Whereupon he continues with the altogether sensible assertion that apothecaries, in Copenhagen and in Danish market towns and in foreign cities as well, are wont to pound with pestles, so that the only thing left is, "that a person who has traveled both in Denmark and abroad once lived side by side with an apothecary's shop in the exact moment when the strange event occurred that an apothecary made use of his mortar and pestle." Perhaps a plot for the "Letters" can be reconstructed from this basis. The hero, who originally studied theology in Copenhagen in order to become a pastor in accordance with his father's wishes, abandons his studies because of the impression made on him by natural science and its philosophy of life; he becomes a schoolteacher but is seized by a passion for the theater after a performance of *The First Love* and travels to the provinces with a touring theatrical company, to Jutland and abroad, to Germany. Thus the connection to *Faust* and *Wilhelm Meister* is quite clear. (The journey to Jutland in the summer of 1840 should be seen in this perspective.) A letter like the one of July 17, [1838], to Emil Boesen can be both real and fictive. Kierkegaard *was* in northern Zealand in the summer of 1838, and he *was* twenty-five years old, but if Boesen, as is likely, was familiar with the "project," then he also grasped the letter's marked literary flourish and significance. He is one of those to whom "the public school teacher" writes concerning his wanderings through the endless realms of the soul.

The connections to *Werther* are no less visible. According to I.C.66, Kierkegaard must have read Sibbern's *Gabrielis Breve* in March 1835 at the latest:

> One often hears people say that someone is a Don Juan or a Faust, but they don't readily call a person the Wandering Jew. But why shouldn't there be individuals of this sort, after all, who have simply absorbed too much of the Wandering Jew's nature? Is it correct when Sibbern, in *Gabrielis efterladte Breve* [Gabrielis's Posthumous Letters], has the hero say that he would prefer to roam the world like the Wandering Jew? To what extent is that correct in and of itself, that is, to what extent is it to be preferred to the life his hero is leading—to what extent is it correct in this hero's character, or does it contain a contradiction?
>
> March 28, 1835

The first edition, which appeared in 1826, is not to be found among the books that Kierkegaard left at his death, a circumstance which does not allow us to conclude, however, that Kierkegaard never owned it. Sibbern wrote the book in 1813–15, in an effort to free himself from a deep and violent passion for Oehlenschläger's beautiful sister, Sophie Ørsted, of whom Baggesen had also been enamored. Like Werther, Sibbern/Gabrielis sends diary-letters to a friend in the capital, having himself gone down to his old school in southern Zealand, firmly resolved to tear himself loose from his amorous involvement. The novel, one of the finest the Danish Golden Age produced, is an account of the cure of a man in thrall to his imagination, who—refreshed by poetry and nature—returns to reality and practical work in the midst of men. With its subdued and confidential tone, its profound psychology, and its nature scenes handsomely described and deeply felt, *Gabrielis Breve* has remained a classic.

In his book about Kierkegaard and Goethe, Carl Roos makes a great point of the fact that Kierkegaard's early papers do not mention *Werther* at all; using subtle arguments, Roos tries to present " 'Guilty?'/'Not Guilty?' " as a deliberate contrast to *Werther*, a *Trutz-Werther*. This is a hypothesis which overlooks the criterion of improbability: it is unthinkable that a Goethe fan—as Kierkegaard was in 1835—would not have been familiar with *Werther*, the classic model for the epistolary novella and the diary-novella. It appeared in Danish in 1832, but on February 10, 1836, Kierkegaard (who had purchased *Faust* in the Stuttgart edition of 1834) became the happy owner of Goethe's *Werke* in fifty-five volumes, the so-called *Vollständige Ausgabe letzter Hand* (Stuttgart and Tübingen, 1828–33). It is obvious that Kierkegaard read *Werther* at one time or another, but since he was not in the position of having to rid himself of some sort of infatuation (in Goethe's, Werther's, or Sibbern's manner) by writing about it, he was able to get along quite nicely with *Gabrielis Breve*. It offers a surer model than *Werther* does, especially when it is combined with Faust's doubt and Wilhelm Meister's capacity for life. A young man, impregnated with the age's Faustian doubt and engaged in a persistent pursuit of a philosophy by which he can live a true and ethically responsible life—that was a fine framework for a piece of fiction which, to boot, gave Kierkegaard the chance of demonstrating what he had learned from Blicher in style and in color and in the choice of materials.

Among the efforts of the 1830s to create a Danish "novella," it is impossible to choose a more central position than Kierkegaard did. The time's distinction between the (educational) novel and the novella need not be discussed here. From a theoretical standpoint, this distinction was debated energetically in contemporary literary journals and was demonstrated in practice by such older authors as Blicher, Sibbern, Fru Gyllembourg, and Oehlenschläger; by the imitators of Walter Scott in both generations, such as Poul Møller, Ingemann, and Carl Bernhard; by younger prose writers such as H. C. Andersen, who, taking Hoffmann and Heine as his models, created a place for imagination and the lyric caprice; by H. P. Holst, who—like Carl Bernhard—had his eye on France; by P. E. Lind, who could not get free from Jean Paul; and by Carl Bagger, who broke all records of realism with *Min Broders Levned* (1835).

H. C. Andersen turned out to be the one who carried off the prize. With his three large novels, *Improvisatoren*, *O. T.*, and *Kun en Spillemand*, 1835–37 (*The Improviser*, *O. T.*, and *Only a Fiddler*), and with the small volumes of fairy stories from 1835 on, he renewed Danish prose and its genres. He created a witty, subtle, altogether oral style, which went from pathos and edification to cheerful chatter and malicious barbs. Indeed, one may well ask if it is not Andersen who—in the renowned words of *Stages on Life's Way*—has "a delightful, a winsome, a delicious affection for the connecting thought and the subsidiary concept and the small talk of the adjective and the mood, and the humming of the transition." For Kierkegaard surely possesses both the fury of passion and the grandiose simplicity of the myth, but when he is at his worst he is so long-winded, confused, baffling, overornamented, Byzantine, and positively Chinese with his meanings-within-meanings that even a Danish reader can have difficulty understanding what the text intends to say. The explanation does not lie in Kierkegaard's having chosen (unlike Andersen) such old-fashioned models for his prose as Fru Gyllembourg (who followed Rousseau), Sibbern (who followed Goethe), and Blicher (the English novel in the eighteenth century and sentimental German *Lesefrüchte*). It lies in the fact, as Brandes observed, that he wrote in his dressing gown. Without giving the matter further thought, Kierkegaard presupposed that readers possessed all the material which he himself had at his disposal. There is an altogether unironic arrogance in this attitude.

Kierkegaard and Blicher

The extensive quotations from Kierkegaard's "Letters" in this chapter make it unnecessary to analyze the influence of Blicher in detail. It is not farfetched to suspect that Kierkegaard had the hitherto published volumes of Blicher's novellas in his carpetbag. As is well known, Steen Steensen Blicher had begun as a novella writer long before the contemporary novella about Copenhagen, the "everyday story," was developed. He had no connection with the circle around Heiberg. Or rather, he had detested Heiberg and the Copenhagen "clique of silhouette cutters" ever since, in 1825, Heiberg had brushed his tragedy, *Johanne Gray*, into the scrap heap: it had got three performances in November of that year. Between Heiberg and Blicher there is no resemblance save their relationship to the eighteenth century—a century they looked upon, however, from radically different points of view. Blicher, who made his debut with a translation of Ossian's poems in 1807–09 (Catalogue 1873), was firmly anchored in English pre-Romanticism from Richardson to Goldsmith. The latter's *Vicar of Wakefield*, which Blicher translated, comprises—together with those German *Lesefrüchte*—his most important literary model.

    The poet-pastor, eternally debt-ridden, began to write for Elmquist's *Læsefrugter* in 1824–25, a popular entertainment journal larded with translations of such German feuilletonists as Clauren, Contessa, Houwald, and Lafontaine—whom Kierkegaard seems to have known: compare *SV*, XIII:25, of March 15, 1836—and "genuine" poets such as Tieck, Jean Paul, Hoffmann, Körner, Arnim, and de la Motte Fouqué. In his skillful book *Den blicherske Novelle*, 1965 (*Blicher's Novella*), Søren Baggesen has clearly shown that the *Lesefruchtnovelle* was the most important basis of Blicher's efforts in the prose genres. To be sure, it was not Blicher's weakness for acts of violence, exciting events, bizarre states of the soul, erotomania, and perversity which captivated Kierkegaard. It was his depiction of nature, of the common people and exotic milieus. Kierkegaard seems early to have developed a taste for traditional stories, tales, legends, chapbooks, folksongs, and broadsheet songs.

The success of his novellas in Elmquist's *Læsefrugter* made Blicher decide to start a rival undertaking called *Nordlyset*, in which a series of his finest novellas saw the light of day between 1827 and 1829, but mixed in among a variety of second-rate items. On this account Blicher acquired a literary "image" among Copenhageners only when the first volume of *Samlede Noveller* (*Collected Novellas*) appeared on New Year's Day, 1833. The unmistakable Jutland tone established Blicher from the outset as a regional writer, a Danish Robert Burns. One could well imagine that the hosier finally found an author after his own heart here. But Ole Restrup has called my attention to the fact that the only subscriber to the volume in Copenhagen was—Frederik Paludan-Müller. For readers of the Copenhagen "everyday story," Blicher provided a wild sort of exoticism, like that of Walter Scott's highlanders and Hugo's gypsies, but his stories must have meant an immersion in the memories of childhood for Kierkegaard senior. The latter had seen the so-called Tatere (gypsy half-breeds), and perhaps he had also been on Himmelbjerget, which gave its name to the Blicher novella describing one of Jutland's most beautiful regions; at any event, his birthplace, Sæding, was not very far from the location of "Jøderne paa Hald," ("The Jews at Hald"). It is a story whose plot is just as unlikely as those of "Josepha," "Præsten i Thorning" ("The Pastor at Thorning"), and "Fruentimmerhaderen" ("The Misogynist"); but if Søren read the novella, he came across the authorial trick by which pages from a diary are discovered—compare Victor Eremita's story about the bureau. In "Kjeltringliv" ("Rogues' Life") and "Røverstuen" ("The Robber's Den") Blicher mixed Jutland exoticism with a celebration of the pariah—compare Kierkegaard's "little robber's colony" in the Gilleleje sketch. The poacher Black Mads can have inspired the attempt at a drama about the master thief, a Robin Hood type.

Yet the pièces de résistance of the collection were "En Landsbydegns Dagbog" ("The Journal of a Parish Clerk") and "Hosekræmmeren" ("The Hosier") from, respectively, 1825 and

1829, two of the Golden Age's masterpieces which meet international competition. Blicher's weakness for crass effects did not fail to assert itself—the noble woman sinks to the dregs of society and the peasant girl cuts the throat of her lover—but both novellas possess the artistic concentration which Blicher (like Kierkegaard) otherwise so sadly lacks. With their depiction, at once resigned and unassuming, of the destructive forces of the age, of the absurdity of existence and the inevitable blows of fate, they can bear comparison with the works of those contemporary masters Kleist and Mérimée. Kierkegaard had read the latter's Don Juan novella toward the end of 1834.

The second volume, of July 1833, did not maintain the standard the first had set. The efforts to achieve realism are obvious in "Sildig Opvaagnen" ("Tardy Awakening"), the story of an erotic triangle which betrays Blicher's rather limited view of woman. With its pastiche form, "Præsten i Vejlby" ("The Parson at Vejlby") reminds one of "En Landsbydegns Dagbog" but fails to approach it in either stylistic mastery or human insight. "Telse" and "Den svenske Major" ("The Swedish Major") are historical novellas, exciting accounts of war with gripping scenes in a bold, popular style. Blicher was very poorly suited to attempt an "everyday story," the moralizing "Eva," where the virtuous fisher-girl is rewarded by marriage to the noble Vilhelm, while the flirtatious Laura ends up as an apple vendor. "Jordbærret" ("The Strawberry"), with its vulgarly masculine view of woman, and "Peer Spillemands Skibsjournal" ("Peer the Fiddler's Logbook") add nothing to Blicher's artistic stature, although "Stakkels Louis" ("Poor Louis"), an epistolary novella, draws a fine portrait of a French emigrant's fate in Jutland.

The third volume scraped bottom with the reprinting of the weakest novellas from Nordlyset of 1827–28, horror stories and ghost stories with German and Italian settings, spanning the centuries from the Crusades to Napoleon. Jutland is the scene only for "Fire Perioder" ("Four Periods"), whose manor house interiors once again underline the author's hatred of women from the upper class, and for "Ak, hvor forandret" ("Alas, How Changed!"), a title which Kierkegaard could have used instead of *Repetition.*

The fourth volume, of 1834, included three new novellas, "Hævnen" ("The Revenge"), a colorful piece of entertainment literature à la Scott, with a medieval setting, "Eneboeren paa Bolbjerg" ("The Recluse of Bolbjerg"), with cleverly developed natural descriptions, and "Juleferierne" ("The Christmas Vacation"), a bull's-eye, a cheerful and lighthearted manor house tale with extremely witty and ironic portraits of the teachers in Jutland's Latin schools. The four novellas that are reprints, the Ossian-like "Gyldenholm," the tale from the French revolution, "Letacq," the gruesome story about the Inquisition, "Leonore," and the piece of robber romanticism, "Krybskytten" ("The Poacher"), with a Robin Hood motif, did not reach the same artistic level.

It is these four volumes which Kierkegaard had or could have had with him on his literary trip in the summer of 1835. They are a part of his library (Catalogue 1521–23) in a five-volume edition (the first volume and a supplement are in a second edition). The fifth volume was purchased on January 19, 1836, and so it may be guessed that he had acquired the four preceding ones earlier. Kierkegaard continued his buying of Blicher with *Samlede Digte,* vols. I–II (*Collected Poems*), among other things, purchased on July 10, 1836. Blicher's unmistakable tone in the two "letters" from Gilleleje quoted above does not speak against a time of composition very late in 1836; on the contrary, it is reasonable to believe that, in principle, Kierkegaard shared the Heibergs' view of Blicher, as it was evidenced by Madvig's review in *Dansk Maanedsskrift* (1835). Denmark's internationally famed philologist characterizes Blicher as "an extremely fine talent, but one limited to a certain sphere," a statement which has elicited posterity's scorn; yet the novellas Madvig likes are the same ones that posterity has taken unto its bosom. Madvig the Heibergian comes down hard on the bad habits acquired from the *Lesefrüchte,* on Blicher's use of Gothic horror and of wildly incredible effects. He regards "Hosekræmmeren" ("The Hosier") as a little idyll, not grasping its tragic pathos.

It was hardly for the tragic element's sake that Fru Heiberg, in February 1834, delivered "Hosekræmmeren" from the stage of the Royal Theater. Together with her husband, she had met Blicher on a tour of the provinces in July 1833 and had no understanding of Blicher's failure to understand that Heiberg bore him no ill will whatsoever for the old affair of 1825. For the Copenhageners, Blicher was a literary genre painter who regarded Jutland and its inhabitants, among them its half-breed gypsies and its riffraff, from the exotic-picturesque side. Kierkegaard's depiction of the "little robber's colony," presenting husband, wife, and daughter in a kind of triptych, is strikingly reminiscent of the peripatetic Blicher's description of the peasant couple with their daughter Cecilie in "Hosekræmmeren." As a matter of fact, it was from Blicher that Kierkegaard filched the trick of having the characters busy themselves with something concrete: here, the knitted stocking is turned into the schnapps-glass and bottle.

What Kierkegaard learned from Blicher in particular was the Ossianic sense for the romanticism and the melancholy of vast space—compare I.A.131, a note about the technique of writing which probably comes from 1834 rather than 1836:

Should not the romantic element actually lie in the absence of a relative standard of measurement, an absence which is important in this precise connection: for if one merely wanted to behold that which is manifold, then something which after all is romantic could not be subsumed under this latter concept—I mean the broad expanses of the desert, which in accordance with Ehrenberg's description [in the essay "De nordafrikanske Ørkener" ("The North African Deserts"), *Dansk Ugeskrift*, 1834, vol. IV, pp. 153–54, which is quoted at length in a note without a date, but which, according to I.A.132 was read and commented upon in March 1836] is very romantic, as is the Jutland heath (Blicher); the beginning of the novella "Telse."

The novella begins:

The earth was covered with snow; the sky with stars; the moon had done its work; all the winds had gone to rest. There was no life below, but the firmament above was in unending movement; the countless small lights in the darkness glimmered, glittered, trembled, sparkled—and smiled—in the darkness like angels' eyes from a dim and distant eternity.

Kierkegaard's "Letters" obviously try to find the same basic poetic tone of melancholy absorption in nature. From Blicher he has learned to contrast the repose below, that is, on earth or on the sea, with the unending movement in the firmament. Where Blicher uses the golden plover's lamenting cry above the heath, Kierkegaard inserts the gull's hoarse cry above the sea. It is a literary pastiche of excellent quality. Kierkegaard did his apprenticeship with Blicher before the German Romantics—Hoffmann, Eichendorff, Brentano, and Heine—got their claws into him.

In *From the Papers of One Still Living* (1838) Kierkegaard pays tribute to Blicher, a tribute which can be understood only when one recalls his contempt for H. C. Andersen and his hidden condescension toward such a Heibergian as Carl Bernhard *(SV,* XIII:65); we do not know if Kierkegaard had made the personal acquaintance of Bernhard or not:

If we turn now from these [Bernhard's] novellas and their arena to that voice in the wilderness, Steen Steensen Blicher, who after all, and that is the most remarkable thing about him, transformed the wilderness into a friendly refuge for an imagination which was exiled from life, we shall meet neither a view of the world which has been tested against life's manifold events nor that set of gymnastic exercises for dealing with life which is so characteristic of those other novellas [of Fru Gyllembourg]; yet here, too, a certain beginning has been made, while the negative side is completely latent, thanks to the fact that a whole positiveness, so to speak, awakes and speaks and, youthful and fresh, renews and regenerates itself with autochthonic originality [footnote by S. K.: "of dust thou

art come!"]. Instead of the view of life contained in the novellas of the author of the "Everyday Stories," that of the individual who has run his race and kept the faith, [Blicher] appears
here as the union of both an individual and a national poetic
ground bass, echoing in the soul's inner ear, and a picture
illuminated by mighty bolts of heat lightning, a picture
spread out in a kind of national idyll before the imagination—a deep poetic mood, veiled in the mists of spontaneity.
Instead of having to admire the masterly technique, as in
those novellas [of Fru Gyllembourg], we are struck here by
simpler dialogues, pregnant with drama, which do not presuppose so much the acuteness of a Cuvier in order for a to-
tality to be constructed out of them but which rather almost
have the profundity of nature as their place of origin. At any
event, there is a unity here, too, which in its spontaneity
points meaningfully toward the future, and which must of
necessity move contemporary readers much more than it has
until now, and thereby perhaps will have a salubrious influence upon the prosaic fashion in which politics has been
treated thus far.

The Heibergian Kierkegaard puts Fru Gyllembourg's masterly
technique on a line with the work of the unsophisticated natural
gifts of Blicher, if not above them. He has correctly perceived that
both these authors began to write late in life and that both of
them—each in his own way and each with his own realm of top-
ics, Copenhagen and Jutland—impregnate their novellas with a
view of life from which the younger generation, utterly devoted to
politics and Hegelianism, can learn something. Kierkegaard's footnote quotes the motto on the title page of Blicher's *Samlede Digte*,
vol. I (p. 5, 1835, purchased July 10, 1836, Catalogue U 23):

> My heath is still and gloomy in its air;
> And yet, beneath the heather, flowers stand,
> Behind the barrows larks have built their nest,
> And send their trills across the empty land.

Kierkegaard read Blicher with his heart, and one can be sure that Blicher would have been a sort of watermark if the "Letters" had ever seen the light of day. Of course, *Either/Or* was produced instead. If one can accept the hypothesis presented here concerning the "Letters," their relationship to *Either/Or* is more or less that of Goethe's *Ur-Faust* to his *Faust*. Kierkegaard's undated sketch, III.B.31, can serve as a fitting final vignette, a sketch in which the original character of *Either/Or*, as an epistolary novella, clearly appears:

> Either/Or
> so reit ich hin in alle Ferne
> Über meiner Mütze nur die Sterne
> a fragment

As I have told you again and again, I shall write to you thus— either/or, and one *aut* is not enough, for the one opinion cannot be subordinated to the other, but it is an exclusive *aut/aut*. Now you may either grow angry with me and break with me as you have many times before, or you may accept it in a friendly fashion; at any event I shall remain: either/or—

The Goethe quotation from the poem "Freisinn" in *West-östlicher Divan* (*Vollständige Ausgabe letzter Hand*, 1828, V:7— Kierkegaard's copy) shows the source of Kierkegaard's original inspiration and what his original plan was: a higher Danish combination of *Werther*, *Faust* and *Wilhelm Meister*.

Perhaps it is best that things went the way they did.

Every thoughtful reader or literary scholar—two categories that do not always coincide—has the right to challenge everything presented in the challenge of this chapter. If one rejects the theory that Kierkegaard's "project" was in reality an attempt to write a Goethean novel, an epistolary Bildungsroman, then one is left only with a headache—the headache of having to make up one's mind about the extent to which those many diary entries and letters, whether they appear in the *Papers* themselves or in Thulstrup's *Breve og Aktstykker*, should be taken at face value. It is an interesting, almost a piquant variety of headache, which opens broad perspectives for the investigation of the religious development of Kierkegaard's youth.

On the other hand, if the gentle reader should accept what we may call the fiction theory, he would escape a plethora of problems. The fall, the visit to the bordello, the irregular taking of Holy Communion, the family curse, the death of the Kierkegaard offspring before or at the latest in their thirty-fourth year (the age of Christ at his death), the thorn in the flesh, the secret note, and many other tidbits . . . , all of this sinks back into the Romantic tradition itself. Like Chateaubriand's improper relationship with his sister, four years older than he was. Like Byron's supposed incest with *his* half sister.

There is something reassuring in the thought that "the great earthquake" can be interpreted in a purely literary way. I still remember my years at Sorø Academy toward the end of the 1930s, where the teacher of religion, Gorm Hansen (who lived in Ingemann's house, by the way), kept his class at least partly awake by his frightening tales, taken from the work of Eduard Geismar, about all the terrible things that had befallen Kierkegaard in the past hundred years.

Now I can sleep well of nights. *Tout n'est que du vent et de la littérature.*

The latter in particular.

5: HEGEL, KIERKEGAARD, AND NIELS THULSTRUP

My view of the *Papers'* first three volumes was fairly clear to me when, on June 1, 1967, I dared to make an opposing statement *ex auditorio* at Niels Thulstrup's public defense of his dissertation, *Kierkegaards Forhold til Hegel og den spekulative Idealisme indtil 1846 (Kierkegaard's Relationship to Hegel and Speculative Idealism until 1846).* Earlier I had presented his book to the public with a long review in *Politiken*, consisting for the most part of praise. It is available in print. My opposing statement, which many people asked me to publish, has not appeared, and it will not be provided in this chapter. But a series of arguments which could not be included in chapter 4 will be presented here. They are not aimed at Thulstrup's "fundamental chief thesis," that Hegel and Kierkegaard have nothing in common as thinkers, "as far as object, goal, or method are concerned" (p. 21), although I cannot subscribe to this thesis for a number of reasons. It appears to me that this main thesis was the point of departure for Thulstrup's work on the dissertation and not the objective result of an unbiased investigation, although he repeatedly emphasizes the investigation's "historical quality."

The Relationship to the Source Material

My attack will be launched against Thulstrup's second thesis, which is untenable from a scholarly point of view—that is, a postulate without an evaluation of the source material. On page 21, the text says:

> Seen historically, the insight of Kierkegaard into this funda-
> mental inconsistency was the result of a process of clarifica-
> tion which he had undergone, as far as both his own
> problems and his whole world of thought were concerned,
> and their relationship to Hegel and the whole of speculative
> idealism, a process of clarification which in essence was com-
> pleted at about the same time as the publication of *Either/Or*.

My (hypo)thesis is the direct opposite of Thulstrup's, to wit: that the years 1835–43, thus up to and including *Either/Or*, are a period of extreme ferment, in which Kierkegaard's attitude toward Hegelian philosophy by no means becomes clarified. That happened *after* the publication of *Either/Or*, thus in the great productive period of 1843–45, and the ferment subsides only with the *Postscript*. In contrast to Thulstrup, I base my postulate upon an analysis of the sources. What I said from the floor, in a brief form, has been explained to some extent in chapter 4, that is, that the sketches from Gilleleje are fictive in every essential detail, that it is not proper to employ fictive materials in the same way as one does actual letters and diary entries, a problem which must have already been apparent to Thulstrup even in 1953, when he published *Breve og Aktstykker* (see above, p. 94). This problem, moreover, is not without its ironic aspects. It obviously makes those notorious statements with a certain pantheistic tenor in the Gilleleje sketches less odious to Christian theologians, but at the same time it deprives the theologians of an important weapon, namely, Kierkegaard's religious statements—all of those which can be interpreted as expressions of feelings of sin and guilt, repentance, decisions to be converted and to live a moral Christian life with church attendance, communion, and so forth. If those statements, or at any rate a good part of them, are fictive, and thus intended for inclusion in the "Letters," how great a value do they have, then, for the elucidation of Kierkegaard's faith? Should he be judged by those statements or by his actions? The statement of May 19, 1838 (II.A.228), so strongly emphasized by Brandt and Heiberg, has an unmistakable literary bouquet:

> There is an indescribable joy which likewise burns through us inexplicably, even as the outcry of the apostles appears without motivation: "Rejoice, and again I will say: Rejoice." Not joy at this or that, but the soul's full-bodied outcry, "with tongue and mouth and from the bottom of the heart": "I rejoice at my joy, of, in, with, within, on, at, and with my joy"—a heavenly refrain which suddenly, as it were, cuts off the rest of our song; a joy which, as it were, cools and refreshes us like a breath of wind, a blast of the trade wind which blows from the oaks of Mamre to the eternal dwelling places.
>
> May 19, 10:30 o'clock in the morning

If it is possible to interpret this sketch in a religious fashion, why then does Kierkegaard omit the most important part of Paul's letter to the Philippians, in the fourth verse of the fourth chapter, *"Rejoice in the Lord always:* again I will say, Rejoice!" Why is the watchman's prescribed midnight verse mixed with Kingo's rendering of King David's fourth Psalm of Penitence from Kingo's *Psalmer og aandelige Sange (Psalms and Spiritual Songs*, in P. A. Fenger's edition of 1827, Catalogue 203) so that the three u-sounds (*tung, mund, grund*) are clearly heard? Why is the homemade "quotation" repeated in the introduction to *From the Papers of One Still Living*, undoubtedly written after his father's death in August 1838 (cf. *SV*, XIII:45)? Why is there this strange "quotation" with all its prepositions, underlined in the following: "I rejoice *at* my joy, *of, in, with, within, on, at*, and *with* my joy?" It sounds more like a student's joke than an intensely emotional religious outburst.

The literary meaning which is attributed to the watchman's verses appears in II.A.325, where the dating is given in the same way, at the end, and with a precise indication of time:

> . . . for what hope is there indeed for the Christian teacher in our time, or what prospects are there for the preacher of the

gospel in our development, when the servants of the word will soon stand with their Christian dogmas like watchmen with their edifying verse ("forgive us for Jesus' wounds our sins, oh gentle God," what a marked contrast to all the deeds and dealings of our highways and byways) to which no one pays attention, and whose song has interest only because it tells the time of day—disregarded as watchmen, except to the extent that the statistical information about whose banns should be read for a first, a second, and a third time would give them an additional year of grace in which they can continue vegetating.

> January 9, at exactly 9 o' clock
> in the evening, to the extent that
> the watchman on the square here
> called out the time precisely

It appears probable to the nontheological observer that these outbursts can be fictive diary entries meant for inclusion in the "Letters," perhaps from the period when the Faustian doubter, later the A. of *Either/Or*, is a teacher in Copenhagen. For that matter, Kierkegaard's attempt to find his way back to Christianity after his father's death—and his resumption of communion on July 6, 1838, shows that he means it in earnest—can be supported with many quotations which point toward the torments he experienced in finding his faith again.

To be sure, Thulstrup is right in saying that Kierkegaard was never an orthodox Hegelian, but consciously or unconsciously he overlooks the fact that Kierkegaard was truly a Heibergian of the purest water, something which is supported, and more than supported, by a body of primary sources, the writings in *Flyveposten*, the aesthetic studies, the homage to Fru Gyllembourg and Fru Heiberg, and, as well, by the later statements of contemporaries, people who knew what they were talking about: Sibbern, Brøchner, and H. P. Holst. And it is even supported by Kierkegaard himself in the anti-Heibergian pamphlet, *Prefaces*, of 1844, in which he unsuccessfully tries to conceal his hate-love for the inner circle which had not wanted to sanction him, although it was thrown open to his friends D. G. Monrad, P.´ E. Lind, and H. P. Holst, not to mention the aesthete Paludan-Müller, of whom so much was made. Here Kierkegaard talks nostalgically about how flattered the younger generation felt at the honor of being allowed to contribute to *Flyveposten:* "Something no younger person understands better than I do, for often I still recall how, at that time, a youthful mind was intoxicated by daring to realize that a contribution had not been scorned, and how no young cadet could look up with more enthusiasm to the famous general under whose banner he would fight than I did to the unforgettable editor of *Flyveposten*" (*SV*, V:52).

Kierkegaard's literary contributions to *Flyveposten*, like his lecture of 1835 in the student association concerning "Our Newest Periodical Literature," had long needed a scholarly edition that would put them into the milieu which produced them and also allow their National Liberal opponents, Ostermann, Hage, and Orla Lehmann, to have their say. Such an edition, with extensive commentaries, was published in 1977 by Teddy Pettersen, *Kierkegaards polemiske debut: Artikler 1834–36 i historisk sammenhæng*. These statements of Kierkegaard, flippant and a little impudent, opened the Heiberg home to him. We know this from Hertz's diaries and Fru Heiberg's *Et Liv*, although we do not know how often he visited there; it must have been more than once but less often than Hertz, the close friend of the family, less than H. P. Holst, and much less than Martensen, the only one with whom Heiberg could discuss Hegelianism on an equal footing—that is, after Heiberg and Martensen got to know one another in Paris in 1836. The fact that this did not suit Kierkegaard does not justify Thulstrup in saying (on p. 48), with respect to Kierkegaard's private coaching by Martensen in 1834, "There was no mention of Hegel at that time." Once again, the criterion of improbability should be applied. Thulstrup must bear the burden of the proof, and he also owes us substantiation for his statement on page 58 that Kierkegaard, in the summer of 1835, "acquired a very hasty, superficial, and misleading knowledge of Hegel." True enough,

Kierkegaard had scarcely any familiarity with Hegel's own writings, but he surely knew Heiberg's popularizing versions, and whatever else of Hegelianism was in the air at the time, before Martensen held his lectures in November and December 1837. Poul Møller deserves some attention here, for his orientation in Hegel was better than Thulstrup (and Vilhelm Andersen before him) will concede. (For more details, see Uffe Andreasen's fine study *Poul Møller og romantismen* [Poul Møller and the Romantic Movement], 1973.)

It can very well be that Heiberg did not understand Hegel. After all, who does? Poul Møller, Sibbern, Kierkegaard, Brøchner, Brandes, Høffding, or Thulstrup? After the master's death the breach between a Hegelian right and a Hegelian left demonstrated quite clearly that various conclusions could be drawn from the Hegelian writings, of which—at any event—the *Aesthetics*, in H. G. Hotho's three-volume edition (Berlin, 1835, Catalogue 1384–86), appears to have come rather belatedly into Kierkegaard's hands. He proceeds from Heibergian premises when he concerns himself with the aesthetic categories in the middle of the 1830s. Martensen's posing as a heavyweight Hegelian aesthetician with his essay on Lenau's *Faust* (June 1837), and his claiming to have gone farther than Hegel did, threw Kierkegaard into a rage—and gave him various complexes, for the simple reason that he still had not done his Hegel reading properly. It was Martensen who, as the first and most gifted of Hegel's Danish disciples, called down Kierkegaard's contempt upon his head. When Martensen's lectures from November 1837 and later caused an intellectual stir among the students, bearing comparison with Steffens's lectures in 1802 and Brandes's in 1871, the scene was set for Kierkegaard's damning judgment. Yet, his wrath was directed only at the Danish disciples with their all too facile minds, not at Hegel himself, not at Heiberg, and not at "the system." Their turn came later, in 1843–45. There is no basis for Thulstrup's declaration on page 100, after a depiction of the summer of 1835 (and on to November of that year), that "Kierkegaard is in very early opposition to Hegel." Kierkegaard's intellectual standpoint during the period was that of the Heibergi-

ans, including Poul Møller, with their admiration of Hegel and
Goethe.

Thulstrup concerning the Years before the Dissertation

In his third chapter Thulstrup depicts the period from November
1837 (Martensen's lectures) to September 1838 (*From the Papers of
One Still Living*) and is of the opinion that Kierkegaard was funda-
mentally at odds with the right-wing Hegelians whose acquaintanceship he had made. Nevertheless, it is the Hegelian parrots—
Rasmus Nielsen, Carl Weiss, Frederik Beck, Hans Brøchner, P. M.
Stilling?—whom Kierkegaard pursues; but since almost none of
them had made any public statement, his attack had to be directed at the violent Hegelian ferment in the student association and
in the various colleges, not least in Regensen (Regency College).
Hegelianism had taken possession of the good minds of the time,
just as structuralism in the 1950s and Marxism in the 1960s took
such a strong hold on young academics that they lost the ability to
engage in impartial thought.

Thulstrup believes that Kierkegaard's religious revival in the
spring and summer of 1838 had a decisive influence on his relationship to Hegelianism. This "revival," for anyone who accepts
the hypothesis about the "Letters," continues to be a *quod erat
demonstrandum.* The proof of Kierkegaard's rallying round Danish
Hegelianism in its Heibergian form can be found in the circumstance, minimized by Thulstrup, that *From the Papers of One Still
Living* was written for Heiberg's *Perseus*: "On the other hand, in
this connection one should not attach too much importance to the
fact that Heiberg's journal represented Hegelianism" (p. 145). Yet
that is precisely what one should do: *Perseus* was a "journal for the
speculative idea," whose columns were thrown open only to those
writers who subscribed to the journal's program, "To the Readers," of the first issue (June 1837)—which has never been
reprinted.

Heiberg's nine-page introduction, "To the Readers," is a genuine
manifesto of Hegelian philosophy, alias the speculative idea. After

a prologue concerning the journals existing at the time and their task, the text continues:

> On the other hand we lack a journal which is exclusively consecrated to ideal undertakings, and not merely in a single direction but in their whole range: for the more culture, in its ascendancy, divides and particularizes the various intellectual interests, the more important the task becomes of assembling them once again in a highest unity, where all of them, after having put aside their empirical differences, can meet in the service of the idea, stay side by side with one another, and profit from a mutual union. In order to redress the ever more perceptible absence in our literature of such a refuge for ideal undertakings, the undersigned dares to make a beginning by establishing herewith a *journal for the speculative idea*.
>
> This more precise definition of the idea as "speculative" will demonstrate the plan of the present journal.

It could scarcely have found clearer expression. The message is spooned into the readers. The list of subscribers, an interesting document for literary sociologists, naturally includes among its numbers "Mr. Kierkegaard, S[øren], Cand. Phil." together with a whole series of outstanding academicians, members of the clergy, military men, noblemen, and estate owners, as well as two actors, C. N. Rosenkilde and J. H. Jørgensen. That the journal means to include only those contributions dedicated to Hegelian, that is, speculative philosophy, becomes equally clear from the section dealing with the arts—poetry in particular, which is compared to a bird, "even though it may land upon a branch, [it] does not cease on that account to be a denizen of the air":

> Yet it is not on the branch that we wish to see the bird of poetry, but in its flight through the sky. Only such poetic contributions which have the speculative idea itself as their content, or in which that idea at least comprises its "Gehalt," its material, and in which poetry thus, as it were, directs its glance toward its own source, not toward the interests and

objects of the outer world, will gain admission to this journal. This speculative poetry (in the word's narrower sense), which does not wish to separate itself from the process of comprehension but furthers the process in its own way, will be able to harmonize with the journal's intention: of spreading speculative knowledge in general.

The same is true, of course, of "popular religious reflections" and in particular of philosophy, which "is the speculative idea itself," and of "aesthetics and theology (the latter field in the word's restricted meaning, namely as dogmatic theology). Because of their relation to art and religion, great things already enclosed within the circle of the speculative idea at the outset are, by the very force of their inherent nature, speculative philosophy." The empirical and the realistic are excluded as a matter of principle, yet as far as the aesthetic contributions are concerned, "certain details of aesthetics which are empirical of themselves can be accepted without jarring against the speculative intention of the journal," and moreover, neither the reviews nor the essays themselves have to conform to fixed outer forms:

> Externally, these can be either independent or critical, all in accordance with the author's taste, and in any form whatsoever, to the extent that they can express a positive and independent thought whereby they will serve to explain the idea in one or another of its tendencies, or at least move in the direction of such an explanation.

One can rest assured that Kierkegaard thoroughly studied these guidelines before setting to work on his paper, *From the Papers of One Still Living*, for *Perseus*.

It was only because *Perseus* ceased to exist in August 1838 that Kierkegaard did not get his savage attack on H. C. Andersen published there, where it would have found a natural home, partly by its clear adherence to the Goethe tradition in Danish literature as Poul Møller (who died on March 13, 1838) had formulated it in his review of Fru Gyllembourg's *Ekstremerne* (*The Extremes*), and

partly by its effort to dissociate itself from the growing politiciza-
tion of Denmark's young poets: it was quite in agreement with
Heiberg's attitude toward the National Liberals. Now Kierkegaard
himself had to pay the costs of publishing his treatise, the very
structure of which was Hegelian. It appeared less than a month
after his father's death on August 9, 1838, a fact which ought not
to be overlooked by the scholars who regard the father's death as
the definitive factor in Kierkegaard's "conversion." The work is Hegelian in its struggle against the Romantics' errors, especially
against that irony which caused the personality's solid view of life
to dissolve. Kierkegaard knew very well what he was talking
about: in 1838 he was firmly anchored in political and religious
conservatism and had certainly not left either Hegel or Heiberg, let
alone Goethe, behind.

This is not the place to discuss Thulstrup's interpretation and
localization of the herostratically famous "Feud between the New
and the Old Soap Cellar," a further proof—after "The Master
Thief"—that Kierkegaard the playwright lacked the talent to write
dialogue and to create figures for the stage. "The Soap Cellar" is a
puzzle the pieces of which can be put in their proper place only
after a carefully study of the primary sources, in particular the
dailies and weeklies of the time. With a devotion worthy of a better cause, Thulstrup has followed in the footsteps of his predecessors, Brandt, Hirsch, and Carl Roos. He has not made any
independent effort to interpret the models of the persons who appear in the play. If one proceeds from the assumption that the
comedy was written for use in the student association, one can be
sure that the public would have been able to tell who was who.
Only Orla Lehmann as Holla Hastværksen and Martensen as von
Springgaasen have been firmly identified. That Phrase was meant
to be Heiberg is pretty well out of the question, and Thulstrup's
own uncertainty appears with utter clarity on page 162: "Hr.
Phrase is very likely Martensen and von Springgaasen Heiberg, but
it must be added that Kierkegaard has somewhat changed the latter in particular, putting statements into his mouth which histori-
cally must be referred to Martensen instead." No! As it appears

from the notes (reprinted by Thulstrup himself in the second edition of the *Papers*) which Kierkegaard made during Martensen's lectures, Kierkegaard merely needed, surely, to quote and to twist Martensen's words a little in order to produce his caricature. Thulstrup has failed to adduce any proof that the Heibergian Kierkegaard, who at that time had not achieved any sort of mastery of Hegel's system, did not entertain strong sympathies for Heiberg as well as for Hegel. It is Danish intellectuals and their political and philosophical jargon that Kierkegaard parodies—just as he does in *From the Papers of One Still Living* of September 1838. The drama and the debut book coincide in one of their aims, and neither work is hostile toward Hegel himself. They also form a chronological entity. That Thulstrup follows Brandt's dating does not speak favorably of his sense of source criticism. Nothing indicates 1839, everything indicates the spring and summer of 1838.

De omnibus dubitandum est

There are also unmistakable signs of a mutual relationship between the Andersen book and the unfinished philosophical novel *Johannes Climacus*, or *De omnibus dubitandum est*. The novel has been exploited in the crudest sort of way by Kierkegaard scholarship, which has used it as a biographical source; but, to date, this same scholarship cannot be said to have solved three difficult problems: the novel's time of composition, its actual usefulness as a biographical source, and its plot. The first two problems are closely related to one another.

Employing extremely shaky criteria from Kierkegaard's own hand, Heiberg and Kuhr have placed it in 1842–43, and Thulstrup puts it (according to his chapter 7, section 3) in the time after November 1842, thus after *Either/Or* had left Kierkegaard once and for all on its way to the typesetter and to proofs. But Kierkegaard's statement that the work was begun "a year and a half ago"—at a time when he had not "read the least bit of Aristotle but, to be sure, a part of Plato"—together with the introductory description of "the storm during the past winter" (IV.B.1, p. 104, crossed out with pencil!), does not make much sense and proves nothing. It is an indication, rather, that a correction was made by the P. V. Christensen mentioned above (see p. 7), the copyist of *Either/Or*.

When, indeed, would Kierkegaard have had time to undertake such a large project in 1842–43? Even if one takes his altogether remarkable industry into account, there remains only the period during which he had finished *Either/Or* and Christensen was busy making the fair copy, in other words the late summer and autumn of 1842 and perhaps two or three months in the winter of 1842–43, that is, until the carefully planned propaganda campaign for *Either/Or*, which got under way on February 18, 1843, or until Kierkegaard's change in mood upon receiving Heiberg's review on March 1. From then on he was fully occupied. But is it not most likely that the fragmentary novel *was written down* in the autumn of 1842, that is, that the corrections and the copy are from this period? At any event, *De omnibus dubitandum est* has roots going back into the 1830s and more precisely to the intellectual situation in Copenhagen in 1838, after Martensen's Hegelian lectures and the ensuing stir in the academic duck pond. These lectures which, with the support of Hegel, depicted the philosophical development of modern times from Descartes (whom Kierkegaard always calls Cartesius) to Hegel, put Kierkegaard into an emotional state very close to frenzy. The two expressions into which he sank his teeth, sucking blood from them like an insect, were Martensen's turn of phrase concerning the necessity of "going beyond Hegel" and the quotation borrowed from Hegel: "De omnibus dubitandum est." This quote can be found in Kierkegaard's account of Martensen's lecture on November 29, 1837, but also goes back to Martensen's review of Heiberg's "Det logiske Cursus" ("The Logical Course") in the December 1836 issue of *Maanedsskriftet*. For some unknown reason Thulstrup does not believe that Kierkegaard had acquainted himself with Hegel by means of this first and partly popularizing account of his *Logik*. And Thulstrup will certainly *not* have it that Kierkegaard originally regarded Hegel with deep respect: see the sketch IV.B.8, piece 11, "to go further than Hegel—that was a dangerous matter." Nor does Thulstrup wish to concern himself with the circumstance—which speaks after all for a Christian interpretation of Kierkegaard's early development—that the Hegelian left, and Strauss in particular, were by no means unfamiliar to Martensen, something Martensen later on tried to conceal. One can read more about this matter in S. V. Rasmussen's admirable book *Den unge Brøchner,* which unfortunately was never finished. S. V. Rasmussen, universally regarded as Denmark's leading Hegel expert, died in 1963 and did not have the opportunity to evaluate Thulstrup's four theses, alas.

If the narrative goes back to 1838, which various ideas and turns of phrase in the text would make us suspect, it shows Kierkegaard's mighty irritation at Denmark's young Hegelians. It can hardly be determined with any certainty who in particular it was that Kierkegaard had in mind, since very few of them indeed had made any public statements at the time, but, apart from Martensen, one may be allowed to guess that he thought of Carl Weiss, P. M. Stilling, F. Beck, Rasmus Nielsen, and perhaps (but it is more doubtful) Hans Brøchner. These were the post-Hegelians, who wished to outstrip Hegel before they had completely understood him, the soap boilers, who doubted everything, although they had no notion of what there was to doubt. And this was what he, Kierkegaard, intended to demonstrate with unparalleled irony, by depicting how sorry the lot of poor Johannes Climacus was when he took the young Hegelian lions at their word and began to doubt everything.

If the theory about this philosophical-polemical purpose holds water (a close equivalent to the campaign, two years before, against the National Liberals), it is a little difficult to see why Kierkegaard combines it with the famous overture, "Please observe . . .," with its pointing finger and its depiction of the father. The two things do not have terribly much to do with one another; but the thought of raising a literary monument to his father—whom he himself had caused so much worry and care—is quite in keeping with the psychological pleasure Kierkegaard took in writing about the dead and, as he wrote, in transforming them. One must wonder, of course, if the hosier would have recognized himself as Climacus senior, an exceptional person, almost a dialectical genius.

Is Johannes Climacus Kierkegaard?

Now we have arrived at the question whether or not we should identify Johannes Climacus with Kierkegaard. Thulstrup seems to entertain no doubts in the matter, "In the narrative's first part we get an (autobiographically) striking and clear characterization of the hero, Johannes Climacus alias Kierkegaard, in the home, at school, at the university among people of his own age but not of the same mind" (p. 255). And further, on page 256, "Both these pieces of information fit the young student Kierkegaard quite perfectly." Goodness gracious, it's Søren as he lives and breathes!—if I may be permitted to use the Kierkegaardian dressing-gown style.

It is possible that Climacus/Kierkegaard began to read rather late in life. But the novella, at any rate, jumps over the essential and verifiable activities of the 1830s: the early study of Heiberg and his writings; the countless visits to the theater, with *Don Juan* and *The First Love* as epoch-making impressions; the break with Grundtvigianism, which had captured his brother and was on the point of conquering his father; the change to an aesthetic way of life; reorganizing the personality into that of a foppish literary dandy; the interrupted participation in Holy Communion; the more or less ostentatious break with his home, which was healed only when economic factors forced Kierkegaard to return; the interest in the natural sciences and the philosophers . . . , one could continue if one so desired. It seems to me that there is considerably more Kierkegaard in the Faustian doubter of the "Letters" than in Johannes Climacus. The novella is not a scantily camouflaged autobiography but a considerable and, for that matter, imposing transformation of facts into literature.

In the sketches there is also an inclination to put a distance between Johannes Climacus and Kierkegaard. Concerning the knowledge the former had of extraordinary people, the original says, "but he knew only four, after all," which in the finished text is changed to "Yet he knew so few after all" (IV.B.1). Who were they? My guess would be Mynster, Sibbern, Poul Møller, and Heiberg. Was he thinking of his father, too? The portrait of the sweetly melancholy Johannes simply has nothing to do with the young, aggressive, and ambitious aesthetician Kierkegaard, who confronts us in the middle of the 1830s. The character in question is a literary figure, the first of Kierkegaard's pseudonyms, the first in the list of kings, admitting his identity just as much and just as little as the later pseudonyms do.

Kierkegaard's own interpretations of the "plan" in the narrative are from 1844, when he was already busy with his statements about how one should read and interpret him. It is a case of autoexegesis. The original plan can be found among the sketches and shows a development that moves in reverse, in four chapters: 1: (Danish Philosophy) Traditional Conceptions, 2: Hegel, 3: Kant, 4: Cartesius—Spinoza. Consequently Kierkegaard wished, it seems, to trace Danish Hegelianism back to its source, something which he—for a very good reason, his lack of broad and systematic reading in the great philosophers—was in no position to do in 1838, at a time when he felt impelled, for decency's sake, to take the official theological examination and the conference examination for the master of arts. He acquired the necessary information by means of philosophical studies after the completion of *Either/Or* in the summer of 1842. One can read about this in Thulstrup. The large and sarcastic reckoning with the Danish Hegelians, "Open Confession," appeared in *Fædrelandet* of June 12, 1842 (*SV*, XIII:397–406).

Kierkegaard's open and definitive break with Hegel, Heiberg, and the whole system cannot be detected, as far as I can see, in *De omnibus dubitandum est*, no matter when one thinks the novella was conceived and written down. It is still more difficult for me to follow Thulstrup's cheerful invitation, uttered on page 185 of his chapter "Concerning the Concept of Irony," to "make an attempt for the time being to ignore Kierkegaard's personal and private standpoint, and merely to contemplate the name Kierkegaard as a pseudonym, which represents a certain standpoint, a standpoint from which the book is written, a pseudonym which plays a role as a Hegelian historian of philosophy." As a historian, one can also read Kierkegaard's dissertation as a piece of Hegelian writing which—without following Hegel in all its details—must be regarded all the same as a respectable piece of work in the spirit of the Hegelian school. The final section especially, settling accounts with Romantic-Schlegelian irony and paying homage to Goethe and Heiberg, has a basic point of view like that of the Andersen book of 1838 and the drama about the Soap Cellar. Thulstrup has the right to regard Master of Arts Kierkegaard, writing his dissertation, as a Christian wolf in Hegelian sheeps' clothing. The consequence must be that one will likewise regard the whole of Kierkegaard's life as a gigantic play in which Kierkegaard acted a profusion of roles, among them that of Søren Kierkegaard in countless versions.

Contemporary Opinion

The contemporaries, Sibbern, Heiberg, Brøchner, and others, were convinced that Kierkegaard—in 1841 as well as two years later with *Either/Or*—was in a Hegelian stage; and so the process of ferment, begun by Hamann and Socrates in particular, had simply not quieted down yet. In this retrospective work of his, a work facing backward, Kierkegaard is constantly up to his neck in Heibergianism—the Heiberg couple is showered with compliments in such essays as those about *Don Juan* and *The First Love*—and the Assessor undeniably has a serious streak of Hegelianism. The sermon which ends his share, the second part, can be interpreted as the higher religious unity of the aesthetic and the ethical. About Hegel himself there is not a single word.

It was Heiberg's review of March 1, 1843, which set Kierkegaard off. After having stood as a courageous cadet at the general's side for eight years, he now had to be content with a few condescending words for a brilliant work: in his wrath, Kierkegaard seems to have overlooked Heiberg's admiration altogether. The *Papers* show

how his fury swells, turning into a regular tidal wave. Sometimes it takes very witty form, as in the undated IV.B.36, which deserves to be reproduced in extenso:

> Professor Heiberg is a peculiar man
> Dum-didi-dum-boom-boom.

Kierkegaard's about-face can be traced in his subsequent production, which turns not merely against Heiberg himself, the *Rector magnificus* of literature. (See especially *Prefaces* of 1844, the settling of accounts with Heiberg's old guard.) From now on, the torpedoing of Goethe and Hegel became a mission for Kierkegaard. He carried the war into the foe's own territory by destroying the main supplies from its two most important allies. As for himself, he sought support from whatever auxiliaries he could find, and both Sibbern and Poul Møller are now held in the highest esteem by him. From May 16, 1843 (when *Two Edifying Discourses*, with the dedication to his father, introduces the religious element under Kierkegaard's own name), to the *Concluding Nonscientific Postscript* of December 1845 (where the enormous production is signed or, at any rate, acknowledged by Kierkegaard), Kierkegaard's effusions, which do not have their like in world literature, are a gigantic reaction against the Heiberg circle and its ecclesiastical, philosophical, and literary adepts. They astonished and frightened the Heibergians by their lack of balance, their fury, and their personal tone. Heiberg retorted only once, in *Urania* of 1844, and then kept silent, letting Kierkegaard run to the end of his tether in the *Postscript*, which attempts the slaughter of *both* Hegel and Heiberg, and systematic thought in general. A religious and existential philosophy of universal importance was the result of this conflict. P. L. Møller entered the lists in December 1845, and in January 1846 the *Corsair* joined him. The affair pushed Kierkegaard in the direction of a constantly more fervent and more demanding philosophy, to which no one, and hardly even Kierkegaard himself, could measure up.

Either/Or cannot be regarded as the end of a process of ferment, inasmuch as the process continued. But after Heiberg's review,

Kierkegaard made his choice as a good existentialist should. He declared open war on Heibergianism with all its Goethean-Hegelian substance, and in his attack on the church he ended by pulling down the whole edifice of established state religion in Denmark, with Mynster at its head.

There is a magnificent pathos about the final phase of Kierkegaard's life, an unearthly, cold, and inhuman rage, which impresses us by its very lack of humanity. We are in the world of the Old Testament.

The beauty and the savagery of Kierkegaard's career are not apparent if one reads him, and the sources, from a preconceived hypothesis about his never having been a Hegelian.

It is a sin to transform a grandiose tragedy into an edifying sermon. An aesthetic sin, at any event. Perhaps a religious one as well.

It is also a sin (and, frankly speaking, a dreadful pity) that Niels Thulstrup undertook the interpretation of the Kierkegaard material he had collected over so many years in the firm and preconceived notion that Kierkegaard never had a relationship—shall we call it a compliant or a promiscuous one?—with Hegelianism.

One gets the answer one asks for. Seek and ye shall find. *Qui cherche, trouve.*

Let us stop the quotations here.

Sat sapiendi.

6: SØREN KIERKEGAARD'S
FIRST LOVE

*The first love is the true love, and one
loves only once.*

It is an accepted part of the
general Kierkegaard mythology
to date Kierkegaard's attachment to Regine Olsen from the month
of May 1837 and to make that little lady into Kierkegaard's first
and only love. The sole "proof" for this is taken from Raphael Meyer's authorized book with the official title *Kierkegaardske Papirer,
Forlovelsen, udgivne for Fru Regine Schlegel af Raphael Meyer*, 1904
(*Kierkegaard Papers, the Engagement, edited for Mrs. Regine Schlegel by Raphael Meyer*): "She recalled having seen Søren Kierkegaard for the first time when she was quite young, and not yet
confirmed; that day she was in the company of others of her own
age at the house of Fru Cathrine Rørdam at Frederiksberg when
Kierkegaard happened to pay a visit. He immediately made a very
strong impression on her, but she did not show it, of course."
More than sixty years after the meeting Fru Schlegel read the *Posthumous Papers;* her attention was particularly caught by what is
now reprinted as II.A.68:

> Today the same scene again—I got to the Rørdams' after all—
> Good God, why should that inclination awaken just now—
> Oh, how much I feel that I am alone—Oh, a curse upon that
> prideful satisfaction of being by oneself—Everybody will de-
> spise me now—oh, my God, do not remove your hand from
> me—let me live and reform—

Meyer writes, "She believed that the passage in the *Posthumous
Papers* [quoted in abbreviated form] referred to this first meeting,
where he thus got a first impression of her, even as she did of

him." The entry, II.A.68, is not dated, so we have only the old lady's *assumption* that it was concerned with her. Yet that is just as improbable as the fact is sure that Kierkegaard and Regine met for the first time at the Rørdams'. The preceding entry, II.A.67, dated May 8, is placed in the year 1837 by Heiberg and Kuhr:

Oh God, how easily one forgets such intentions! I have once again been returned to the world for yet a while, deposited within my own self to rule there. Oh, but what did it profit a man that he gained the whole world but forfeited his life. Today too (May 8) I have tried to forget myself, yet not by means of boisterous sound—that surrogate does not help— but by going out to the Rørdams' and talking with Bolette, and (if possible) by forcing the devil of wittiness to remain at home, the angel, who with a flaming sword, as I deserve, places himself between me and every innocent girlish heart— when You overtook me, oh God, accept my thanks for not having let me go mad directly— I have never been so afraid of it, accept my thanks for having turned Your ear to me once more.

In this entry "the Rørdams' and talking with Bolette" was originally crossed out in pencil by Kierkegaard himself, together with the whole of II.A.68. But even if one proceeds from the premise that Kierkegaard consciously wished to erase the traces of his first affection for Bolette Rørdam, the two entries, which are assumed to be correctly dated to May 1837 and connected with one another, are still difficult to interpret.

I shall refrain from any interpretation other than the banal one that Kierkegaard knew Bolette Rørdam before May 1837 and was taken with her, that he tried to withdraw from the world—his infatuation?—in order to consecrate himself to his religious life, no doubt to find his lost way back to God, that he still could not resist the temptation of seeing the young girl, and that he knew very well how his devil of wittiness could run away with him, something that damaged him in the young girl's eyes. What Kierkegaard writes in his otherwise quite undependable document

"My Relationship to 'Her'," of August 1849, agrees with this interpretation; "Regine Olsen—I saw her for the first time at the
Rørdams'. I really saw her there that first time, when I did not go
to the family." The statement is mysterious, unless it is to be interpreted as referring to later and closer associations with members
of the Rørdam family. The continuation has a very telling parenthesis: "(In a certain sense I have some responsibility toward
Bolette Rørdam, just as I, as a matter of fact, also got an impression of her earlier, no doubt, and perhaps made one upon her too,
even though in all innocence, in a purely intellectual way.)"

It is to Kierkegaard's credit that, at a time when he was busy
confessing to posterity about something he regarded as one of humanity's great love stories, that is, his own, he still had enough
love of the truth to recall his infatuation with Bolette Rørdam.
There is every reason to believe that Kierkegaard's first attachment
was to Bolette Rørdam and that afterward, when he had immortalized his love for Regine through his literary works, he wished
that Regine, and Regine alone, had been his first and only love. He
not only erased the traces of Bolette—I beg the gentle reader to
forgive me for taking the liberty of using first names with these
two ladies—but also tried to insert Regine into the story at a point
in its course when she perhaps could not make any claim at all to
being the first and only and great love. The most famous of all the
Regine statements (II.A.347) goes as follows (I almost refrained
from quoting it, since all Kierkegaardians know it by heart):

> You ruler of my heart, "*Regina*," concealed in the deepest hid-
> ing place of my breast, in my fullest thought of life, there, at
> an equal distance from heaven and from hell—unknown dei-
> ty! Oh, can I really believe the tales of the poets—that, upon
> seeing the object of love for the first time, one believes one
> had seen her long before, that all love, like all knowledge, is
> recollection, that love, even in the simplest individual, has its
> prophets, its types, its myths, its Old Testament. Everywhere,
> in every girlish face, I see the traits of your beauty, but I feel
> that I must have all girls in order to extract your beauty from

theirs, as it were; that I must sail around the whole world to find the continent I miss, and toward which the deepest secret of my being points, as though it were the pole;—and in the next moment you are so near to me, so immediate, filling my spirit so mightily, that I am transfigured in my own eyes, and feel that it is good to be here.

Oh blind god of love! You, who see into secret places, will you make a revelation to me? Shall I find what I seek here in this world, shall I experience the *conclusion* of all my life's eccentric premises, shall I *enclose* you in my arms,—or:
Does the order say, Onward?
Have you gone ahead, oh you my *longing*, transfigured, do you wave to me from another world? Oh, I will cast everything from me in order to be light enough to follow you.

February 2, 1839

This passage presents two interesting matters, one, that the word *"Regina"* is an addition, the other, that the style is 100 percent poetic. Two conclusions must be obvious. First, that the text can refer to Bolette as easily as to Regine. And second, that it can be a part of the epistolary novella, "Letters." Who can say that its hero did not fall in love on that rambling odyssey of his? Even as Faust did. And Wilhelm Meister. In this case the date is fictive and does not coincide with the period during which Kierkegaard, the student of theology, sat cramming, his mind's eye fixed on his certificate.

If the date is not fictive, Bolette Rørdam is still not out of the picture, in any case. II.A.617 has an unmistakably Heinesque ring to it: "Like a lonely fir, egoistically closed within myself and aimed at higher things, I stand here, casting no shadow, and no wood dove builds its nest in my branches.—Sunday, July 9 [1837] in Frederiksberg Park after a visit to the Rørdams." In his memoirs Goldschmidt tells about having been introduced to Kierkegaard while visiting the same family in 1837–38, but since he simultaneously reports that, on the way home, he and Kierkegaard discussed *From the Papers of One Still Living*, which had just appeared, he has misled Goldschmidt scholars into believing that his *first* meeting with Kierkegaard must have taken place shortly after the book's publication, on September 6, 1838. Of course, nothing prevents the two young lions from having met one another earlier, but it was the walk and the literary discussion which made a special impression upon Goldschmidt's memory. Perhaps it would be appropriate to call attention to II.A.273—from October 11, 1838, and thus undoubtedly written after the literary promenade:

> Of course, the interesting time is the period of infatuation, in which, after the total impression that the first stroke of the magic wand produces, one takes something home from every meeting, every glance (no matter how quickly the soul, so to say, conceals itself behind the eyelid)—like the bird which busily carries one piece after another to its nest, and yet constantly feels itself overwhelmed by great riches.

In the years 1837–38 an attachment to Bolette Rørdam, born in 1815 and thus two years younger than Kierkegaard, would have been a more natural thing for him than a passion for Regine, born on January 23, 1823, and confirmed on April 22, 1838, in Holmens Kirke. Of course, the time itself had a weakness for nymphets, but just the same . . .

Bolette was the youngest of four daughters left by Pastor Thomas Schatt Rørdam (1776–1831). His widow, Cathrine Rørdam (July 20, 1777, to December 31, 1842), kept open house at Frederiksberg, and both Peter Christian and Søren Kierkegaard visited the home. The oldest daughter, Elisabeth, born in 1809, died unmarried in 1895; the next, Emma (1812–97), got married in 1857, forty-five years old, to Pastor Søren Johan Heiberg (1810–71) in Kjeldby, who in 1839 had married number three, Engelke Rørdam (1814–55). Bolette Rørdam herself got married in 1857, also at a rather advanced age, to Pastor Nicolai L. Feilberg (1806–99) in Helsinge-Drosselbjerg. She died in 1887. Kierkegaard appears to have maintained contact with the Rørdam home, and the four daughters, until at least 1841, when he loaned them the books of his half cousin, Hans Peter Kierkegaard—which books we do not know. One can read about the Rørdam home, moreover, in Goldschmidt's *Erindringer*, 1877 (*Memoirs*), where one finds, on page 240:

It was around the time of my editorship [of *Næstved Ugeblad*], in the summer of 1837, . . . that I encountered Søren Kierkegaard for the first time. I met my former teacher [at the von Westen Institute] P. Rørdam, and he invited me to visit him, or, more precisely, his mother, who lived at Frederiksberg. Søren Kierkegaard was there, among others. I was certainly not a calm and careful observer, but an internal photograph has stayed with me. He was about seven years older than I, of course. At that time his face had a healthy color, but he looked frail, with shoulders that stood out somewhat; his eyes were wise, lively, and haughty, with a mixture of geniality and malice.

Here follows the account of the walk home along Gamle Kongevej with the discussion of *From the Papers of One Still Living*, which had just been published. Goldschmidt's remark, "I had read it and remembered best something about H. C. Andersen," shows clearly that his powers of memory are not dependable, since the book treats of nothing but H. C. Andersen: the acquaintanceship between Kierkegaard and Goldschmidt can therefore very well date from the summer of 1837—indeed, it most likely does.

I was surprised that he talked so much about his own book, but he did not become ridiculous in doing so; for he constantly spoke at a much higher intellectual level than my own. There was a long pause, and all of a sudden he made a little hop and struck himself along the leg with his thin rattan cane. There was something in the movement that called an errand boy to mind, but quite different from the sort of errand boy one customarily sees. The movement was comical, and yet it almost hurt to see it. I am quite aware that I am in danger of recalling the scene with an admixture of subsequent knowledge, but I am sure that there was something that hurt—something of this sort: that the frail, learned man wished to take part in the joys of life but could not or would not. I heard later that people in the region of Lyngby thought at the time that he was in love with a young lady (who then married one of his cousins) or found some special pleasure in her company. He often visited the family and liked to be present when there was dancing, taking delight in it, although he did not dance himself. Perhaps it was with a happy thought of the Lyngby region that he made that movement of his.

Even if one takes into account a shift of memory and later literary additions on Goldschmidt's part, a sum of convincing truth remains. In these final years of the 1830s Kierkegaard was in an erotic stage, not like the cynical and reflective Johannes the Seducer but like stud. theol. S. A. Kierkegaard, who wanted very much to find himself a wife. But neither Bolette Rørdam nor Regine Olsen got married later on to a cousin of Kierkegaard. Thus a certain Jane Doe from the Lyngby region will lead a ghostly existence in our minds, presumably residing in the parsonage of Pastor Peter Diderik Ibsen (1793–1855), who, after pastoral duties in Lunde (1825–31) and Svendborg (1831–33), received the call to Kongens Lyngby on September 4, 1833. (In the summer of 1839 Ibsen had tried to arrange a meeting between Kierkegaard and Christian VIII, crown prince at the time, and so Pastor Ibsen and Kierkegaard must have known one another earlier.) When Ibsen lost his wife, Dorothea, née Falckenthal, on July 8, 1844, Kierkegaard wrote him a somewhat artificial letter of condolence (Thulstrup, no. 109):

And I have spent many pleasant hours in your home, and in your home I have always found a generous reception, a hospitality with which your wife received everyone, a courtesy, an indulgence for my odd wishes and my odd manners. Your home has been one of the few where I could count on these things, and I still count on them.

For good reasons, no mention is made of the circumstance that it was at Ibsen's that he presumably realized the nature of his feelings for Regine. But how human it makes him after all—the possibility that one girl, or perhaps even two, had entered his life before the queen of his heart appeared. Kierkegaard is often his own worst enemy.

Strictly speaking, he cannot be blamed for the fact that, after his death, he would cause Kierkegaard scholars to deprive him of some of his humanity.

7: THE SUMMER OF 1840
IN JUTLAND

The time I was a little lad, and went and
herded sheep.
Blicher, "Den jydske Landsoldat" ["The
Jutland Militiaman," 1829]

Among the many amusing episodes in Kierkegaard scholarship—which has been very generous in this respect—there is the journey to Jutland in the summer of 1840. It has occupied the attention of Jørgen Bukdahl, Flemming C. Nielsen, and—altogether in the spirit of Kierkegaard—a policeman of high rank, Arthur Dahl. They have all made their accounts in good faith, something which is laudable—and suspect only in the instance of the policeman, to whom the case-files are bound to be of utmost importance. The problem is the same as in the affair of the difficulties, now over twenty-five years old, between another genius, Céline, who has little more in common with Kierkegaard than the acquisition of a martyr's rank *à tout prix*, and Denmark, official Denmark, the jurists' Denmark. Now what is fiction, and what is fact?

Barfod versus Heiberg and Kuhr

Let us begin with Barfod, for whom I have the same sincere sympathy as I do for the child in *The Emperor's New Clothes*, a story printed for the first time on April 7, 1837. Quite naively, the child says what he thinks he discovered as he sat with Kierkegaard's mighty pile of paper before him.

From the first half of the year neither a diary nor random dated entries in diary form are extant; they almost seem to

have been intentionally destroyed, like most of the other entries touching more personally upon S. K. from this and the
following year, together with the close of the previous one. A
little pocket notebook, in octavo and with partly unconnected
and therefore often meaningless notes, several of them in
pencil, has the following material on its first page:

whereupon Barfod, on pages 244–45, prints what then will be
III.B.211 and 212 in the *Papers*. It emerges much more clearly
from Barfod's typographical arrangement than from the later *Papers* that the material is a letter, bearing the date "Copenhagen,
June 14, 1840." The quotation "All is new in Christ," 2 Corinthians
5:17, is from the diary note of July 6, 1837 (II.A.102), a day in the
period during which Kierkegaard was working on the "Letters."
That the work on his "project" continued until 1840 is unlikely,
although possible.

One's suspicions are aroused when one finds that Barfod, after
providing the information that Kierkegaard became a theological
candidate on July 3, 1840, writes, "[Loose sheets, marked: 'From
an old journal']." These sheets comprise two entries from July 4,
two from July 5, three from July 10, one entry each from July 11,
15, and 18, and August 9 and 10, with one undated entry. These
thirteen entries are printed in Group A of the *Papers* as III.A.1–13,
which means that Heiberg and Kuhr, who omit the information
that the entries are from an old journal, have taken them as being
factual, not fictive. They seem to stem from Journals DD and EE
(the originals of which are not extant), pages which are referred to
in III.A.5; according to this, they would originate, respectively,
from December 2 and 3, 1838 (DD), and July 30 and August 1,
1839 (EE).

We do not know if Kierkegaard copied out these notations
before or after his trip to Jutland, and we get no explanation in
Heiberg and Kuhr's introduction (III:vii):

Within Group A (composed of sketches having the character
of entries in a diary) there are four sections in the volume,
one from the journal of 1840, July 4 to August 10, one for the

sketches from the Jutland trip of 1840, July 19 to August 6, one for the journals in the period 1841–November 20, 1842, and one for random papers from the whole period.

These pieces of information are distinguished by neither their clarity nor their comprehensibility. The placing of III.A.1–13 as a special group among the diary materials excludes interpreting them as fiction, but III.A.12 from August 9, 1840, the anniversary of the father's death, undeniably provides a signpost—pointing backward toward the "Letters," forward toward *Either/Or:*

When one understands the words of Brorson:
  When the heart feels most marooned,
  Then the harp of joy is tuned,
not as though written in a religious but rather in an aesthetic sense, then one will have in them, as it were, a motto for every poetic existence, which must of necessity be unhappy.

One must be extraordinarily obtuse in artistic matters not to perceive in these words an aesthetic-religious poet, for whom the trip to Jutland possesses or possessed a significance other than the purely private one of visiting distant Jutland relatives in the father's home parish. There is still no help to be had from Heiberg and Kuhr, whose account of the source material is reproduced here in concentrated form without, however, distorting the text:

After the total interruption in S. K.'s notes from the end of the year 1839 and thereafter, brought about by the intensive reading for the examination ... in the year 1840, the journal (A.1–13) begins again on July 4, the day after S. K. finished his official theological examination. When it was registered in Catalogue B [of Barfod] this journal consisted, as it does now, of only six loose sheets which were originally bound together; with an interruption corresponding to the period of S. K.'s journey to Jutland, the notes on these sheets conclude with the date August 10.

Kierkegaard was back in Copenhagen on August 6. It is not immediately apparent why he should have kept a diary before and after the trip to Jutland and then stopped his entries from August 10 on, far into 1841. That would indeed cause a blank to appear on P. A. Heiberg's clockface (see chap. 2). After a reference to such imposing sources as *Stages on Life's Way* and Kierkegaard's own five-act production of "My Relationship to Her," of 1849, Heiberg and Kuhr arrive at the following conclusion, which might well be altogether unique as a historical presentation of the sources—in the year 1911, thus after Erslev, Seignobos, Langlois, Bernheim, Gustave Lanson, and several others had demonstrated the most elementary demands of historical source criticism.

In all probability the remainder of the volume, of which now only the six sheets are left, contained journal entries from the time of the [Regine] story's first three sections, and S. K. himself destroyed this part of the volume; from November 15 and 16 there existed on "loose sheets" two entries (III.A.217 and 218) from which we may be permitted to draw conclusions with respect to the character of a part of the destroyed journal entries, at any event; but otherwise we do not have the slightest basis for forming an idea about the extent of these entries—indeed, to be exact, not even for the assumption that anything at all has been destroyed.

That is true as true can be. Why, after all, should Kierkegaard have destroyed entries of the nature of III.A.217 and 218, which could be handsomely fitted in among the diapsalmata? Experience shows that men of letters, even the greatest, are parsimonious with their gold. Is it too profound to conjecture that Kierkegaard preferred to wipe out the traces of his extremely complicated connections with Regine Olsen? But here, thank heavens, the "Wednesday letters" are extant. Our Lord takes care that even the tallest trees . . .

Heiberg and Kuhr's description of the Jutland journey must indeed be reproduced:

Of the two pocket notebooks listed in Catalogue B with entries from this journey, only one (III.A.14–50) is in the library's collection; it lacks any dating whatsoever, but its
connection with the journey of 1840 is certain enough. Among
other things, it contains entries whose composition in the
stagecoach is revealed not only by their content but by the
handwriting itself, which in several instances shows signs of
the coach's bumping; a reason for Kierkegaard's sudden
switch from Danish to Latin at one point in the entries (see
III.A.23 and 24) can perhaps be sought in the prying glances
of his fellow travelers. These notes from the stagecoach logically stem from the beginning of the journey, the part
through Zealand to Kallundborg. S. K. himself has cut out
eight sheets from this pocket notebook, and their stubs, next
to the binding, do not allow any sort of definite conjecture
about the content at any point.

This is just as exciting as Victor Eremita's discovery in the bu-
reau! Unfortunately, only one historical fact is sure, namely that
Kierkegaard sailed on the ferryboat from Kalundborg to Aarhus on
July 19. Theoretically speaking, he could have walked to
Kalundborg. On his hands. Or spent the night on the way. And
experienced   strange   adventures.   The   thirty-four   entries
(III.A.15–49) smell of literature, even at a distance, and they have
roots going far back in time—to 1838, perhaps to the "Letters."
Even III.A.15, with the title "Fantasies for a Posthorn," reminds
one of a loose sheet, II.A.683, dated without hesitation by the editors to January 2, 1838: "I would like to write a novella with mot-
toes by myself. Motto: Fantasy for a posthorn." If this date is
fictive, as is quite conceivable, reference is made nonetheless in
the same note to the Echo, or the person Echo, who plays such a
large role in the drama about the Soap Cellar. The only concrete
clue for a dating is III.A.35, which speaks of the reading for the
examination as the longest parenthesis Kierkegaard has ever experienced. His preoccupation with postilions and posthorns is understandable in the extreme if this journey to Jutland, his second one

"abroad," was going to be incorporated into the "Letters," like the one to northern Zealand and Sweden of 1835. The posthorn novella, if this was an independent work and not just a component in the "Letters," was meant to treat of a man who becomes a teacher of children (see above, p. 119) and discovers the meaning of childhood by reproducing his own. The idea is repeated in the second, the "real" Jutland diary (III.A.51–84) in III.A.57, about "the vagrant, the vagabond," whose main personage, after all, is a teacher.

This second pocket notebook, III.A.51–84, is known only through Barfod, who under the heading "The Trip to Jutland" writes, naively and briefly, "The sketches from this journey are kept, sometimes in pencil, in a little pocket notebook," a statement which earns him the following stern reproof from the supreme court judges, Heiberg and Kuhr:

> Of the contents of the second pocket notebook (A.51–84), which begins in Kallundborg, we now possess only what was printed by Barfod: if one compares the printed material with the detailed table of contents in Catalogue B, only three entries (III.A.58, 60, and 74) seem to be wholly omitted (among them, unfortunately, one whose opening words—"I'd like to know what a young girl"—*could* point in the direction of Regine Olsen), while the rest have evidently been included in their entirety, even though with a change in the order the pieces had in the pocket notebook, according to Catalogue B, the interspersion of pieces from other places (A.89 from the journal of 1841 and [III] A.35 from the first pocket notebook), and the presence of a sketch (III.A.70) whose opening words are not adduced in Catalogue B—this causes some misgivings.

This report from the schoolmaster P. A. Heiberg would be exceedingly comical if it did not reveal his own editorial principles in such a depressing way, his weakness for unfounded guesses ("I'd like to know," etc.), and his incomprehensible hatred for Barfod, which has its source in Heiberg's pedantry. Whether the entry

III.A.70—consisting of four lines and quite unimportant in the present connection—was included in Barfod's catalogue or not should be irrelevant. The *Papers'* reprinting of Barfod is far from faultless. At first glance, no one can tell that III.A.53 undoubtedly is a compression of at least one entry each about Aarhus, Kallø, and Knebel, the last town of which had Emil Boesen's elder brother, Carl Ulrik Boesen, as parish pastor from 1835 to 1849. III.A.64 does not respect Barfod's italicizations, which are Kierkegaard's own. III.A.65 and III.A.53 are printed by Barfod in brevier: there must have been, then, a good deal more in Kierkegaard's manuscript. The notation about the "evening light" reminds one of the notations from Gilleleje. III.A.66 appears to be inserted—it is not to be found in Barfod's *Posthumous Papers*, at any event—from page 22 in the so-called Catalogue B. It is included without further explanation and without the underlining of the place-name, Sæding, as given by Kierkegaard/Barfod. Other place-names were underlined too, such as Holstebro and Idum: compare the practice in the "Letters" of emphasizing the place where the writer (or author) was. III.A.69 inserts, instead of "One," the name of the person in question: Hundrup, a teacher at the school in Randers, who was still alive when Barfod published his first volume.

III.A.73 is very strange, without a date; it is included here in Barfod's original version (according to the *Posthumous Papers*, p. 262), thus with the underlinings and notes of Barfod that were not reprinted by Heiberg and Kuhr. The entry must have been made a few hours before the final part of the trip with the postilion to Sæding:

> I am sitting here quite alone (of course, I have frequently been just as alone, but I did not grow as aware of it), counting the hours until I shall see *Sæding*. I cannot remember any change in my father, and now I shall see the places where he herded sheep as a poor boy, the places for which I feel nostalgia as a result of the descriptions he gave. What if I fell ill now and was buried in Sæding's churchyard! A strange thought. His last wish for me is fulfilled—is it possible that

my whole purpose on this earth has really been subsumed in it? In God's name. The task was, after all [Barfod's footnote: "In the manuscript a 'not' is inserted here, which however must be a mistake in this context"], so small in relation to what I owed him. I learned from him what a father's love is, and I thereby grasped that divine father's love, the only thing in the world which cannot be shaken, the true Archimedean point.

Heiberg and Kuhr reprint the opening of the last sentence correctly: "The task was, after all, not so small in relation to what I owed him." Should this be interpreted as though the task, the fulfillment of the father's last wish to Kierkegaard, that is, to take the official theological degree, was not so terribly small, after all, in relation to what Kierkegaard himself felt he owed his father? Better proposals for an interpretation are requested.

The Consistency of Heiberg and Kuhr's Datings

After the entry, as it is printed in Barfod, which ends with "the true Archimedean point," Heiberg and Kuhr have III.A.74– 76, of which the first is the unimportant "I'd like to know what a young girl ..." (see p. 163), the second is four lines about "the pest house," and the third, III.A.76, is a literary mood picture in "evening light": "If only I might remember the impression of this evening properly." But after "the Archimedean point" (Barfod, p. 262 and III.A.73), Barfod adduces a good half page to which Heiberg and Kuhr have paid no attention. It concerns the question whether or not Kierkegaard preached in Sæding church during his visit there. After "the Archimedean point," Barfod has the following passage on page 262:

I had thought of preaching for the first time in *Sæding* church, and it ought to occur this Sunday (August 2, seventh Sunday after Trinity); to my by no means small amazement I see that the text is Mark 8:1– 10 (the feeding of the four thousand), and these words, "Whence shall one be able to fill

these men with bread *here in a desert place*," struck me, since
I shall speak in what is the poorest parish in Jutland in the
heath region.

The expression *heath region* is not italicized (that is, underlined
by Barfod, in accordance with Kierkegaard) in III.A.66, the strange
location of which—outside the order established by Barfod—undeniably must inspire mistrust in the *Papers*, that is, in Heiberg
and Kuhr, for whom it seems to have been a matter of principle
that Kierkegaard did *not* preach in Sæding church on Sunday, August 2, 1840. The "demonstration of proof" is to be found in the
preface to the third volume of the *Papers*, pages ix–x. It is depressing to quote it in extenso, because it so painfully reveals P. A.
Heiberg's unwillingness—I recognize that it is a postulate of mine
to make Heiberg and not Kuhr the one genuinely responsible—to
accept Barfod's "trip to Jutland," actually the only extant source:

> From the year 1841 we have in the first place a journal which
> very likely was begun toward the end of June and concluded
> before S. K. undertook his journey to Berlin on October 25.
> The entries (A.85–145) have no datings at all, to be sure, and
> the cover itself was "without year and marking," according to
> Catalogue B, but the second entry (A.86) consists of a prayer
> with the title "The Seventh Sunday after Trinity" and a refer-
> ence to "my diary from my trip." Presumably on the basis of
> this reference, Barfod has placed the entry in the year 1840
> (when the seventh Sunday after Trinity fell on August 2), in-
> serting it at that point in the entries of the pocket notebook
> from the journey with which the reference has to do
> (III.A.66); nor is there anything to prevent the prayer and the
> entries directly following, with sketches for a sermon
> (A.87–89) connected with the text of the prayer, from having
> been written down in the year 1840, after the return from the
> journey, but the subsequent entry says:

I shall break the quotation off here, feeling a little worried
about ending a quotation with a colon. Yet the quotation which

follows after the colon, III.A.90, is connected by Heiberg and Kuhr with "the fourth section of the history of the engagement," which, in accordance with their opinion and that of all other Kierkegaard scholars (except myself) ended with "the first break" at the beginning of August 1841. Whereupon the firm of Heiberg and Kuhr presents its arguments for *not* wishing to accept the idea that Kierkegaard preached in Sæding church in 1840:

> In the chronology it would be consistent to place the notes for the sermon in 1841, when the seventh Sunday after Trinity fell on July 25, and therefore we have chosen to put the starting point for this volume of the journal in July 1841, something which is also in better agreement with the view [whose?] of the journal's history for the year 1840. A corroboration of this chronology is offered by the journal entry from a little further on (III.A.111) with the heading, "An effective piece of advice for dull authors"; it can naturally be associated with S. K.'s reading of the proofs of his dissertation, which were sent from the printer's on September 16, 1841. The last entries presumably point with considerable clarity toward the time of the final break, which took place on October 11. [Preface to *Papers*, III:x]

The long and short of it is that Heiberg and Kuhr choose to employ an undependable, secondary source as their support, that is, Kierkegaard's sketches from 1849, "My Relationship to 'Her'," when they have the job of arranging the papers from 1840. Thus one must be permitted to advance the hypothesis that Kierkegaard could in any case have given a sermon in Sæding church on August 2, 1840, that is, the seventh Sunday after Trinity.

Consequently, there is also no reason for accepting the editors' assumption that the undated sketches, III.A.85–145, "very likely [were] begun toward the end of June and concluded before S. K. undertook his journey to Berlin on October 25," that is, in 1841. They can just as well have been written and doubtless *were written in the last five months of 1840*, thus during the first and relatively happy part of the engagement (see chap. 8, where my chief argu-

ment for placing the journal almost a year earlier than in the period chosen by Heiberg and Kuhr is precisely its unmistakable
resemblance to the first Wednesday letters).

The commentary of Heiberg and Kuhr on III.A.90 is revealing,
as far as their principles of dating are concerned: what in the
world does this undated statement, which they place in 1841, have
to do with the letter in " 'Guilty?'/'Not Guilty?' " and the return
(taken for granted by the editors or alleged by Kierkegaard) of the
engagement ring? III.A.95, with its quotations from Poul Møller's
poem "Den gamle Elsker"("The Old Lover"), points directly toward 1840, the autumn in which the poem plays a role in the
letters to Regine—see in particular Thulstrup's letter Number 27,
undoubtedly from November 4, 1840. III.A.105, concerning the
Jewish jeweler, points to the period of the engagement. III.A.121,
concerning the pitiful horses which Kierkegaard used on his excursion to Fredensborg, points to Thulstrup's undated Number 23,
which lies in the vicinity of November 13, 1840, that is, Martinmas
Eve, when Kierkegaard drove out to Fredensborg in a hired carriage. III.A.133 and 134 have a clear connection with Regine, with
the "R"of the first one inserted above the line; and III.A.144, with
its reference to Christian Wilster's translation of Euripides, is a
new piece of evidence for the placing of these sketches in 1840.

If this theory about III.A.85–145 holds water, that is, if these
sketches are to be placed in 1840 and not, in accordance with
Heiberg and Kuhr, in 1841, the conclusion will not be catastroph-
ic. It is quite simple. *For a period of a good ten months, the first ten
of 1841, we have no sure entries*—apart, perhaps, from some letters to Regine, and these not of the most charming kind. The letter
to his half cousin, Hans Peter Kierkegaard (1815–62), a son of
Kierkegaard's father's cousin Mikael Andersen Kierkegaard
(1776–1867), is reprinted as Number 47 in Thulstrup's *Breve og
Aktstykker.* It is not plain why it should be dated 1841; the books
loaned to Fru Rørdam's four daughters would rather lead one's
thoughts to 1837–39.

This blank on the clockface of Kierkegaard's life offers no cause
for alarm. Kierkegaard had enough to do with his pastoral semi-

nar, which he began on November 17, 1840, and his dissertation, *Concerning the Concept of Irony with Constant Reference to Socrates*, which on July 16, 1841, was declared by the philosophical faculty as worthy of being defended for the master's degree. The printers had it ready on September 16. The defense took place on September 29. If Kierkegaard, in the summer of 1841, had the energy to compose his large treatise on "The Aesthetic Validity of Marriage," which was then included in *Either/Or* among B.'s papers under another title and perhaps in a revised form, he was certainly up to his ears in work—not to mention the broken engagement, which, in the amount of psychological chitchat and gossip it caused, far outdid a divorce of the 1970s. In 1841 it was a sensation, a scandal.

A great deal happened during the Copenhagen *saison* of 1840–41. Kierkegaard's friend H. P. Holst went south in October, with the "enemy"—Kierkegaard's, not Holst's—hot on his heels, H. C. Andersen. The *Corsair* put to sea on October 8, 1840, and both God and man knew who stood behind it, the twenty-one-year-old student M. A. Goldschmidt, whom Kierkegaard had become acquainted with in 1837 or 1838. The campaign against Kierkegaard's friend H. P. Holst culminates in Grimur Thomsen's leaflet (on Holst's plagiarism). In its repertoire the Royal Theater has Scribe's *The Sheriff* and *The Bath at Dieppe*, both in September, together with Heiberg's vaudeville-monologue *Grethe i Sorgenfri (Grethe in Sorgenfri)*, written for Fru Heiberg, Donizetti's light opera *The Daughter of the Regiment*, which became a great success only later on, H. C. Andersen's *Maurerpigen (The Moorish Girl)*, which immediately failed, like Scribe's operetta *Queen for a Day*, Ancelot's *The Mazarin Family*, Sille Beyer's five-act drama *Ingolf og Valgerd*, with Fru Heiberg as Valgerd, and Hertz's now-forgotten Romantic play in three acts, *Svanehammen (The Swan's Slough)*. Bournonville's ballet *Toreadoren (The Toreador)* had its premiere on November 27, 1840, and with its fifteenth performance, of March 14, 1841, caused an unprecedented uproar. This magnificent production, one of Bournonville's finest ballets (which Harald Lander staged in 1929, dancing the title role himself), gave rise—on March 14, 1841—to a first-rate intrigue, a concert of whistles arranged by Count Schulenburg, which made Bournonville—in the toreador's costume—turn toward the royal box and ask Christian VIII what he should do. He received the royal answer, "Continue, my dear Bournonville." As a result, Bournonville got two weeks' confinement to his quarters and six months' involuntary exile—in Italy. There is no reason to weep: Naples had its premiere on March 29, 1842.

Kierkegaard's Sermons, 1840–41

It is not possible to state with utter certainty that Kierkegaard preached in Sæding church on the seventh Sunday after Trinity, that is, on August 2, 1840, but nothing, nothing at all, speaks for Heiberg and Kuhr's placing of "the prayer and the entries directly following, with sketches for a sermon connected with the text of the prayer" (III:x) under July 25, 1841. Why should Kierkegaard (who must have been quite tired after his work in the pastoral seminar and on his dissertation, which he had just submitted) have undertaken the composition of the sermon in July 1841, when he had problems enough on the home front—that is, with Regine?

Undeniably, the passage misfiled by Heiberg and Kuhr, III.A.66 (*Posthumous Papers I*, p. 262), "I had thought of preaching for the first time in Sæding church, and it ought to occur this Sunday,"speaks for Barfod's theory of a sermon in Sæding, even though it seems strange that Kierkegaard would not have known beforehand that the text was Mark 8:1–10, concerning the feeding of the four thousand. "And these words, 'Whence shall one be able to fill these men with bread *here in a desert place*,' struck me." Of course, Kierkegaard was aware of the poverty of the parish, thanks to his father and the family's letters, and he must have known before he left home on what Sunday in Trinity he would arrive in Sæding. The prayer, however, is difficult to interpret without reference to the background of a poor parish:

O Lord our God. All creation looks up to You and awaits food
and nourishment from You; You open up Your generous hand
and feed with Your blessings everything that lives. You hear
the animal's cry, You heed *the lament of man*. They lift up
their thoughts to You—they to whom You gave much, because they know that everything comes from You, and that no
abundance will give nourishment if You do not bless it; they,
to whom You gave little, because they know that no gift from
You is so small that it with Your blessing is not abundance.

It is Kierkegaard's lack of preparation, before all else, that
speaks against a sermon in Sæding. If he had intended to present
himself as the son of the parish's great benefactor, he would have
been thoroughly prepared and would not suddenly discover the
identity of the text for that particular Sunday. It is also difficult to
understand how this sermon in particular, which would have been
Kierkegaard's first, could have disappeared. But would he have
been allowed, in fact, to enter the handsome pulpit in the
towerless granite church on the heath before he had completed
the pastoral seminar, which he entered on November 17, 1840,
and as a member of which he gave his test sermon in Holmens
Kirke at noon on January 12, 1841? *That* sermon, preserved in extenso in III.C.1, and the opinion entered in the records by the two
younger theologians who had just finished their studies—Rasmus
T. Fenger (1816–89) and Ingvard H. L. Linnemann (1818–92)—
are reprinted in Thulstrup's *Breve og Aktstykker*, I:14–15. Here it is
called Kierkegaard's *first* sermon. That *can* be right.

A literary interpretation still has to be made of the prayer in
III.A.86, and the many later sketches for sermons, both in Section
A (III.A.129–31, 135, 137, 139, 140, and 143) and in Section C
(III.C.1–25, among them the sermon of January 12, 1841). Those
in Section C have been connected by the editors with Kierkegaard's
participation in the pastoral seminar in the winter of 1840–41 and
the summer of 1841, and that will not be disputed here. But to a
literary historian it seems obvious to ask if any of these sketches
was intended for the "Letters," the "project" on which Kierkegaard

had been working these many years. The sketch which immediately attracts attention is, of course, III.C.5, with the heading "Concerning the Edification Which Lies in the Thought That against God We Are Always Wrong." There is no need for a closer analysis either of this sketch, which is only half a page long, or of the sermon, which the ethicist B. sends to the aesthete A. in *Either/Or*. The decisive factor is merely that, both in III.C.5 and in "Ultimatum," we have entered the world of fiction. Thus one can also interpret the prayer III.A.86, "The Seventh Sunday after Trinity," as a purely literary document belonging to neither the one nor the other of the calendar Sundays that have been proposed, respectively August 2, 1840 and July 25, 1841. It is simply the poet Kierkegaard's use of a literary motif, the feeding in the wilderness, which was superbly suited for application to the sections in the epistolary novella dealing with the Jutland heath.

In accordance with this hypothesis, the prayer can have been written at any time in the period from the summer of 1840 to the autumn of 1841, and it has its most fundamental interest as evidence of what Kierkegaard had planned to do in his "project." Since he plainly intended to include writings from persons other than the Faustian doubter in his "Letters"—the Danish Faust gradually vanishes into the background amidst the Ossianic mists of Jutland—it is logical to believe in the existence of a Christian ethicist with the name of B.: B. for Boesen, whether Kierkegaard thereby meant his dearest friend, Emil Boesen, or the latter's brother, Carl Ulrik Boesen, the parish priest in Knebel. If it is *he* whom Kierkegaard depicts or caricatures in *Either/Or's* final section, "Ultimatum," then the friend B., the ethicist, would be Emil Boesen, who sends the aesthete A., Kierkegaard, one of his brother's sermons, not given as yet, concerning the edification in always being wrong against God.

This is a hypothesis just as plausible as the many theories about syphilis, visits to the bordello, conversions in May, and God knows what, which are forever buzzing in our ears. It deserves a whole book. A pretty book from Reitzel, the foremost publisher of the Golden Age.

Blicher's Shadow

Kierkegaard's journey to Jutland is in Blicher's style. Inaccuracies in dating are unimportant. Kierkegaard left Kalundborg with "the smack," or ferryboat, on July 19 (not July 17), and he returned with the hypermodern steamship, "Christian VIII," which left Aarhus on August 6, 1840; thus he was away from Copenhagen for a good three weeks. He traveled in a literary way, collecting material for his "project" even though one may be permitted to think that the "Letters" were now on the point of turning to dust in Kierkegaard's hands. That he continued to collect material ought to be plain from III.A.57, which falls into two parts, one depicting a vagrant, a member of the Moravian Brethren, born in Christiansfeldt, who cannot settle down on Fyn and who later ends up on the highways of Germany, and the other a scene describing five or six gypsies, to whom Boesen's wife, Anthonia Frederikke Frechland (born in 1801, the same year as her husband), gave religious instructions while they were confined in Viborg Penitentiary. In the prison they were evidently also taught by a convict-teacher, "a prisoner, who in earlier days had been a tutor, but who had embezzled some money. . . . Now, I'd like to think that this teacher was my vagrant," that is, the vagabond mentioned in the heading.

Blicher's influence is most readily seen in III.A.67:

> The visit at Hald; the old man I met, lying without a care on his back in the heather, only his stick in his hand. We kept one another company as far as Non Mill. We passed some running water, called Koldbæk [Cold Brook]; he assured me that it was the liveliest water in the whole region, whereupon he went down to it, stretched out full length on his stomach, and drank of it. We continued now, and he confided to me that he actually had set out to beg.

II.A.68, the scene from the woodland district near Hald, with the shy woman and the little boy, bears an unmistakable Blicherian stamp at its very end:

I got lost; far away a dark mass rose up, waving back and
forth in constant unrest. I believed it was a forest. I grew
quite surprised since I knew that there was no forest in the
vicinity save the one I had just left; alone on the torrid
heath, surrounded on all sides by the most complete monoto-
ny, except, right before me, that waving sea, I actually grew
seasick and desperate at not being able to get any nearer to
the forest, despite my exertions. Nor did I ever get there, for
when I came out onto Viborg Road, it continued to be visible,
but with the difference that now, since I had the white high-
way to judge by, I saw that it was the hills covered with
heather on the other side of Viborg Lake. Because one has
such a wide view on the heath, one simply cannot judge dis-
tances; one walks and walks, the objects do not change, since
there is really no *object* (for, in order for there to be an object,
that *other thing* is constantly required whereby it becomes an
object, but that is not the eye; the *eye* is what combines).

The descriptions, or the observations, scarcely have their roots
in Kierkegaard's own wanderings on foot in the heath regions
around Viborg and Hald; they stem rather from his literary attempts in the summer of 1835 at Gilleleje and from the introduction to Blicher's "Telse," quoted above (see p. 127f.). Jutland was
literarily fashionable just then, and as usual, Andersen had gotten
ahead of Kierkegaard. As early as 1830 he had published "Vand-
ringsmanden i Ørkenen: En Skizze" ("The Wanderer in the
Wilderness: A Sketch") in *Læsning for den fine Verden*. The June
issue of *Læsefrugter* the same year contained his "Maleri fra Jyl-
lands Vestkyst" ("Painting from Jutland's West Coast") (*SS*,
XII:165), and in July he had no fewer than two poems in the appendix to Iversen's *Fyens Stifts Avis*, "Den jydske Hede i Regnveir"
("The Jutland Heath in Rainy Weather") and "Aftenvandring paa
de jydske Vange i godt Veir" ("Evening Walk on the Jutland Fields
in Good Weather"). In January 1831 Andersen issued "Phantasier
og Skizzer," which was originally planned for publication under
the title "Jydepotte" ("Jutlander's Pot") in *Flyveposten*. It was

Kierkegaard's misfortune in general that he so often arrived too late, something one can find demonstrated with melancholy clarity in his opposition to J. L. Heiberg.

Whether or not the same feeling of arriving too late caused Kierkegaard to abandon his "project," that Faustian- Wertherian-Wilhelm-Meister-like *Bildungsroman*, "Letters," is a question that may be left in abeyance. It was in the beginning of the 1840s that the novel in its French form (as represented by Hugo, Musset, Mérimée, and Alexandre Dumas)—not to mention the grisette literature of Paul de Kock and Henri Murger—came into vogue. Goethe was no longer the star. If Kierkegaard had continued on the paths he had begun to walk in 1835, he would have appeared, literarily speaking, in clothes just as much out of date as those his father, merchant M. P. Kierkegaard—the title or job-designation "hosier" had passed away with the years—had had him wear in the Borgerdydsskole and, presumably, during the first years at the university, that is, until 1835.

There is nothing in Kierkegaard's *Papers* which allows us to establish firmly that on such and such a date he threw the whole "project" overboard in order to collect his powers instead for one novel, one piece of writing, one work, one project, in which the epistolary form and the romantic fiction of Jean Paul, Heine, Eichendorff, Hoffmann, Brentano, Hotho, and many other German Romantics played an immense role. We know only that the engagement and its deplorable conclusion in 1841 were of great importance for Kierkegaard, so it is logical to believe that, at some point or another in 1841, he broke with what was old—the past, the engagement, the project, etc.—in order to leap out, as a poet, over a sea 70,000 fathoms deep, with a great new work.

This statement can be excellently supported by quotations from Kierkegaard's letters to Regine and the many unmistakably personal elements in Kierkegaard's drafts of sermons from the pastoral seminar. It would not be hard to write a whole book about it. Learned and with footnotes and with a superfluity of cross-references. One can also say, think, assume, or assert that Kierkegaard chose a poet's existence at a certain point in the autumn of 1841—

from about August 11, 1841, when according to his own statement, he returned the engagement ring to Regine Olsen, past October 11, when he, likewise according to his own statement, made
the final break, to October 25, when he, after having played the
cynical, indifferent, and icy aesthete for two weeks, took the
steamship and the steam train to Berlin.

There is no reason to make fun of Kierkegaard. He must have
had a dreadful time for two full months. The Jutland interests
were lost beyond the horizon. Yet Kierkegaard did purchase
both Steen Steensen Blicher's collection of poetry, *Trækfuglene:
Naturconcert*, 1838 *(Birds of Passage: Concert in Nature)*, and
his *Vestlig Profil af den Cimbriske Halvøe fra Hamborg til Skagen
1839 (Western Profile of the Cimbrian Peninsula from Hamburg to Skagen 1839)* (Catalogue 1524–25). Kierkegaard could
not manage to include Blicher in the "project," which came
out in 1843 as *Either/Or.* Above the hillock from which
Kierkegaard's father had cursed God as a child after having tend-
ed his sheep on the heath—the everlasting heath, in Blicher's
words—one can still sense Pastor Steen Steensen Blicher's melancholy physiognomy in an Ossianic chiaroscuro. Looking more
closely one can spy the hunter Blicher with his dog, his muzzle-
loader, and his gypsy half-breeds, decoratively placed, as he is
presented in Christen Dalsgaard's painting *St. St. Blicher on
the Heath.*

For if there is any time when the ethical standpoint tempted
Kierkegaard, it had to be then. In Jutland. During the visit in
Sæding. And the weeks thereafter.

He had his theological degree behind him, and he knew that
upon finishing the pastoral seminar he could apply for a pastorate
whenever he pleased. He had a powerful and influential protector
in Christian VIII, who even as crown prince had demonstrated his
interest in him. He had finally digested enough Greek philosophy,
Plato in particular, and enough of the aesthetics of German Romanticism, to be able to look his dissertation calmly in the eye: it
was something which could be taken care of within a limited
amount of time, a year or so. When he had done so, not only the

possibility of a pastorate but also the way to a chair at the University of Copenhagen would be open before him.

Finally, he had received an inheritance and in the process had become a good catch, a particularly good catch, who would have no trouble at all in finding a helpmeet to share his future.

The last was a problem which must have bothered him. The two-year-old infatuation with Bolette Rørdam had evidently vanished during the intensive preparations for the examination, but at the Rørdams' house in Frederiksberg he had met little Regine Olsen, who in the meantime had grown up to be a very pretty young lady. To be sure, she was half engaged to Frederik Schlegel, but she had not been indifferent when she and Kierkegaard met in the summer after his examination, at Pastor Ibsen's in Kongens Lyngby.

Perhaps she was the right one, the girl for him. It naturally required an official application to her father, Councillor of State Olsen, but he would like to see the father-in-law who would want to turn down such a brilliant match. The theological degree and the considerable fortune were already in his hands. The dissertation, which would earn him a reputation as a scholarly aesthetician and philosopher, could be taken care of easily, he was sure. He knew from his preparation for the examination that he was in good intellectual form and *could* concentrate, when it was a matter of importance. The long years as an aesthetic *Taugenichts* and boulevardier *were* over. Now the future was what mattered, and it was going to be all right. After all, he enjoyed the favor and protection of Heiberg, Sibbern, Mynster, indeed of the King himself, and so his sky was cloudless, filled with sun.

Let me, collapsing, confess that I have no idea if Kierkegaard really thought this way in August and September 1840. No diary notations or passages from letters support such a hypothesis, which nonetheless can be just as reliable as other ships which Kierkegaard scholarship has launched.

Thus I may be permitted to stick to my guns: if the ethical stage ever presented itself to Kierkegaard as a real possibility, it was now.

There was only one hitch. A young girl came along, Regine Olsen, who was merely herself, delightful, natural, and uncomplicated.

Thus things were doomed to go awry.

8: THE WEDNESDAY LETTERS TO REGINE OLSEN

Die eine ist verliebt gar sehr,
Der andre wär' es gerne.
Eichendorff

The delicate problem of whether Johannes the Seducer is an exemplary figure or a bogeyman will not be discussed in detail in this chapter. It is sure that Johannes's letters to Cordelia offer remarkable similarities to Kierkegaard's letters to Regine Olsen. The resemblances are all the more striking if one can make a correct dating of the letters from the time of the engagement, undated letters by and large, but which go—according to Kierkegaard's own statement—from September 10, 1840, to October 11, 1841. There is scarcely any reason to doubt these dates, since an engagement with a ring, as is well known, can be dated between the putting of the ring on the finger and its return, the external signs of the beginning of the engagement and its end.

The Extant Letter Material

Georg Brandes, who in his Kierkegaard book of 1877 was the first to undertake a thoroughgoing psychological interpretation of Kierkegaard's literary production, was also the first to perceive the engagement's enormous significance for Kierkegaard's great leap, into the realm of literary creation. Previously, Kierkegaard had published only scholarly works on aesthetics, the book about H. C. Andersen of 1838, and the dissertation on irony. In 1843 he dared to launch a fictional work of huge proportions, quite anonymously, to be sure. Brandes finds Kierkegaard's own yearnings in the refined home life of Judge Wilhelm and perceives Regine in *Either/Or's* chorus of lamenting women. On page 78 he writes about

Either/Or: "He reaches down into the town's malicious gossip about him, which depicted him as a cold and ruthless experimenter and seducer, and it amuses him, it gratifies him to paint this devil on the wall in a fashion somewhat better than the town could—'The Diary of the Seducer' is the result—and it fills him with satisfaction to give public opinion this straw man to prod." Thus Brandes finds—as Heiberg did before him, in his review of *Either/Or* in *Intelligensblade* of 1843—that the urge to annoy the moralists of the time is an essential motive in the genesis of the work.

In 1880 the publication of volume IV of the *Papers* took place, containing Kierkegaard's many entries from 1849 about the engagement, its history and its human and religious aspects. "My Relationship to 'her' " is dated August 24 and bears the subtitle "Somewhat Poetic" with good cause. In this fashion the engagement, so to speak, had entered the public domain, and it was natural that Regine Schlegel also felt an urge to have her say in the matter. In 1893 she asked Henriette Lund to take the Kierkegaardian papers that had been entrusted to her and to conceal them; but when, in the autumn of 1896, she heard the Lund version of the engagement, she became anxious: it had turned out to be something of a flight of fancy, a little novel with the original documents woven into it more or less casually.

In October 1898 Regine Schlegel turned to librarian Raphael Meyer at the university library and asked him to take down what she had to say. A couple of months later she got her papers back from Henriette Lund: thus Regine Schlegel herself played a part in providing both of her historians with material. After her death on March 18, 1903, the way was open for the publication of the two books, and this occurred in 1904. Henriette Lund's half-fictitious work bears the title *Mit Forhold til hende. Af Søren Kierkegaards efterladte Papirer ved Henriette Lund (My Relationship to Her. From Søren Kierkegaard's Posthumous Papers by Henriette Lund).* Meyer's book has the more official title *Kierkegaardske Papirer, Forlovelsen, udgivne for Fru Regine Schlegel af Raphael Meyer (Kierkegaard Papers, The Engagement, edited for Mrs. Regine Schlegel by Raphael Meyer).* Finally, in Hjalmar Helweg's book of 1933 there are various passages inspired by Regine, things she had told Hanne Mourier in March 1902. Regine Schlegel obviously nourished a wish to be heard, on her own behalf, as a party to the case.

We can ignore Henriette Lund's arrangement and dates altogether, since she is quite devoid of any philological and historical method. Meyer's edition, on the other hand, deserves our respect for its exact reproduction of the text, which even aroused the applause of A. B. Drachmann himself; Meyer's contributions in the field of dating are also worthy of attention.

Emanuel Hirsch was the first to make a serious and astute attempt at bringing order into the dates, but the task is difficult, perhaps even hopeless. Hirsch's closely reasoned attempt was printed in *Theologisk Tidsskrift*, series 5, volume 2, 1931, as the second part of an article with the modest title "Nogle Smaa-Bidrag til Kierkegaardforskningen" ("Some Small Contributions to Kierkegaard Scholarship"). Hirsch's arrangement was followed by Niels Thulstrup in his edition of *Breve og Aktstykker vedrørende Søren Kierkegaard.*

If I cannot subscribe to Hirsch's findings, despite my admiration for his learning, acuity, and pioneering contribution to the field, it is the fault of his method. His analysis of the four or five kinds of paper is meritorious and in accordance with the techniques of modern source criticism, but he himself was compelled to confess that the results of the paper analysis were unhappily negative. In any event, it did not provide any firmer basis for datings than we possessed before. Nor can I follow Hirsch in the layout of his work: "The following arrangement is made in accordance with Kierkegaard's own division of the engagement's development into five stages. To be sure, Kierkegaard has stylized the course of the story, reducing Regine's lively emotions to a few basic traits; but there is no other way to do it, and his own emotions appear to me to be described with precision."

However, another way does exist, the way of modern source criticism. It alone deserves to be called "the only way." One transgresses against it if one takes Kierkegaard's words at face value, without further ado. Kierkegaard is undoubtedly a witness for the

state, but he is also, just as truly, a party to the case—even the
accused, since "cultured Copenhagen" took it for granted that he
was guilty, and he thus had a clear interest in turning his deposi-
tion of evidence into a defense. This factor must be taken into account in any evaluation of the source material, which falls into
four groups: (1) Kierkegaard's letters and notes to Regine Olsen,
which certainly constituted primary material, but which, on a
number of accounts, must be regarded at the same time as literary
texts. (2) Kierkegaard's letters to Emil Boesen from his first so-
journ in Berlin, thus after the engagement was dissolved and
before the publication of *Either/Or*. These letters have the effect of
being a direct echo of events, and they seem to possess a quite
special value as sources, since Kierkegaard at this time still did not
clearly perceive the poetic role he would undertake to play after
the publication of *Either/Or*. (3) Kierkegaard's own recapitulation,
from 1849, of the relationship and his reflections about his motives. He himself characterizes these statements as being "somewhat literary," and that is unquestionably true of *all* the entries
about Regine in his journal. They have the typically manic Kierkegaardian tone; events are twisted this way and that, and religious
and psychological themes of an unfathomable and subtle sort are
inserted into the story. Any sort of check of these entries is out of
the question, but it is plain for all to see that Kierkegaard "recalls"
or poeticizes the relationship, and that it is important for him to
put the broken engagement into a religious perspective. (4) Regine
Schlegel's accounts to Henriette Lund, Raphael Meyer, and Hanne
Mourier. Although her statements are from sixty years after the
engagement, they must be vouchsafed a not inconsiderable value
as sources. They do not betray any wish for self-extenuation;
Regine Schlegel seeks to present the objective truth, to the extent
that it was possible for the old lady to do so.

Everyone familiar with Kierkegaard's mentality, where recollection plays such an outstanding part, must surely acknowledge that
Kierkegaard is frequently a mediocre witness on his own behalf. In
this he resembles such great egocentric authors as Rousseau, Chateaubriand, Strindberg, Johannes Jørgensen, and Céline—no one

would dream of taking *their* recollections as the historic truth. As a rule, Kierkegaard's process of recollection is a poetic reworking, and sometimes a kind of autosuggestion. That is particularly true of his relationship to the dead. Thus, in his relationships to Poul Møller and his father, he created states of intellectual dependency and subtle involvements about which the contemporary source material is absolutely silent; indeed, at times it directly contradicts these notions.

As for essentials, therefore, we must ignore Kierkegaard's later and obviously colored reports, keeping to the letters themselves. There are thirty-one of them in all, of which twenty-six can actually be called letters while five are simply notes. We can exclude the latter. All undated, they have to do with purely practical matters: with visits to his brother-in-law on Købmagergade (Number 37 in Thulstrup, whose numbering will be used in the following discussion), with Kierkegaard's being "prevented from coming this evening" (Numbers 43 and 44), with Regine's having to be satisfied with letters instead of the perfume he would have preferred to put into the box, and with theater tickets (Number 46). Apart from the last one, which leaves her unsure as to whether he can go to the theater with her that evening or not, these notes contain nothing whatsoever of psychological interest. They are brief and to the point.

The first striking thing about the remaining twenty-six letters is that they are not letters in the usual sense, that is, not the kind of amorous letters which we could imagine were exchanged between two lovers in Copenhagen of the Golden Age. To detect the difference, one needs merely to compare them with the letters between Oehlenschläger and Christiane Heger before the poet's trip abroad in 1805. Only in exceptional cases—that is, in the notes mentioned above—do the letters serve practical purposes. They distinguish themselves by their literary tone and style, and it is difficult to rid oneself of the suspicion that Kierkegaard saw them as exercises of the pen, as literary experiments. But they also have another significance. Hirsch discovered that most of the letters were written on Wednesdays and that Wednesday, in Hirsch's phrase, was "the memorial day of Kierkegaard's love." In other words, the letters have a meaning as ritual: during the first part of the engagement their day of love, Wednesday, was celebrated with a weekly visit by letter. One must not forget that they lived only a few minutes from each other and that the letters were delivered by Kierkegaard's servant.

What Wednesday is it that Kierkegaard and Regine Olsen treat with such solemnity?

Which Wednesday Is the Memorial Day of Kierkegaard's Love?

The letter Kierkegaard dated "Wednesday, December 30" (Number 29), which is thus from 1840, will help us make a little progress:

> Today I shall remind you of that Wednesday when I approached you for the second time in my life. The very weather called forth this memory in my soul, just as sometimes, by means of a certain resemblance growing out of its very lack of resemblance, a winter day can quite vividly revive the thought of a summer day. I had such an indescribably light feeling. I drove out to Lyngby, not in the usual way, not huddled in a corner of the coach, gloomy and out of sorts. I sat in the middle of the seat, unusually erect, not keeping my head bowed, but looking around me, happy and filled with confidence. Everyone I met was infinitely welcome. It was with mixed feelings that I greeted them; as if each and every one of them simultaneously possessed the holy solemnity of an old friendship and the seductive magic of a new acquaintanceship. At the rectory I showered everyone with flattery, we swam in its profusion. It was a pleasure for me to be prodigal, for I felt myself touched by something which was raised above flattery.

Here Kierkegaard pauses with the observation that this recollection, today, had a painful effect on Regine: "You misunderstood me." No doubt the memory of the Wednesday at Lyngby, very likely the first time that both of them became conscious of their feelings, grew painful for Regine when various troubles emerged in her relationship to her fiancé. Therefore Kierkegaard continues, "So let me tell you another old story, which also took place on a Wednesday. This event falls into the historic time, and so I shall give it a date. It was Wednesday, November 18, when you told me you expected a letter from me."

One must be allowed to proceed from the assumption that in the "historic time"—that is, the period of the engagement—Regine had become accustomed (up to Wednesday, November 18, 1840, at any rate) to receive a letter from Kierkegaard every Wednesday in commemoration of their love's special day. The following reconstruction of the Wednesday correspondence must stand or fall on the accuracy of this hypothesis.

Unfortunately, it is well-nigh impossible to discover on precisely which "prehistoric" Wednesday the love affair began; but there is no doubt that the visit in Lyngby, described in the above letter, was made to Pastor P. D. Ibsen, who had been rector at Kongens Lyngby from 1833 on (see above, p. 156). Kierkegaard's acquaintance with him stems from his student days, and we know that he paid him a visit in July 1839, when Ibsen tried to get Kierkegaard a position at the court of Prince Christian. Concerning this matter, II.A.520, dated July 28, 1839, says, "At this time I felt disturbed and pained by my singing master Don Basilio [a character in *The Marriage of Figaro*]. Pastor Ipsen's [*sic*]lecture about the advantages of a position at the prince's court." In 1839, July 28 was a Sunday, and so it is natural to think that Kierkegaard, in the midst of his preparations for the examination, allowed himself the luxury of taking a hired carriage to Lyngby in order to hear his friend Pastor Ibsen preach. On Sunday, July 14, Kierkegaard's big brother, Peter Christian, had set out on a trip to Jutland that lasted until August 10, taking him to Sæding, where he, as the head of the family and its best-known member, wanted to visit his poor Jutland relatives, whose Maecenas the recently deceased hosier had been. In a touching letter of March 24, 1840, written in Jutland dialect and with great orthographic awkwardness, Else, the fa-

ther's sister, thanked Peter Christian for the great honor her nephew had bestowed upon her, the family, and the parish:

> We have meant to write for a long time but troublesome and
> toilsome circumstances made us put it off I see by your dear
> letter that your journey went nicely and pleasurably and you
> came back in Copenhagen in good shape to your dear family
> and friends.

While the big brother was thus embarked upon his charitable
and philanthropic journey to Jutland, little brother Søren could allow himself some relaxation in Lyngby. No doubt Kierkegaard—
having received his inheritance just a few months before—had
waited until his brother's departure before engaging in the extrav-
agance of a tour in a hack to Kongens Lyngby. But there is nothing
which says that it absolutely had to be 1839 when he went to
Lyngby for Regine's sake. Bolette Rørdam often visited the Ibsens,
she seems to have spent vacations there, playing the part of that
strange concept which still existed in my youth, of a "young girl in
the house." In addition, there is that mysterious Jane Doe, whom
Goldschmidt mentions (see above, pp. 155–56). Strictly speaking,
nothing prevents Kierkegaard from having fallen in love with
Regine only in the summer of 1840, when the young thing, after
all, turned seventeen. Proceeding from the thesis—hardly a rigor-
ously scientific one—that no one can fall in love while he or she is
preparing for an examination, two weeks are still left in July,
namely from July 3, when the degree was taken with distinction,
to July 19, when Kierkegaard set out for Jutland in his brother's
footsteps, to visit his father's native parish.

Logically, one ought to be able to regard these two weeks as a
likely period for falling in love. In particular since Kierkegaard
probably felt that the pretty young girl was about to pledge herself
to another, namely to the man who later became her husband,
Frederik Schlegel. One of the undated letters, Number 27, sum-
mons forth a picture from memory: "And when I stand in the
midst of the crowd, surrounded by noise and bustle which has
nothing to do with me, then I see the open window and you stand

there, in your summer dress, as you did once upon a time at Schlegels [Head clerk W. A. Schlegel, Gammel Torv, No. 5]."

This interpretation, which places the time of falling in love in the summer of 1840, deviates from the theory I presented in 1968 in the Publications of the Japanese Kierkegaard Society, but upon closer reflection about Bolette Rørdam and Jane Doe, it seems more plausible to me than putting the start of the love affair in the summer of 1839. The few Wednesdays coming into question for the summer of 1840 become fewer still if one assumes that Kierkegaard had time to fall in love only after taking his examination (it is terrible, of course, to feel a compulsive urge toward such pedantry)—they are reduced to the three Wednesdays of July 1840: the 3rd, the 10th and the 17th.

The Wednesday Problem

After the necessary digression about the Wednesday problem and Kierkegaard's relationship to Bolette Rørdam and Regine Olsen, I shall now return to the problem of dating the letters. The hypothesis about a Wednesday correspondence gives rise to a sort of game of solitaire: it is a matter of putting the right letters on the right Wednesdays. Regine's letters have not been preserved. Judging by Number 29, she had greater troubles in getting them delivered than she did in writing them.

The following letters have firm datings, that is, they are dated by Kierkegaard (who, like all other mortals, could of course put the wrong date on them). Letter Number 20 bears the date Wednesday, the 28th, which naturally must be October 28, 1840; the letter's contents presuppose the coming of winter, and so Wednesday, April 28, and Wednesday, July 28, are out of the question—they are the only other possibilities during the period of the engagement. Number 26 is dated Wednesday, December 9, and thus must be from 1840, like the letter of Wednesday, December 30, quoted above. Number 30 is undated, to be sure, but it contains good wishes for the New Year and can be fittingly dated to Thursday, December 31, or Friday, January 1, 1841. Thus it falls outside the Wednesday correspondence, which seems not to have been continued in 1841. Of dated letters from this year there is only a note of September 11, 1841, Number 41. But Number 35 is written for Regine's birthday, Friday, January 23, 1841, and Number 36 can be dated to March 1841 on the basis of other criteria, presumably on Thursday, March 9, 1841, since Kierkegaard was supposed to review a sermon by T. Thomsen in the pastoral seminar on that date. Number 40 must be from May 1841, probably from Thursday, May 6, 1841; at any event, it is a thank-you note for a birthday present. A total of eight letters can thus be dated with a goodly amount of confidence.

It is quite clear that the fiction or the ceremony of the Wednesday letters belongs to 1840, no doubt to the beginning of the period of the engagement and of love itself. For this reason, Number 24 can also be accurately put in 1841; it starts, "It is Saturday, and I cannot come to you," and its mildly erotic tone makes it a likely candidate for the more problematical part of the engagement. Other letters can be dated with some accuracy, that is, within certain weeks, months, or seasons. Letter Number 18, which begins with the quotation from Arnim identified by H. P. Rohde, "Es endet Schmerz, So wie der Scherz, So wie die Nacht, Eh' man es gedacht," must be from the first phase of the engagement; it accompanies a bottle of lily of the valley, *extrait double de muguet*, and reference is made to it in the undated letter Number 42: "You recall, perhaps, that I sent you a bottle of this essence about a year ago." Number 16 is from the same time: "It is Indian summer, toward evening." Number 22 starts with the words "Now it is winter" and refers to the "Feast of the Tabernacles"; it must have been written in the first cold days of the year, presumably toward the end of October, the time of the Feast of the Tabernacles. Since there is also a reference to the coming of winter in the Wednesday letter dated October 28, it is logical to place Number 22 on the previous Wednesday, October 21.

Letter Number 23 is an intentional mystification:

My Regine! This letter has no date nor is it supposed to have one, for its principal content is an awareness of a feeling which is no doubt present within me at every moment, even though in all the various keys of love, but which is not present, however, in any single moment in contrast to others (not ten o'clock on the dot, or eleven o'clock pure and simple, not November 11th in contrast to the 10th or the 12th). . . . Today I was on Knippelsbro, this day does not have any date either, as there is not a day on which I do not undertake this expedition.

Regine Olsen's parents lived at Børsgade 66, where the main office of the Private Bank now lies, thus in the immediate vicinity of Knippelsbro, and the letter must be dated Thursday, the 12th, or Friday, the 13th of November. It seems to be Kierkegaard's first break in the pattern of the Wednesday correspondence: "That Martinmas Eve, when I was absent until 8:00, I was at Fredensborg, I cannot say whether it was yesterday or the day before yesterday, since I have no today as a point of departure." I agree with Hirsch that the letter must have been written right after the excursion to Fredensborg described in the letter.

On the other hand, there can be little doubt that Hirsch misdated letter Number 19—"Three weeks ago today you expected me to have written to you, and I did not do so"—for the unwritten Wednesday letter is mentioned in another letter, Number 29, dated December 30 (1840), in which Kierkegaard, after having talked about their first happy meeting at the Ibsens in Lyngby, continues, "Yet this recollection had a painful effect upon you today. You misunderstood me. So let me tell you another old story, which also took place on a Wednesday. This event falls into the historic time, and so I shall give it a date. It was Wednesday, November 18, when you told me you expected a letter from me." Letter Number 19 must therefore be placed three weeks after the unwritten Wednesday letter, on Wednesday, December 9, 1840, the same date as Number 26, which is dated by Kierkegaard himself.

Hirsch's evidence for his dating, the mention of the fresh sunflower (heliotrope), seems to be quite unconvincing.

Little more can be done in dating the letters by internal criteria, but, employing them in connection with external evidence, one gets a total of thirteen letters which can be more or less accurately placed. If one abides by the hypothesis of a Wednesday correspondence beginning with the first week of the engagement and continuing up to the blank of Wednesday, November 18, it is not impossible to place the remaining letters, using psychological grounds. Naturally, absolute certainty can never be achieved—that exactly the right letter has been placed on exactly the right Wednesday—but all the same it is possible to follow the course of the relationship.

The Wednesday Letters of 1840

According to his own statements, Kierkegaard asked for the hand of Regine on September 8, 1840, several weeks after his return from the journey to Jutland. During that interval he seems to have prepared the ground by "getting near to her": "The time from August 9 to the beginning of September can in a stricter sense be regarded as the time in which I got near to her." Regine Olsen, who at that time was attracted to Frederik Schlegel—indeed she regarded herself as being unofficially engaged to him—seems to have said nothing at all, whereupon Kierkegaard went directly to her father, Councillor Olsen. A decisive conversation with him was held on September 10, and Regine, who in the meantime seems to have been prepared by her parents, answered yes, although we have no idea what her feelings toward Schlegel were in the matter. One may well assume that the father's evaluation of the two sons-in-law turned out in Kierkegaard's favor; after all, he was a candidate in theology, was on the point of writing his dissertation, and had inherited a fortune that was considerable by the standards of the day.

Thus it is reasonable to set the letters betraying a certain insecurity at the beginning of the engagement. The first Wednesday after the engagement is September 16, and Number 15 fits nicely here. The mildly ironic putting-Regine-at-a-distance, "To our own little Regine," and the excessive use of student humor show that Kierkegaard still had not found the appropriate tone. It is likely that the letter accompanied the gift of a book, the first volume of Poul Møller's *Efterladte Skrifter (Posthumous Writings)*. Poul Møller's poems were destined to play a large role in the Wednesday correspondence; they are quoted both directly and indirectly.

Letter Number 17 is perfectly suited to Wednesday, September 23. An air of academic joking still clings to it, as it does to the drawing of the man with a spyglass on Knippelsbro, who acts as if he were examining Trekroner, but who in fact has a mirror in his telescope, so that he can keep an eye on Børsgade 66, Regine's home, with his back turned. The close, the underlined phrase "Yours forever," lacks any great personal warmth and is itself almost a joke; the allusion to Poul Møller's poem "Attempt to Make a Heavenly Letter in Grundtvig's New Historical Taste" can have been understood by Regine only if she had already begun the study of Møller's poems.

It would be quite difficult to put Number 18 later than Wednesday, September 30. The gift it mentions was destined to play an unhappy role in the relationship:

> You told me the other day, when you were up visiting me, that at your confirmation your father had given you a bottle of lily of the valley *(extrait double de muguet)*. Perhaps you thought I didn't hear you, or perhaps you thought that it had gone past my ear like so many other things which find no echo within. But no, by no means! Yet even as that blossom conceals itself so delightfully in the large leaf, so at first I let the plan to send you the gift which accompanies this letter conceal itself in the half-transparent mists of oblivion so that it then, freed from every external request (no matter how distant it was), reborn to a new life in comparison with which the first existence was merely an earthly one, could spread that aroma for which longing and recollection ("from

the spring of my youth") are rivals. However, I was on the very brink of being unable to find such an *extrait* in Copenhagen. Yet even in this respect Providence is supreme, and love's blind God always spies solution. That you receive it in this moment (just before you go out) is because I know that you too are familiar with the infinity of the moment. I hope only that it will not arrive too late. Hasten, my messenger, hasten my thought, and you, my Regine, stop a moment, only a moment, stand still. Yours eternally. S. K.

It is a pretty letter and a tender one. The student humor has given way to an adoring and poetic tone. Having made do with one bottle of perfume since April 1838, Regine Olsen had revealed to her fiancé that it was now used up, and he hurried all over town looking for exactly the same brand, sending it to her with a letter in which we hear the poet Søren Kierkegaard for the first time. He is ever so tactful because he fears she might believe she had squeezed the gift out of him, and he sends his servant to her with it before a meeting they have arranged—so that she can have it on when they meet. The letter's pronounced literary air emerges not only from the introductory quotation from Arnim, "Es endet Schmerz," but also in the allusion to Møller's poem "From the Spring of My Youth," which is quoted indirectly in Number 19: "I feel a fervent longing for you, you sun among women." Kierkegaard made generous use of these quotations in paying court to Regine.

Letter Number 16 fits Wednesday, October 7: "It is Indian summer, toward evening." In his diary Molbech reports that the weather on October 8, 1840, was fine, sunny autumn weather. Here Kierkegaard essays a poetic tone in earnest, and the moods he strikes recall the tenor of "The Diary of the Seducer": "But how swift the thought is, when, like an arrow from the drawn bow, it is let loose with the whole power of the tensed spirit, when longing is the bowstring and a glad certainty the arm which tightens it, and the eye which aims it an unfailing hope."

The poet mounts his Pegasus, and it is his voice one hears in

Number 21, a letter filled with the same infatuation and thus neatly suited to the next week, Wednesday, October 14. It is the collection's most beautiful letter. After reading Plato, Kierkegaard writes a letter to love, its sweetness and its melancholy pain. In the letter's introduction and close, Eichendorff's poem "Musikanten-gruss" is quoted; it is to be found in the novel *Dichter und ihre Gesellen*, which Kierkegaard himself owned (Catalogue 1633). The first stanza goes:

> Zwei Musikanten ziehn daher
> Vom Wald aus weiter Ferne,
> Der eine ist verliebt gar sehr,
> Der andre wär' es gerne.

The last two lines reappear in "The Diary of the Seducer," in the section about the zephyrs, where Kierkegaard (or, more precisely, Johannes) has had enough of letting the winds play with the girls' clothes and hair. "That is enough, it is too much: one of her curls has fallen down . . . try to behave yourselves. A whole regiment comes marching up:

> Die eine ist verliebt gar sehr,
> Die andre wäre es gerne."

The feminine form shows that a school for girls may be involved, not a squad of soldiers.

Wednesday, October 21, must be furnished with Number 22, on the basis of the line, "It is winter now, but the Feast of the Tabernacles was celebrated in the winter season." No doubt it was inspired by the traditional October moving day, the day of stoking the furnace and hanging the winter curtains. The letter is filled with sheer goodness, tenderness, and love; but despite the thanks it offers to nature's marvels it is by no means as carefully worked out as the great hymn to love in Number 21.

Kierkegaard himself dated Letter Number 20, and so its location on Wednesday, October 28, cannot be disputed. It is quite brief and a little mysterious. Do the withered flowers indicate a first clouding of the relationship?—"they died, but a drop remained,

which has given painful birth to an immortality in itself which
only the aroma of flowers and old melodies possess." The final
words are a hidden quotation from *Erik og Abel* of
Oehlenschläger, whose *Aladdin* is quoted directly. Is Kierkegaard
ready even now, a month and a half after the engagement's beginning, to transform it into recollection?

Number 27 contains both a wintry mood and an image recalled
from the past; thus it would be logical to place it on Wednesday,
November 4. The contents of the letter, which was accompanied
by a neckerchief, are not easy to interpret. It begins with a quotation from Poul Møller's "The Old Lover," the third quotation from
this poem in the letters. The image recalled from the past seems to
have been inspired by a picture belonging to Regine, now in
Kierkegaard's possession: he returns it with the letter—a picture of
a young man and a girl with a flower in her hand. "With the picture my thought also returns to its beginning, and I tear myself
away from everything, flee from everything which would hold me
prisoner with the chains of care, and I cry out more loudly than
cares themselves . . . yet, yet, yet, I am happy in the midst of all
this, indescribably happy: for I know what I possess." It is as if
Kierkegaard must force himself to appreciate his fiancée properly.
Nor does it bode well that he now recalls Regine, "in [her] summer
dress, as once upon a time at Schlegels," thus presumably from
the summer of 1840, when he fell in love with her.

The celebrated letter Number 23, which can fairly be put on
Thursday the 12th or Friday the 13th of November, has already
been quoted. It is Kierkegaard's first break in the pattern of the
Wednesday correspondence, and on that day Regine had expected
not merely to get a letter but also to see her fiancé at her parents'
house, for the traditional feast of Martinmas goose. For two
months Kierkegaard had spoiled and coddled his beloved with regular letters every Wednesday, often accompanied by presents. But
on Wednesday, November 11, she had to wait. Both for the letter,
which did not come, and for her fiancé, who came too late—in
their middle-class circles customary dinner time was four or five
in the afternoon. She had good reason to feel it was a transgression

against their amorous rituals, and it is plain enough that she did not get an explanation from her fiancé that Martinmas Eve; for it is an explanation, to be sure, that he sends her in a letter (which he, to boot, does not even take the trouble to date correctly)—but what an explanation!

> Earlier, you know, I never rode alone, but care and worry and sadness were my faithful companions, now the band of travelers has grown smaller. When I go for a ride I am accompanied by the memory, the recollection of you, and when I return, by longing for you. And in Fredensborg these companions of mine meet and embrace one another and kiss. It is this moment which I treasure so highly, for you know that I love Fredensborg indescribably for a moment, a moment, but only a moment, which is priceless for me.

It is handsomely conceived and handsomely phrased, yet I wonder if Regine would not have preferred that her fiancé had arrived in time for dinner? And his excessive praise of the recollection of her can scarcely have satisfied a young girl in love.

But now, having thrust the dagger in, Kierkegaard continued to twist it in the wound. On Wednesday, November 18, Regine does not get a letter but a gift, Carl Bernhard's novel with the ironic title *Gamle Minder (Old Memories)*! It was published on November 16, 1840.

On Wednesday, November 25, Number 31, Kierkegaard comments upon this omission. "My Regine! Perhaps, together with *Gamle Minder*, you expected to get a future memory in the form of a letter. There was no chance for it, thus accept these lines which, who knows, perhaps can soon become a representative of a vanished time." That is a rather rough sort of joke, and one wonders if the relationship had so badly deteriorated that the couple simply had not been on speaking terms since Martinmas Eve. Why did they not straighten out these misunderstandings by word of mouth, seeing that they lived so close to one another? Kierkegaard's merciless ridicule of their erotic correspondence would not make it any easier for Regine:

But freedom is the element of love. And I am convinced that you have too high an opinion of me to wish to see in me a serviceable gentleman-in-waiting, who performs the ceremonies of love with the scrupulosity of a bookkeeper, or to wish that I should compete for a medal for perseverance in Chinese handicraft, and I am convinced that *my Regine* is too poetic to detect—when a letter is missing—in this fact a lack of "obligatory attentiveness," to use an official expression, and too poetic—even though there never came any letter at all—to think back with longing to the fleshpots of Egypt, or to wish to be circled constantly by the enamored windmill-like turning of a sentimental swain.

Doubtless that is just what Regine would have liked very much to see, and all Kierkegaard's elaborate stylistic embossments can scarcely have convinced her that their relationship was not in decline. Before, she had received sweet and loving letters, often with gifts, every Wednesday, but now!

My letters are not a succession of bleedings to death, slowly exhausting themselves; each letter is the fruit of a visit which the God of Love bestows upon me, and into which I, with my letter, initiate the one from whom the God always sends greetings, and in whose name he comes; for love is nothing at all, or vapid flattery, when it does not have a definite form. The God assumes this form, or rather, he lets a holy sleep fall upon you, and he leads you to me, and you do not know it, my letter gives you the first news of your visit to me, and we both thank him, that God, to whom we owe so much, that God who gives such generous gifts to all those who pray but do not demand. Your S. K.

This, of course, is a touch of gallant chastisement: she will get love letters only if she does not ask for them or expect them on the stroke of the hour. But the continuation suddenly whisks us to the world of Johannes the Seducer: "In this moment I go past your window. If I look at my watch, that indicates I have seen you; if I

do not look at my watch, I have not seen you." Thus Kierkegaard
has accompanied his servant from Nytorv, probably going along
Strøget over Højbro Plads to Børsgade, while trying carefully to
figure out how long it would take for his servant to deliver the
letter and for Regine to read it. If he spies her in the window, he
will look at his watch. If not, he will not. Obviously, he does not
have the slightest intention of going up to her door. One recalls
Johannes the Seducer, directing the course of a dinner conversation
so cleverly that, at a point he has carefully worked out, the talk
will fit the content of the letter which his servant delivers.

One can well imagine that Letter Number 25 was written on
Wednesday, December 2. It is brief and apologetic: "And when it
sometimes seems to you that I evade you, it is not because I love
you less, but because it has become a necessity for me to be alone
in certain moments." *Qui s'excuse, s'accuse.*

The motif of loneliness is elaborated in Number 26, dated
Wednesday, December 9, the day Regine—in accordance with
what has been adduced above—must have received the undated
Number 19, with its reference to the missing letter of three weeks
before: "So you expected me to write to you three weeks ago, and
not to come—today, you expect that I shall come and not write."
After the harsh letter of November 18, making fun of the regular
love letters, Regine—naturally enough—had decided that the
Wednesday correspondence was over, but Kierkegaard plainly
wished to please and surprise her, probably because a reconciliation had taken place at the beginning of December. Apparently
Regine had assured him that she "loved [him] from the innermost
abundance of [her] soul," and this outburst of affection on the
young girl's part stirred Kierkegaard and touched him. He excuses
himself with a reference to his melancholy, and now he regards
Regine as his angel of salvation. The two letters fit together perfectly in their line of thought: in the former, Number 26, he compares himself to the merman at the bottom of the sea, and in the
latter, Number 19, he says that she can save him with her love. It
is plain that the merman symbolism was a favorite of the two
lovers. On the back of a picture, enclosed with one of the letters

(we cannot determine which one), Regine wrote out the following
stanza from Ewald's romance "Liden Gunver" ("Little Gunver"):

> And if my arm gives you such peace and rest,
> > Such pleasure fair,
> Fair merman, hasten, and come and take
> > Of them the pair!

The reconciliation is further stressed by Number 33, which
Kierkegaard dated "Tuesday evening–Wednesday morning," and
which presumably was written on the evening of Tuesday the 15th
and delivered on Wednesday morning, December 16. The letter
begins with a quotation from Christian Winther's "Henrik og
Else," and Kierkegaard's intention is quite transparent:

> I'll try you no longer, I know you are true,
> Christ grant that all maids were as faithful as you,
> For I shall reward you: you spoke to my heart,
> We'll start fresh tomorrow. God's peace as we part.

With these words, Kierkegaard naturally meant to indicate that
the episodes in November had been intended only as a test of
Regine's loyalty, and that everything was all right now, because
she had passed the test so brilliantly.

There can be very little doubt about the dating of the next letter,
Number 28. It begins with a quotation from Novalis, emphasizing
how fitting it is that those who love and understand one another
should be together: "It is Tuesday today. You know that. But
Christmas comes before New Year." Thus the letter must be from
Tuesday, December 22. And with it Kierkegaard approaches the
conclusion of the Wednesday letters. He had toiled with them
since Wednesday, September 16, and there had been only two ir-
regularities: no letter on November 18 and two letters on December 9.

The great New Year's letter of Wednesday, December 30,
Number 29, provides the real key to the Wednesday correspon-
dence. As already shown, we hear in it the story both of the
Wednesday custom's origin, at Lyngby in July 1840, and of the

missing letter of Wednesday, November 18. The letter, moreover, is loving and uncomplicated. It recapitulates the course of the relationship in the autumn with the words, "I came, I saw, *she* conquered," and the sentiment can naturally not have been displeasing to Regine.

Thus I have tried to reconstruct the Wednesday correspondence of 1840, to the extent that a reconstruction is possible. The correspondence consisted of sixteen letters, to be found between Numbers 15 and 33 in Thulstrup. Number 24 falls outside the series—it is a Saturday letter with a piece of practical information, to the effect that Kierkegaard cannot come—and so does Number 32, which accompanies the gift of a music stand. They are both undated and undatable; their practical content removes them from the pattern of the Wednesday letters. The sixteen letters can and should be regarded as a mixture of reality and fiction. After the fumbling attempts of the first two letters to find the proper tone, attempts smacking of student humor, each individual letter represents the conscious effort of a poet to create an epistolary work of art. The letters are not merely intended to tell Regine about his feelings toward her—even when these feelings, as in Number 23, turn out to be extraordinarily complex. They are also meant to immerse her in poetic moods, that is, to get her to vibrate in the same rhythm as the letter's author. For this purpose Kierkegaard uses quotations on a large scale, both direct and indirect ones. It is plain that, in the course of the engagement, Kierkegaard got Regine to read his own favorite poets, Ewald, Baggesen, Oehlenschläger, Christian Winther, and in particular, Poul Møller. We cannot be sure that she also read the works of Novalis, Eichendorff, Arnim, and *Des Knaben Wunderhorn*, all of which are also quoted. Many letters begin with a quotation, and it is plain that these letters subsequently attempt to maintain the mood and the tone of the quotation. One can see that Kierkegaard uses poetry as a tuning fork for putting his own prose into the proper key.

If the Wednesday letters are read in the order proposed here, they form a coherent work of art, where reality and fiction are woven together in an impressive way. Do they point backward to the epistolary novella, "Letters," which occupied Kierkegaard for such a long time? There is no answer to the question. On the other hand, it can readily be established that they look forward to *Either/Or* and " 'Guilty?'/'Not Guilty?' " All are written by the same supreme artist-in-prose. And the same personality, complicated and complex-ridden, stands behind the artist.

The Letters of 1841

The letters of 1841 are of another kind and have no ritual function. Number 30 is a New Year's letter which, according to one's taste, can be dated on the last day of the old year or the first of the new. It accompanies a little gift, a handkerchief, which is compared in a somewhat macabre fashion to the linen cloth with which pious Veronica dried away the tears of Christ, and it closes with the ominous words, "Oh but do not summon me, restless and troubled, like unto him whom gloomy thoughts grant no peace, whom secret care pursues like an unsettled spirit in its flight, but summon me as someone who is mild and friendly, filled with hope and confidence. In either event I hope that this linen cloth may not leave your couch. Your S.K."

The birthday letter, Number 35, must be from January 23, 1841. It is charming enough but seems to have a presentiment of troublesome clouds on the horizon: "God grant that no one may take your happiness from you—not you yourself with restless yearning, with ill-timed doubts, with self-consuming despondency—nor I with my melancholy, and my self-made anxieties—not the smile of prosperity—not the tears of adversity—not the impatient haste of longing—not the deceptive drugs of recollection." Kierkegaard sends as a birthday gift a "painter's apparatus," whatever that may be, and a couple of candlesticks: "Let them shine for you, even as your music has often diverted my gloomy spirit."

Letter Number 36 appears to have been written in a rather exhilarated mood, after Kierkegaard on March 9, 1841—which incidentally was a Wednesday—had sent off his review of a sermon at the pastoral seminar. This is perhaps what inspired the sentence, "You certainly won't think, will you, that I take advantage of the occasion, as it were, and write to you *occasionally*, just because I have my pen in hand?" Surely he must have guessed at Regine's thoughts upon getting a Wednesday letter after a two-month pause. Compared to the love letters of 1840, the fall in temperature is already quite perceptible.

In Number 38, which cannot be dated, it is apparent that a scene had taken place between them on the morning of the day the letter was written. Kierkegaard sends Regine a copy of the New Testament, "to show you that I chastise myself in the same way."

Number 40 is dated by Hirsch on May 5, 1841, thus on Kierkegaard's birthday, but Thulstrup thinks that the withered rose (described in the letter) speaks for a somewhat later dating. Since May 5 was a Wednesday in 1841, and since the letter both mentions a gift (a letter-case) and thanks Regine for her good wishes on Sunday afternoon and Tuesday morning, it is undoubtedly correct to place it on Wednesday, May 5. After all, the withered rose can very well have been a hothouse flower. The rose, moreover, plainly has a symbolic function, and one not particularly flattering to Regine: "I have been a melancholy witness of its gradual decline; I have seen it suffer; it lost its aroma, its head grew tired, its leaves were bent in the struggle with death, its redness vanished, its fresh stalk grew dry; it forgot its splendor, it believed it was forgotten, and it did not know that you preserved a recollection of it, it did not know that the two of us, together, preserved its memory." The letter's tone and the following lacuna in the correspondence make it all too clear that things were drawing to a close.

According to his own statement, Kierkegaard returned the ring on August 11, together with the note inserted in " 'Guilty?'/'Not Guilty?' " The original is not preserved. The note is reproduced here as evidence of spiritual affinity.

In order not to demonstrate once again what must inevitably happen, and what, when it has happened, will indeed provide the strength which is required: let it happen now. Above all, forget the one who writes this; forgive a man who, whatever he might be able to do, still would not be able to make a girl happy. In the East, the sending of a silken cord means a sentence of death for the recipient; here, to send back a ring will be a sentence of death for him who sends it.

However, Regine was unwilling to accept the break forthwith, and the engaged couple continued to meet for two more months. We know what happened in this period only from Kierkegaard, on whose statements I dare not depend. But Number 41, from September 11, 1841, has such a brusque tone that it is easy to see, at any rate, how Kierkegaard's charm has ceased to function: "My Regine. Are you going to Ordrup today? Should your answer be no, then perhaps—in the absence of your letter of yesterday—you will send me your no of today. However, I ask about it only to find out if I can find you at home today. Your S. K." This can be interpreted as follows: "Yesterday I waited for the information which you didn't think it was worth the trouble to send me, and I'd prefer not to make a visit for nothing. Therefore please tell me what is happening." Hirsch thinks that "the letter breathes the meaningless gossipiness of two months of deceit." In it I perceive only Kierkegaard's irritation; it is difficult for him to maintain even the veneer of politeness.

Nonetheless, Number 41 is kindliness itself in comparison to the undated letter which Regine received in late September or early October, Number 42; for, of all Kierkegaard's letters, this one is the most diabolic:

My Regine! Perhaps you recall that, about a year ago, I sent you a bottle of this perfume, adding the message that I had intentionally let several days go by after you had mentioned your predilection for it, in order to conceal the delicate flower in the veils of recollection. Now I recall this once again. Thus I recall that you made the statement then, I recall that I recalled that you said it. The recollection of it has thus become dearer to me, not backward but forward. That is the blessing which time has. Thus I am sending you a bottle of it, swathed in a plethora of leaves.* But these wrappings are not of a sort that one hastily tears off, throwing them away in annoyance in order to get at the contents; on the contrary, they are precisely what gives one pleasure, and I see with what care and solicitude you will unfold each single sheet, and recall thereby that I recall you, my Regine, and may you yourself recall your S.K.

Hirsch thinks that Kierkegaard wrapped the perfume in Regine's own love letters, and if he is right, the letter undeniably acquires a fearful air of irony. But I cannot say that I am convinced by his argumentation: "There is no other explanation of what wrappings Regine might otherwise undo with care and solicitude, in the process recalling that Kierkegaard recalls her." After all, there is the possibility that the bottle of essence of lilies of the valley was in a box with one or two dozen red roses, whose stalks and leaves were so entangled in one another that they could be untwisted only with gentle care. The rose blossom was directly symbolic of their love, of course, and the motif of recollection, brought up in the letter and sadly familiar to Regine, would thus be given a particularly ironic frame.

The irony becomes still crueler, still more savage, if one can imagine that it was on a Wednesday in October, for example, Wednesday, October 6, 1841, that Regine, who must have guessed how near the relationship was to its final collapse, received the undated Number 39, a superb prose-hymn to recollection, whose splendor is praised at the cost of the moment and, by implication, the moment's misery. "My Regine! The moment will not favor us. Very well, let us recollect. Recollection is my element, and my recollection is eternally fresh, it meanders like a running water through the heath of my life, humming and narrating, narrating and humming, always the same thing, lulling cares to sleep, beckoning to me, luring me to follow its course to its spring, where it

---

*Danish "Blad-Omslag": "Blad" means both a leaf of paper and the leaf of a plant. (Trans.)

bubbles forth from the obscure memories of childhood." The beautiful prose-poem can be regarded as a preliminary study to the section on recollection in *Repetition* (*SV*, III: 193 and 198ff.), but it is doubtful that Regine perceived the letter's aesthetic qualities. The two connected letters and the first letter's symbolic gift, the perfume of lilies of the valley in the bouquet of roses, must have been a slap in the face for the poor girl, engaged in her painful struggle to keep her melancholy fiancé—she was fond of him, we know, in an altogether artless and uncomplicated way. Besides, a broken engagement in the Copenhagen of that day could give rise to a scandal which a middle-class family would not gladly swallow.

Was it these last two letters which made Regine give up? She can certainly be forgiven if such was the case. What help was all her goodness, her affection, her care, and her forbearance vis-à-vis a fiancé who fled from her and their engagement, showing her quite plainly that the recollection of their love was enough for him and that he entertained no intention at all of turning their engagement into a marriage? She told Raphael Meyer about their parting. "At their last meeting she said, 'I can't stand it any more; we must part; now you are free; do not come to me any more.' They shook hands and gave one another a final kiss. But the very next day Kierkegaard's servant brought her a letter from him." This final epistle seems not to be extant. It can scarcely be one of the printed letters. Perhaps it would be understandable if Regine tore it to pieces when she got it, tired of words and nothing but words. She herself thought that it was *she* who had broken the engagement.

Kierkegaard and the Marquis de Sade

I have dwelt on Kierkegaard's letters to Regine because I think that, in the sequence presented here, they can cast a light on Kierkegaard's relationship to Johannes the Seducer. It goes almost without saying that a genuine seduction was out of the question, as far as Kierkegaard was concerned. Kierkegaard does not aim at preparing the girl erotically in order to realize a plan laid from the beginning, that is, a sudden and unmotivated withdrawal which would get the girl to employ erotic means in the struggle to win her beloved back. Of course, in the Wednesday letters Kierkegaard lulls Regine with erotic moods, but he is honest to the extent that he himself shares in these moods, or at any rate participates in them as their poetic creator. But the object is not to make Regine erotically interested in him. She appears to have been that from the outset. The mere circumstance that she visited him alone in his apartment was a bold matter in 1840, a patent transgression against the middle-class moral code.

In other respects, the resemblances between Kierkegaard and Johannes are unmistakable. First, Kierkegaard spoils Regine with gallant and emotional Wednesday letters, and when, after two months, she has become accustomed to them, he makes an abrupt about-face. He is absent from the Martinmas dinner, at which he was obviously expected. He leaves without explaining why he came too late. He fails to send her the Wednesday letter. He takes a very long time to explain his behavior. The next week he does not send the customary letter but rather a book with the malicious title *Gamle Minder.* Simultaneously, he employs his servant as a go-between in about the same calculating way that Johannes does—compare the episode in which he says he will look (or not look) at his watch before her window, depending upon whether or not he catches sight of her, while never thinking of paying a call.

It is difficult, in the midst of these subtle pranks, to ignore a good deal of teasing, a sick sort of teasing, and a by no means inconsiderable element of intellectual sadism. Even if we do not wish to accept the chronology constructed here, the two letters about the perfume bottle (Numbers 42 and 39) will hardly admit an interpretation that is flattering to Kierkegaard. A kind and uncomplicated letter would have merely needed to contain a few lines of the following sort: "My Regine! Even if the relationship between us these last weeks has not been what it could and should be, you still must give me the pleasure of presenting you with this perfume, which I know you like so much. Your S. K." This would have been the natural and the tender thing to do, altogether understandable in a critical situation in which the two partners do not know whether or not the engagement will survive. But Kierkegaard obviously sent the perfume in order to have the chance to ride his hobbyhorse of recollection, and he cannot have been unaware that all his glorification of the recollection of Regine would necessarily fill her with painful emotions. After all, *she* was thinking about the present moment and the future marriage.

Unlike Cordelia, Regine did not surrender herself, let herself be seduced, although there are various indications in Kierkegaard's notes to the effect that she would not have shunned such a solution, if she could thereby have kept him and avoided a scandal. But the resemblance between the situations of the two girls is clear. Both have been brought to the very highest emotional pitch, and both are left in the lurch. The one by a cynical seducer, who clings the whole time to his minutely detailed plan of battle, and the other by a—yes, by whom?

We can obtain some excellent information about the matter from the letters which Søren Kierkegaard—after the final break with Regine on October 11, 1841, and the following two weeks of playacting in Copenhagen—sent home from Berlin to Emil Boesen, his only intimate friend. These letters are sources of a high value. Of course, Kierkegaard does not appear in them without a mask—the whole affair with the Austrian actress Mademoiselle Schulze, of whom it is said that her resemblance to Regine makes her suitable for a liaison, is a transparent sort of comedy—but just the same, Kierkegaard is surprisingly open and honest here. For once we get the impression that he is not writing with arrière-pensées about the judgment of posterity, but that he is in fact putting his cards on the table.

At the time Emil Boesen himself was involved in a love affair, and it is actually Kierkegaard's advice in this connection which tells us how he, Kierkegaard, saw himself. On October 31, 1841, directly after his arrival in Berlin, he writes, "For my sake, practice the art of being in command of every expression, of keeping chance under your control, of being able to spin out a tale, immediately and without fear or anxiety. Oh, one can fool people as much as one wishes, I know that from experience, and I, at least, have a boundless foolhardiness in this respect." On November 16, 1841, he writes about Emil Boesen's own love affair: "And now let's take you. Do you bear any responsibility, have you transgressed against any obligation, and is it really worth all the trouble, just to go past her window and see her smile? Conjure her up in your imagination, and she'll sit all the more prettily in the window, and smile and weep and do everything you desire." The advice was repeated on January 16, 1842, with the personal addition, "You are not accustomed (I think you will agree with me and not grow angry at my saying it) in the same sense as I am to hold your life literarily in your hand." There then ensues a clear manifestation of the aesthetic program of life, which Kierkegaard himself had followed in his relationship to Regine:

> You see, it will result in a misunderstanding if you connect your love affair with this. I know nothing of these melancholy shivers, my relationship to her has an altogether different reality and has been brought before a much higher forum, and if I had not had the courage to bring the case before this forum, then I'd regard myself as an effeminate aesthetic half-human, as a worm; for it was terrible to play a game with such high stakes for the sake of a whim. Obviously you are a novice, you have emotions, I have passion, but my reason rules over my passion, but my reason is once again passion. Let me be frank here. Is it proper to abandon oneself in this way to an emotion [?] I don't understand you. Let a girl make as strong an impression on me as this one has made on you, and then I'll declare war, and then I'm in my element, waging war is sheer pleasure for me. I have never been able to get the thought into my—if you will—four-cornered or proud head that a girl should be invincible. Don't you hear the music of war, isn't your soul pure movement—it's inconceivable.

Doesn't it seem that one hears Johannes the Seducer before he has the tocsin rung for the final attack? Kierkegaard did not need to go far to find the model for Johannes the Seducer. The difference between them is merely that Johannes wants to seduce the girl, while a seduction is exactly what Kierkegaard does not want. He wishes to break off before matters come to that. Kierkegaard is afraid of the erotic, anxious lest he not be man enough to meet the situation around which his thoughts and feelings have circled for years. It is difficult not to regard a fear of sexuality as a main factor in the break with Regine. Always superior, he instinctively felt that here she would have the upper hand. The result was an urge to assert himself, and to this end he mobilized his rich resources of intelligence, wit, and acting skill. Now, it is only a small step from self-assertion to revenge. Despite the difference in their relationship to sexual matters, Kierkegaard and Johannes the Seducer are cut from the same cloth. The decisive feature they have in common is the strong desire to dominate and to rule by means of intellectual power and strength, to subjugate another human being. Cordelia, abandoned by her lover, and Regine, deserted by her fiancé, have both been victims of a treatment in which one cannot help seeing a certain sadistic element.

On the whole, the resemblances between Kierkegaard and the Marquis de Sade are really not so few in number. Their two oeuvres resemble one another in that they have never been regarded as 100 percent poetic or fictive. No one has thought of claiming that the two authors wrote primarily in order to create art. They have other intentions: those of the Marquis are sexual, those of Kierkegaard philosophical and religious. But they resemble one another in having used art in the service of these ends.

Naturally, a direct link is out of the question. The Marquis de Sade was born in 1740 and died in 1814, the year after Kierkegaard's birth. Kierkegaard never mentions his name, and so, at the most, one can speak only of a roundabout relationship. In 1795 de Sade's *La philosophie dans le boudoir* appeared, a little tale of seduction where everything is in dialogue form. It is one of de Sade's milder stories, telling how Eugénie, a very willing and quick young lady, is seduced by various male and female libertines. The book's frivolous *pointe* could well bear the signature of Johannes the Seducer: see how easy it is to destroy the morals of a young person!

De Sade's erotic manual did not lack models, Restif de la Bretonne's *La paysanne pervertie* and Choderlos de Laclos's *Les liaisons dangereuses*. The latter, an epistolary novel, is from 1782, but it appeared in Danish translation in 1832, something which can give cause for reflection. Might one propose a connection, backward in time, with the French libertine tradition? That was the case with Friedrich Schlegel, whose *Lucinde*, as we know, played such a large role in Kierkegaard's youth. But in Laclos, de Sade, and Schlegel eroticism is a collective undertaking. That great subjectivist, Kierkegaard, is an individualist on this point.

The resemblances between de Sade and Kierkegaard can be extended further still. Both live in isolation, plagued by obsessions. De Sade's isolation was, to be sure, involuntary in part—that is, his years of incarceration—but he had a comfortable existence in his prisons, with servants at his beck and call, and eating so much that he ate himself out of any possible physical involvement in erotic matters. Kierkegaard's prison was his voluntary retirement from the surrounding world, and he too had an existential relationship to exquisite foods. Both of these isolated individuals must be regarded as persons who were unwell, tormented by a lack of human contact and by loneliness. Both took revenge on the fate which dealt so harshly with them—by dreaming and by making, in literature, the world different from what it was. Both dwelt in that borderline region where fiction and reality collide, and in the clash with their surroundings both felt themselves to be persecuted martyrs. Both are without any sense of reality, without any understanding of social and political life, without the ability to discern reasonable proportions. The slightest disturbance from the outside world, upsetting their carefully drawn circles, rolled along like a snowball, eventually turning into an avalanche. They suffered from being the victims of their own strong imagination, but since they, as dreamers, were unsuited for a normal life in society, it was only in their fantasies that they succeeded in wholly realizing themselves.

The great and utterly decisive difference between Kierkegaard and the Marquis de Sade, of course, is that Kierkegaard never went beyond the limits of his fantasies, while the Marquis undertook a palpable realization of his dreams. He got, as a result, those years at the penitentiary, while Kierkegaard was the prisoner only of his own thoughts, in whose webs he was caught. He received an almost sensuous revelation in the Royal Theater's performance of *Don Juan*—presumably in the autumn of 1834 (as I tried to show in 1972 in a paper in *Orbis Litterarum*)—and for almost ten years he had daydreams about himself as Don Juan. Even when he was absorbed in serious Faust studies, he perceived in Faust the tragicomical figure of Don Juan. Tragic, because Don Juan never found the great love among his thousands of mistresses, comical because he, defying common sense, took the trouble to keep up the search. As an eroticist, Kierkegaard, like the Marquis de Sade, was bound to his imagination, but in contrast to the Marquis, he lived his erotic life at his desk, with pen in hand. That is, if he did not—as a kind of voyeur—make voyages of discovery along Copenhagen's "Path of Love" and in Frederiksberg Park.

And so fate—or the true part of his own nature, which was pure intellect and not physical at all—willed that he should confront eroticism in the shape of a young, natural, and graceful girl from the better sort of family. Immediately, he indulged in evasions. He transformed their engagement into an epistolary game of a ritual kind and with an unmistakable air of intellectual sadism. That Kierkegaard played with Regine, tormented her, and enjoyed his intellectual superiority—the letters bear witness to this with distressing clarity. It goes almost without saying that they also tell about Kierkegaard's own sufferings, his melancholy, his torments, and his fear of sex. Like the Marquis de Sade, Kierkegaard wished to reign in eroticism's realm, and, as in the Marquis's case, pleasure and pain were mingled in him in a strange world of fiction and reality. It is difficult to say where the one ends and the other begins; but it is agreed that for Kierkegaard pain was mixed with a certain form of pleasure. An *algolagniac* is the label, I think, that learned men would give him.

The Wednesday letters look even beyond *Either/Or* and *Stages on Life's Way*. They portend the Christian martyr who sought pain and suffering in the relationship to God and established suffering as a model for others to imitate. Kierkegaard's tormented and crucified Christ has nothing save the name in common with the anarchistic-pornographic Jesus Christ Superstar of our days.

I have often been struck with astonishment (but not struck dumb, something that would have been appropriate) at the failure of Kierkegaard scholarship to take a serious interest in the subsidiary figures in that work of art which has, as its sole title, Søren Kierkegaard. Thus, like Elith Reumert and Johannes Hohlenberg, one can conceive of it as a novel (in several volumes) or as a play in several acts, where the main character improvises or writes his role as he goes along.

In this dramatic undertaking, which may be regarded as a farce or a tragedy, all according to one's taste or mood, there were other players, acting with or against him, and they cannot be reduced to extras. The aged father with his obsessions from the Old Testament, the older brother with his darkened spirit, the faithful friend and confidant, Emil Boesen—the three can be fitted into the play together with the somewhat younger aesthetic rivals, such as a P. L. Møller or a Goldschmidt.

Regine Olsen, on the other hand, cannot be swept aside as an ingenue, a pious little lamb, who understood nothing whatsoever of what was happening. Nor can Frederik Schlegel be regarded as a comical figure from one of Copenhagen's Biedermeier vaudevilles. They were genuine, whole people, who clearly perceived that they were involved in a desperate situation because of their collision—determined by fate or, perhaps, rather by fate's disfavor—with a personality about whose genius they entertained no doubts.

They bore the situation bravely, behaving with a dignity and a genuine humanity which makes the intrigues and the insinuations, the dubious and the parvenulike aspects of Kierkegaard's character, emerge in a dismaying fashion.

It would be fitting, perhaps, if posterity would send a thought their way now and then. They were moths who entered the circle of light cast by the great egocentric, but they did not burn their wings. That is perhaps more than can be said for many of the Danes who were involved, for example, with Ibsen, Strindberg, or Céline.

As a married couple, the Schlegels never made fools of themselves and never put themselves or others onto pedestals.

9: CONCLUDING NONTHEOLOGICAL POSTSCRIPT

> *"Let God keep His heaven, if I but can*
> *have Gurre." I think it is the fairest place*
> *in Denmark.*
> H. C. Andersen

The many Danes who think (if we are to believe our Danish weeklies) that things are fairest in Denmark, and who therefore are willing to abdicate their claims to heaven (with a little *h*), provided they can keep their Guru (with a big *G*)—these people can hardly profit from this book.

Can the theologians?

After all, it is *they* who must draw the theological (?) consequences from the evaluation of Kierkegaard scholarship which has been presented here. As the book's title indicates in its altogether discreet way, there are plenty of myths in Kierkegaard research, something to be ascribed, perhaps, to the fact that so many scholars of a theological and philosophical persuasion have so readily let themselves be inveigled or coaxed —not to use the ugly word, seduced. They have also let themselves be ensnared by the presentation of the *Papers*, for which the supreme court judge, P. A. Heiberg, must take the main responsibility, even as a second Abraham. To be sure, together with Kierkegaard himself, who was the first to prepare the "correct," religious interpretation of his life. As Kierkegaard's contemporary, the cartoonist and wit Fritz Jürgensen, had his painter say, "One bows before van Dyck."

It is up to the theologians and the nonprofessional Christians to decide whether or not they wish to confront the problems that have been raised here. I am by no means familiar with the entire literature on Kierkegaard, for that would be a man's full task in the years vouchsafed unto him. Presumably for my sins' sake, I

have actually read a good part of the theological Kierkegaard literature in Danish, Swedish, English, German, and French, but I
shall gladly confess that my glance grows a little shifty if anyone
inquires about the actual meaning of all these works of learned
men. I can understand such experts as Løgstrup, Sløk, and Hirsch;
but I throw my hands up in despair at such scholars as Bohlin,
Geismar, Hohlenberg, and many others, something that doubtless
embarrasses me more than it does them.

My efforts run aground each time on the theologians' noncha-
lant treatment of the source material—and is it not they who have
given cause for scandal? The theologians' knowledge of Kierkegaard seems to me to be a matter of faith, for naturally, looking at
the matter from a theological standpoint, there is nothing to prevent Kierkegaard from having found the way to god, or God, exactly as he describes it. The oppressive and depressing childhood, the
sinful oldster of a father, whose intimate confessions were meant
to save the dandy of a son, the religious sacrificing of Regine, the
huge aesthetic-philosophical-religious production of 1843–46, the
paradoxical Christianity, strewn with thorns, which led eventually
to an absurd existentialism in open conflict with the state
church—all this can very well be true.

It can also be partially true. A brilliant work of literature concerning the genius in the market town of Copenhagen, enclosed by
its walls. A poet who, as actor and prompter, every moment becomes so intensely a part of his role that he believes in it and in
himself. For a non-Christian—I left the Danish People's Church
long ago—there is nothing here which reduces Kierkegaard's
greatness, his fascination, or his genius by an inch. He is the Pied
Piper of Hamelin, pulling everything along with him into destruction. If one does not wish to plunge into the river and be carried
away, one must be blooded by the master's sword. That is what
happened to Brandes, Ibsen, and Høffding—three Kierkegaardians
in reverse, but as existentialists, belonging entirely to his school.

Inevitably, one can apply a Marxist method of interpretation to
Søren Kierkegaard. But it will not serve any reasonable purpose.
The circumstances of economic production in the first half of the

nineteenth century will explain nothing of Kierkegaard's life and thought. He was an incurable capitalist, not to say a parvenu. His relationship to the poor, "my poor," was purely capitalistic. Though industry and a working class had arisen in Denmark with responsible spokesmen—Dampe, Goldschmidt, Grüne, Dreier— they had changed nothing in Kierkegaard's world of thought. One does not seek the salvation of one's soul in order to exemplify a theory about class conflict. Marx would have been the first to un- derstand that.

Kierkegaard senior, toward the end of the 1830s, grappled with the sins of his youth, the family curse, and his imminent death. To be sure, between his youth with the Moravian Brethren on Storm- gade and his funeral, conducted by Mynster in 1838, there lies al- most a generation of spiritual cohabitation with Mynster and Grundtvig. Kierkegaard's cult of the father began in earnest with the *Two Edifying Discourses* of May 16, 1843, and *Fear and Trem- bling* of October 16, 1843, the latter of which was published the same day as *Repetition* and *Three Edifying Discourses.* Opposite this production it is useful to place a—I was on the point of saying a witness of the truth but shall correct myself, employing "a con- temporary witness" instead, namely Bishop J. P. Mynster. Of course, he was closely connected to the Heiberg ménage, but he cannot be brushed aside as an undependable source on that ac- count, can he? On January 1, 1844, he wrote an article, "Kirkelig Polemik" ("Churchly Polemics"), signed Kts., in issues 41–42 of Heiberg's *Intelligensblade.* The article considers the relation of the church to "more cultured people." In its course Mynster brings up *Fear and Trembling*, in which he finds a "deep religious founda- tion." Yet his testimony about the hosier is still more important:

> For me, there is something touching in the fact that Mag. S. Kierkegaard always dedicates his Edifying Discourses to the memory of his late father. For I too knew this estimable man; he was a simple and straightforward citizen, went his quiet and undemanding way through life, and had never submitted to any sort of philosophical cure whatsoever. How does it

happen, then, that the son, for all his rich education, as soon as he wished to put his Edifying Discourses on paper, always turned his thoughts toward that man who long since had gone to rest? Whoever has read that beautiful speech—or let us call it a sermon, "The Lord gave, the Lord hath taken away, blessed be the name of the Lord"—will understand. The son, even as I, saw his old father suffer bitter loss, he saw him fold his hands and bow his reverend head, he heard his lips pronounce those words, but at the same time he saw his father's very being pronounce them in such a way that he sensed what he has set forth so beautifully in the case of Job, that "he too is a teacher of men who had no teaching to pass along to others, but who left the race of man his very self as a model, and his life as a guide for every human being" who beheld it; he sensed that the old man in "his pious words had overcome the world, and in his pious words was greater and stronger and mightier than the whole world." And what the son learned from his old father in that house of sorrow was set down in a sermon, a sermon which will appeal to and refresh every sensitive heart, even though it would not lead the reader to some "philosophical cure," even though it contains nothing which everyone could not "say to himself in his own sofa"—but truly not "equally well." It is not because I mean to set a limit to my gratitude for this sermon, but because it is a part of the whole affair, that I shall ask, Will the three following discourses have the same effect? And if not, might it not be in part for this reason—that the "philosophical cure" will emerge all too plainly?

Mynster's last two quotations are from the review of *Either/Or* which Adjunct H. P. Kofoed-Hansen published in the fourth issue of *For Literatur og Kritik. Et Fjerdingsaarsskrift udg. af Fyens Stifts literære Selskab*, 1843.

Mynster's article is thought-provoking on several points. First, it shows that the Heiberg circle, despite the battles that had already taken place, was not of a mind to write off so gifted an author as

Kierkegaard without further ado. Mynster's concluding salute to Goethe is certainly not accidental. Indeed, this great paradigm of the highest culture must not be attacked. On the other hand, one could very aptly use Magister Kierkegaard as a weapon against the Hegelian left, which had Strauss and Feuerbach as its two major prophets. The left was on the verge of winning many a Danish disciple, thanks in particular to the uncomfortably idealistic philosopher whose name was Hans Brøchner.

The article also shows that Mynster has a quite distinctive and a credible view of Kierkegaard's father as a "simple and straightforward citizen." He must have become thoroughly acquainted with Kierkegaard senior in the course of the family's many funerals in the 1830s and during intimate conversations which, above and beyond questions of charity, must certainly have also been concerned with the two gifted sons' problematical future as theologians. Søren, at least, should not be allowed to go the Grundtvigian way of his older brother, with all the official difficulties that path entailed.

Finally, it shows that Mynster saw (or at any rate believed) that it was the cares of his father's old age which had turned Kierkegaard's mind toward God, and that it was precisely father figures such as Abraham and Job which exerted a magnetic attraction on Kierkegaard's imagination—his poetic imagination as well as his religious one.

That Mynster had already perceived what consequences for the state church Kierkegaard's passionate philosophy of paradox would have, with its faith by virtue of the absurd—that may well be a more doubtful matter. Plainly enough, in his article Mynster was concerned only with the third collection of discourses, *Four Edifying Discourses*, eighty-four pages in all, put on sale on December 6, 1843.

Mynster's objection, that the last three discourses are too philosophical, can also apply to the two previous collections, from May and October 1843. Strictly speaking, the same judgment can be rendered on the "Eulogy for Abraham," which follows upon the beautifully embossed mood pictures in *Fear and Trembling*—stylistically among the most distinguished of Kierkegaard's accomplishments. If one makes a comparison with Kierkegaard's sketches for sermons from the pastoral seminar in 1840–41, or with his graduation sermon held in Trinity Church on February 24, 1844, it is difficult—for a layman at any rate—to find essential differences, let alone to detect stronger measures of fervor, among these sermons or edifying discourses, ten in all: "Ultimatum" in *Either/Or, Two Edifying Discourses* from May, *Three Edifying Discourses* (which, like the eulogy for Abraham, are from October), and finally the four edifying discourses from December 1843. In all of them one meets a theological candidate who, firmly anchored in the Mynster tradition, is preparing himself to be a pastor. The fervor and the religious passion of *Edifying Discourses in Various Spirits*, and *Works of Love*, both from 1847, lie far in the future.

The passion one meets in *Fear and Trembling* can undoubtedly be interpreted as "ein seliger Sprung in die Ewigkeit" and thereby also as the definitive break with Hegel, Heiberg, and their German and Danish disciples. That Kierkegaard did not abandon the aesthetic stage on this account would seem to be clear from his many observations about the difference between the tragic hero (Agamemnon, who will sacrifice his child) and Abraham, the knight of faith, in the same situation.

Repetition, of October 16, 1843, of course treats the category of repetition, something which involved Kierkegaard in a polemic with Heiberg in *Urania* of 1844; but it is first and foremost a work of fiction, and so it is entirely appropriate that Aage Henriksen submitted it to analysis in his witty and penetrating dissertation of 1954 on Kierkegaard's novels. *Repetition* demonstrates, for that matter, something which will come as no surprise—that Kierkegaard had not at all abandoned his old love for the stage; during his Berlin stay he was to be found almost every evening in the Königstädter Theater.

At some time or another in 1843, Kierkegaard realized that he could not get Regine back, since she now belonged to another. Was he slow-witted? In the spring of 1843 they had seen one another on

Sundays when they attended Mynster's sermons, and on Mondays they had passed one another between eight and nine o'clock on sidewalks with which they were both familiar. If Kierkegaard was informed in July 1843 about Regine Olsen's engagement to Schlegel, it is altogether understandable from a psychological point of view that he now leaps into faith and glorifies his "sacrifice": his renunciation of Regine becomes a religious act in the service of higher powers. The existential choices are always easier if other people make them for us.

To be sure, Kierkegaard had many other possibilities to choose from in the summer of 1843. He could have continued as an aesthete along the lines of Johannes the Seducer. He could have established himself as an eccentric country parson on the Jutland heath, with only two or three worshipers in the steepleless granite church. He could have applied for the professorship in philosophy as Poul Møller's successor. He could even have indicated his desire to compete for the professorship in aesthetics after Oehlenschläger. Instead of P. L. Møller.

As a martyr, a theologian, a dogmatist, and a philosopher, Kierkegaard will stand securely upon his pedestal. If one wishes to celebrate him as a Christian *poet*, one can make a pastiche—without the smallest grain of irony—out of Paul V. Rubow's homage to Chateaubriand, in which that incorrigible professor of literature—whose inherent and carefully cultivated malice doubtless has assured him of eternal life—imitates Brandes's homage to Hamlet. For the melancholy Dane, the French *vicomte*, and the son of the Jutland hosier are, after all, of the same spiritual stock.

"It is for your sake, Magister Kierkegaard, that we seize upon every publication from the Danish Golden Age, every newspaper, every article whatsoever that you may have read. You are everything that is fascinating and demonic. Just as you are lyric prose and delicious petty chatter with the reader. The private, the intimate conversation contained within the novel and the edifying discourses—these are your discoveries. You are the father of the art of philosophical prose, the master of the art of mood, and the fortunate lover of the description of nature. When I speak of aesthetes, I mean you, for my ability to make abstractions is not very well developed, and for me, you occupy the whole concept of the aesthete. All the same, I hate you almost as much as I love you. That means nothing. I have a tiny share of you, just as you had of my forebears. If I should choose those among your contemporaries with whom I should have most liked to associate, I believe that I would have preferred the company of the Heibergs, Mynster, and Martensen. Not to mention that honored aversion of yours, a certain Mr. Andersen. The thought of meeting you fills me with fear and trembling. It is not given to ordinary mortals to look into the eyes of the gods, and it is not pleasant to be a fool, who beholds only what he deserves in the mirror."

SOURCES

This catalogue of the works and sources on which I have drawn makes no claims whatsoever to being complete or representative. It gives a list of the works and editions most frequently used in the book but naturally does not pretend to exhaust all the literature concerning the Danish Golden Age and the writings of its personages who appear in these pages.

I have employed Kierkegaard's works in the first, collected edition, *Samlede Værker (Collected Works)* in fourteen volumes, edited by A. B. Drachmann, J. L. Heiberg, and H. O. Lange (1901–06), because I prefer it to its two successors. All references to *SV* are thus to this edition; the Roman numeral indicates the volume, and the Arabic numeral the page.

Kierkegaard's *Papirer (Papers)*, to which reference is made in accordance with the customary practice, have been employed in all three editions: H. P. Barfod and H. Gottsched's old *Efterladte Papirer (Posthumous Papers)* in eight volumes (1869–81) (*EP*); *S.K.'s Papirer (Papers)* in eleven volumes edited by P. A. Heiberg, Victor Kuhr, and E. Torsting (1909–48); and the photographic reproduction of the latter edited by Niels Thulstrup (1968ff.) with its two supplementary volumes, XII and XIII, and its index, which is still incomplete.

In all essentials, Kierkegaard's letters have been quoted from *Breve og Aktstykker vedrørende S. K.*, vols. I–II (1953–54), edited by Niels Thulstrup.

In certain instances, further information that the author thought to be relevant has been added in brackets. Asterisked works have been translated into English.

Adorno, Theodor W. *Søren Kierkegaard. Konstruktion des Ästhetischen.* 1933.

Ammundsen, Valdemar. *Søren Kierkegaards Ungdom. Hans Slægt og hans religiøse Udvikling.* 1912.

*Andersen, H. C. *Mit Livs Eventyr*, vols. I–II. 1855. Ed. H. Topsøe-Jensen, 1951.

———. *Hans Christian Andersens Dagbøger*, vols. I–VII. 1971.

Andreasen, Uffe. *Poul Møller og romantismen*. 1973.

Aschengreen, Erik. *Engang den mest spillede*. 1969.

———. *Farlige Sylphider* [on Bournonville]. 1975.

Baagø, Kaj. "Magister Jacob Christian Lindberg." 1958. [Dissertation.]

Baggesen, Søren. *Den blicherske Novelle*. 1965.

Barfod, H. P. *Af Søren Kierkegaards Efterladte Papirer, 1833–55*, vols. I–VIII. 1869–81. [With H. Gottsched.]

Beck, Vilhelm. *Erindringer fra mit Liv*. 1900.

*Billeskov Jansen, F. J. *Hvordan skal vi studere Søren Kierkegaard?* 1949.

———. *Søren Kierkegaard. Værker i Uddrag*, vols. I–IV. 1950. [With an altogether outstanding commentary.]

———. *Studier i Søren Kierkegaards litterære Kunst*. 1951.

Birkedal, Vilhelm. *Personlige Oplevelser i et langt Liv*, vols. I–II. 1890.

Björkhem, John. *Søren Kierkegaard i psykologisk belysning*. 1942. [A lengthy review by Carl Jørgensen appeared in *Kierkegaardiana* III, 1959.]

Bohlin, Torsten. *Søren Kierkegaards etiska åskådning*. 1918. [German translation: Gütersloh, 1927.]

———. *Søren Kierkegaards dogmatiska åskådning*. 1925.

Borchenius, Otto. *Fra Fyrrerne. Literære Skizzer*, vols. I–II. 1878–80.

———. *Litterære Feuilletoner*. 1880.

Borup, Morten. *Breve og Aktstykker vedr. J. L. Heiberg*, vols I–V. 1947–50.

———. *Johan Ludvig Heiberg*, vols. I–III. 1947–49.

———. *Peder Hjort*. 1959.

*Brandes, Georg. *Søren Kierkegaard. En kritisk Fremstilling i Grundrids*. 1877. [German translation: Leipzig, 1879.]

Brandt, Frithiof. *Den unge Søren Kierkegaard. En Række nye Bidrag*. 1929.

———. *Søren Kierkegaard og Pengene*. 1935. [In collaboration with Else Rammel.]

———. *Syv Søren Kierkegaard-Studier*. 1962.

———. *Søren Kierkegaard. His Life—His Works*. 1963.

Bredsdorff, Elias. *Goldschmidts "Corsaren."* 1965.

Brix, Hans. *Mystica om Søren Kierkegaard, Analyser og Problemer*, vol. III. 1936.

Brosbøll, Carl [alias Carit Etlar]. *Minder*. 1894.

Bruun Andersen, K. *Søren Kierkegaard og Kritikeren P. L. Møller*. 1950.

———. *Søren Kierkegaards store Jordrystelse*. 1953.

Brøchner, Hans. *Erindringer om Søren Kierkegaard, Det nittende Aarhundrede*. 1876–77. New edition by Steen Johansen, 1953.

SOURCES   223

Brøndsted, Mogens. *Meïr Goldschmidt*. 1965.

Bukdahl, Jørgen. *Søren Kierkegaard. Hans Fader og Slægten i Sædding*. 1960.

———. *Søren Kierkegaard og den menige mand*. 1961.

Christensen, Arild. *Søren Kierkegaard og Naturen*. 1964.

Christensen, Erik M. *Ex auditorio*. 1965.

Christensen, Villads. *Søren Kierkegaard og Frederiksberg*. 1959.

———. *Søren Kierkegaard i Lyset af Shakespeares Hamlet*. 1960.

———. *Peripatetikeren Søren Kierkegaard*. 1965.

———. *Søren Kierkegaard-Dramæt*. 1967.

Clausen, Julius. *En Kvindes Kærlighed. P. L. Møller og Mathilde Leiner*. 1928.

———. *Mennesker paa min Vej* [on Regine Olsen]. 1941.

Dahl, Arthur. *Søren Kierkegaards Jyllandsrejse*. 1948.

Diem, Hermann. *Die Existenzdialektik von Søren Kierkegaard*. 1950.

Drachmann, A. B. *Udvalgte Afhandlinger* [on the engagement]. 1911.

Fenger, Henning. "Søren Kierkegaard—A Literary Approach." *Scandinavica* III. 1964.

———. "Søren Kierkegaard, P. E. Lind og 'Johan Gordon.'" *Kierkegaardiana* VII. 1968.

———. " 'Mestertyven'—Søren Kierkegaards første dramatiske forsøg," *Edda* 1971.

———. *The Heibergs*. 1971.

———. "Prise de Conscience esthétique de Søren Kierkegaard, 'Don Juan'," *Orbis Litterarum* XXVII. 1972.

———. "Søren Kierkegaards psykologi." *Ugeskrift for Læger*, no. 22, 1972.

Geismar, Eduard. *Søren Kierkegaard. Hans Livsudvikling og Forfatterskab*, vols. I–VI. 1926–28. [German translation, 1929.]

Goldschmidt, M. A. *Livserindringer og Resultater*. 1877.

———. *Breve fra og til Meïr Goldschmidt*, vols. I–III. Ed. Morten Borup, 1963.

Gottsched, H. See Barfod, H. P.

Grundtvig, N. F. S. *Mands Minde* 1788–1838. Ed. S. Grundtvig, 1877. [Contains a reprint, on pp. vi–xi, of Frederik Barfod's article in *Kjøbenhavnsposten*, no. 288, 1838, with a report of the thirty-fourth lecture, Kierkegaard's only written source for a knowledge of these lectures.]

Hansen, Knud. *Søren Kierkegaard. Ideens digter*. 1954.

Heiberg, Johanne Louise. *Et Liv, genoplevet i Erindringen*, vols. I–IV. Fourth edition by Aage Friis, 1944.

Heiberg, P. A. *Bidrag til et psykologisk Billede af Søren Kierkegaard i Barndom og Ungdom.* 1895.

———. *Nogle Bidrag til Enten-Eller's Tilblivelseshistorie.* 1910.

———. *En Episode i Søren Kierkegaards Ungdomsliv.* 1912.

———. *Et Segment af Søren Kierkegaards religiøse Udvikling.* 1918.

———. *Søren Kierkegaards religiøse Udvikling.* 1925.

———. *Registratur over Søren Kierkegaards arkiv, microfilm at the Royal Library*, 1962.

Helweg, Hjalmar. *Søren Kierkegaard. En psykiatrisk-psykologisk studie.* 1933.[With Hanne Mourier's recollections of Regine Olsen, and of the latter's accounts of the engagement. My article "Søren Kierkegaards psykologi," *Ugeskrift for Læger,* no. 22 (1972), is an extensive defense of Helweg. See Ostenfeld, Ib.]

Henriksen, Aage. *Methods and Results of Søren Kierkegaard Studies in Scandinavia.* 1950.

———. "Søren Kierkegaards romaner." 1954. [Dissertation, reviewed by Niels Kofoed in *Kierkegaardiana* I, 1955.]

Hertel, Hans. "P. L. Møller and 'romantismen' in Danish Literature." *Scandinavica* VIII, pp. 35–48. 1969.

Hertz, Henrik. *Stemninger og Tilstande.* 1839. Ed. Johannes Weltzer as *En litterær Nøgleroman fra 1839.* 1948.

Himmelstrup, Jens. "Søren Kierkegaards Opfattelse af Sokrates." 1924. [Dissertation.]

———. *International Bibliografi.* 1962.

———. *Terminologisk Ordbog til Søren Kierkegaards Samlede Værker*, 3rd ed., 1964.

Hirsch, Emanuel. *Søren Kierkegaard–Studien*, vols. I–III. 1930–33.

———. "Nogle Smaabidrag til Søren Kierkegaard-Forskningen." [Contains material on Regine Schlegel and the engagement.] *Teologisk Tidsskrift,* 5 Rk, II. 1931.

———. *Probleme der Abfassungszeit von Søren Kierkegaards Schrift "Uber den Begriff der Ironie."* 1964. [A strongly personal review by Gregor Malantschuk in *Kierkegaardiana*, 1964.]

Hjort, P. *Udvalg af Breve fra Mænd og Quinder*, vols. I–II. 1867–69.

*Hohlenberg, Johannes. *Søren Kierkegaard.* 1940.

———. *To Skuespil om Søren Kierkegaard.* 1946.

———. *Den ensommes Vej.* 1948.

Holm, Kjeld, Malthe Jacobsen, and Bjarne Troelsen. *Søren Kierkegaard og romantikerne.* [Berlingske Leksikon Bibliotek.] No year.

Holm, Søren. *Om Filosofi og Religion.* 1942.

———. *Søren Kierkegaards Historiefilosofi.* 1952. [German translation: Stuttgart, 1956.]

———. *Græsk Religion.* 1963.

———. *Græciteten.* 1964.

———. *Om Humor.* 1964.

Holmgaard, Otto. *Peter Christian Kierkegaard, Grundtvigs Lærling.* 1953.

Hostrup, Christian. *Erindringer fra min Barndom og Ungdom.* 1891.

Høffding, Harald. *Søren Kierkegaard som Filosof.* 1892.

Jacobsen, J. O. "Søren Kierkegaards sidste svære Dage." *Dagens Nyheder,* Nov. 13, 1955.

Jensenius, Knud. " 'Det unge Menneske' hos Søren Kierkegaard." *Nordisk Tidskrift,* 1930.

———. *Nogle Kierkegaardstudier, "De tre store Ideer."* 1932.

Johansen, Steen. *Erindringer om Søren Kierkegaard.* 1955.

Jørgensen, Carl. *Søren Kierkegaard. En biografi med særligt henblik paa hans personlige etik,* vols I– IV. 1964.

———. *Søren Kierkegaards Skuffelser.* 1967.

Kabell, Aage. *Søren Kierkegaard—studiet i Norden.* 1948. [Review by Paul Krüger in *Orbis Litterarum* VII, 1949.]

Kierkegaard, Olaf. *Fæstebonden i Sædding Kristen Jespersen Kierkegaard's Efterslægt.* 1941.

Koch, Carl. *Søren Kierkegaard og Emil Boesen. Breve og Indledning.* 1901.

Kragh-Jacobsen, S. "Indledning" to Poul Chievitz, *Fra Gaden* [1848]. 1943.

Krarup, Per. *Fra mit livs rejse.*

———. *Erindringsglimt og refleksioner.* 1975. [On A. B. Drachmann, H. O. Lange, and J. L. Heiberg.]

Kuhr, Victor. *Modsigelsens Grundsætning.* 1915.

Kühle, Sejer. *Søren Kierkegaard. Barndom og Ungdom.* 1950.

Kyrre, Hans. *Henrik Hertz. Liv og Digtning.* 1916. [With diary excerpts.]

———. *M. Goldschmidt,* vols. I– II. 1919.

Landmark, Johan D. *Fortolkninger til Søren Kierkegaards Ungdomshistorie.* 1926.

Leopold, Svend. *Søren Kierkegaard. Geniets Tragedie, Roman-Biografi.* 1932.

Ljundal, Arnold. *Problemet Kierkegaard.* 1964.

Lukács, Georg von. "Die Seele und die Formen" [on Kierkegaard and Regine Olsen], in *Essays*. 1911.

Lund, H. C. A. *Studenterforeningens Historie 1820–70*, vols I–II. 1896–98.

Lund, Henriette. *Naturforskeren P. W. Lund*. 1885.

———. *Mit Forhold til hende*. 1904.

———. *Erindringer fra Hjemmet*. 1909. [1880]

Lund, Holger. *Borgerdydskolen i Kjøbenhavn.* 1787–1887.

Løgstrup, K. E. *Opgør med Søren Kierkegaard*. 1967.

Magnusson, Rikard. *Søren Kierkegaard set udefra*. 1942.

———. *Det særlige Kors*. 1942.

Malantschuk, G. *Indførelse i Søren Kierkegaards Forfatterskab*. 1953.

———. "Søren Kierkegaard og Poul M. Møller." *Kierkegaardiana* 1959.

———. *Dialektik og Eksistens hos Søren Kierkegaard*. 1968.

Martensen, H. L. *Af mit Levned*. 1882.

Mesnard, Pierre. *Le vrai visage de Søren Kierkegaard*. 1948.

Meyer, Raphael. *Kierkegaardske Papirer. Forlovelsen. Udgivne for fru Regine Schlegel*. 1904.

Møller, P. L. *Kritiske Skizzer fra 1840–47*, vols. I–II. 1847. [Partially reprinted as a Tranebog (Gyldendal, 1971), edited by Hans Hertel.]

Møller Kristensen, Sven. *Digter og Samfund*, vols. I–II. 1942.

———. *Den dobbelte Eros*. 1966.

Nielsen, Flemming Christian. *Søren Kierkegaard og Aarhus*. 1968.

Nielsen, Rasmus. *Søren Kierkegaards Bladartikler*. 1857.

———. *Paa Søren Kierkegaardske Stadier*. 1860.

Nielsen, Svend Aage. *Søren Kierkegaard og Regensen*. 1965. [English summary.]

Næsgaard, Sigurd. *En Psychoanalyse af Søren Kierkegaard*. 1950.

Ostenfeld, Ib. *Angstbegrebet i Søren Kierkegaard: Begrebet Angst*. 1933.

———. *Poul Kierkegaard. En Skæbne*. 1957.

———. *Søren Kierkegaards Psykologi*. 1972.

Petersen, Lars. *Søren Kierkegaard som romanforfatter*. 1972.

Plum, M. N. *Schleiermacher i Danmark*. 1934.

Poulsen, Mogens. *Kierkegaardske Skæbner*. 1955. [Contains material on Emil Boesen i.a.]

Rasmussen, S. V. *Den unge Brøchner*. 1966. Ed. Justus Hartnack.

Rehm, Walther. *Søren Kierkegaard und der Verführer*. 1949.

Reumert, Elith. *Skjøn-Jomfru*. 1909.

Rohde, H. P. *Det litterære Løvstræde*. 1964.

———. *Auktionsprotokol over Søren Kierkegaards Bogsamling*. 1967.

———. *Gaadefulde Stadier paa Kierkegaards Vej*. 1974.

Rohde, Peter P. *Søren Kierkegaard. Et Geni i en Købstad*. 1962.

———. *Søren Kierkegaard. An Introduction to his Life and Philosophy*. 1963.

Roos, Carl. *Kierkegaard og Goethe*. 1955. [See Steffen Steffensen's expert review in *Kierkegaardiana* II, 1957.]

Rubow, Paul V. *Dansk litterær Kritik i det 19de Aarhundrede indtil 1870*. 1921.

———. *Søren Kierkegaard og hans Samtidige*. 1950.

———. *Goldschmidt og Søren Kierkegaard*. 1952.

———. *Søren Kierkegaard og Kirken*. 1955.

Rudin, Waldemar. *Søren Kierkegaards person och författarskap*, vol. I. 1880.

Saggau, Carl. *Skyldig—Ikke Skyldig?* 1958.

Schack, Tage. *Johann Georg Hamann*. 1948.

Schousboe, Julius. "Om Begrebet Humor hos Søren Kierkegaard." 1925. [Dissertation.]

Sjestov, Leo. *Søren Kierkegaard og den eksistentielle Tænkning*. 1947.

Sløk, Johannes. *Die Anthropologie Søren Kierkegaards*. 1954.

———. *Shakespeare og Søren Kierkegaard*. 1972.

Stybe, Svend Erik. "Frederik Dreier." 1959. [Dissertation.]

———. "Symposion Kierkegaardianum." *Orbis Litterarum* X. 1955.

Thulstrup, M. M. *Søren Kierkegaard og Pietismen*. 1967.

Thulstrup, Niels. *Søren Kierkegaard. Bidrag til en Bibliografi* [with Edith O. Nielsen]. 1951.

———. *Katalog over Søren Kierkegaards Bibliotek*. 1957.

———. "Speculative Idealisme indtil 1846." 1967. [Dissertation.]

Toftdahl, Helmuth. *Søren Kierkegaard først—og Grundtvig så*. 1969.

Toldberg, Helge. *Goldschmidt og Kierkegaard*. 1956. [In the *Festskrift* for Paul V. Rubow.]

Topsøe-Jensen, Helge. *Mit eget Eventyr uden Digtning*. 1942.

———. *Omkring Levnedsbogen*. 1943.

———. *Mit Livs Eventyr*, vols. I–II. 1951.

———. *H. C. Andersens Levnedsbog*. 1962.

Troels-Lund, Troels. *Bakkehus og Solbjerg*, vol. III. 1922.

———. *Et Liv. Barndom og Ungdom*. 1924.

Wamberg, N. Birger. *H. C. Andersen og Heiberg*. 1971.

Weltzer, Carl. *Peter og Søren Kierkegaard*. 1936.

————. "Omkring Søren Kierkegaards Disputats." *Kirkehistoriske Samlinger*, 6 Rk, 6 Bd, 1949.

————. "Endnu Lidt om Søren Kierkegaards Disputats." *Kirkehistoriske Samlinger*. 1950.

————. *Grundtvig og Søren Kierkegaard.* 1952.

Winther, Christian. *Breve fra og til Christian Winther.* Ed. Morten Borup, vols. I–V. 1974.

Zeuthen, Lina. *Søren Kierkegaards hemmelige Note.* 1951.

P.S. After the bibliography of the first, Danish edition of this book had gone to press, Professor Henning Schmidt, M.D., gave a lecture on Odense University's Speech Day with the following title: "Where Did Venus Go, When She Went Out?"(printed in *Nyt fra Odense Universitet*, May 25, 1976). The works on venereal diseases mentioned therein, Philippe Ricard's *Beobachtungen über Syphilis und Tripper* (1836) and his *Traité pratique des maladies vénériénnes* (1838), provide strong supporting evidence for Carl Saggau's conjecture that Kierkegaard, around 1840, may have been absorbed by medical theories on syphilis and its consequences—inherited from his father—for him.

INDEX